544 741A

W9-DJQ-597

9988

In Search of Something

Books by Herbert Cerwin

In Search of Something
Bernal Díaz, Historian of the Conquest
These Are the Mexicans

In Search of Something

The Memoirs of a Public Relations Man

by Herbert Cerwin

with an introduction by
Frank H. Bartholomew,
Chairman of the Board,
United Press International

SHERBOURNE PRESS, INC.
Los Angeles, California

Copyright © 1966 by Herbert Cerwin

All rights reserved. No portion of this book may be reproduced without written permission from the publisher, except in the case of a reviewer who wishes to quote brief passages in connection with a review for inclusion in a magazine, newspaper or journal.

Library of Congress Catalog Card Number 66–26076

Manufactured in the United States of America

First Printing

The author and publisher wish to thank Julian P. Graham for permission to use photographs taken by him which comprise the bulk of the photographic section.

Contents

Introduction

You are about to have the unusual experience of reading a book that is amusing and which has depth and a warm understanding of the array of characters marching across its pages.

Here is a top-flight observer who has learned the magic formula of truly great reporting: simple declarative sentences with action words, and not adjectives, telling the tale.

You'll be present when Herbert Cerwin introduces Charlie Chaplin, the sad comedian, to Robinson Jeffers, the sardonically amused writer of tragic poetry.

Here you'll have Cerwin's candid view of Chief Justice of the United States Earl Warren, in earlier days, when he was on the make politically.

In fact, the pages that follow will introduce you to a host of colorful and important people and events, from San Francisco to Rio de Janeiro; some you know, some you don't, some you thought you knew but may not be so sure of after you've read the book.

It should be hard to put this book down after you have read the first ten pages; at least I found that to be the case with the manuscript. I was caught up by the enthusiasm and the nostalgic feeling that runs through it.

Of course I don't claim to have a completely objective view of Herbert Cerwin. The fact that he and his wife,

7

Dagmar, have been our friends for many years, and that we are now neighboring vineyardists in the pleasant little wine town of Sonoma, California (that is, when they and we are not in New York, Mexico or somewhere in Europe or the Orient) disqualifies me from any claims to objectivity.

We first met in the artists' colony of Carmel, California. There were strange goings-on there that were hitting the front pages, including the appearance of Madame Mathilde Baumgardner and her Society of the Sun. I decided I had better see what our "stringer" was up to with those sun worshippers. A "stringer" is a correspondent who covers the news in smaller communities on those rare occasions when there is news. But in Carmel, there seemed to be news all the time.

When my wife, Toni, and I reached Carmel, we drove over a narrow, rutted road through the woods. There were no street signs but I finally found the house we were looking for. My knock was answered by a youngster with red cheeks. I asked him for our "stringer" and to my surprise, he said it was he, and asked us into the house. We ended up staying for dinner and my offering him a full-time job with the United Press. But he was quite happy living in Carmel, he said.

A year or so later, it was from Del Monte and Pebble Beach where news now came—not Carmel. These stories had a familiar ring and, sure enough, it was our ex-stringer, Cerwin, putting Del Monte and Pebble Beach on the map.

We saw quite a lot of him and Dag after that, and when I found he spoke Spanish, I offered him a position in Buenos Aires. It must have been difficult for him to refuse, but he did. Not too long afterward, however, he persuaded United Press to send him as a special correspondent to take part in covering the war in China. He was back in a short time. "We're in for trouble," he said, and rushed to get into the Navy or Army, but eventually affiliated with Nelson Rockefeller and the Office of the Coordinator of Inter-American Affairs.

I was proud of the things I saw him accomplish in Mexico and Central America in the interests of the United States. Later, the diplomatic job he did for the State Department in Brazil was in the best Cerwin tradition. He took on these major responsibilities for our country with his usual good judgment and enthusiasm; wherever they have traveled or lived, the Cerwins have made friends.

In the mystifying business of public relations, he is among the best. I have seen him operate over many years in many places and at work on many problems. I've seen him presiding at cocktail parties for corporation presidents, diplomats, editors, poets, peasants and millionaires, and getting something good out of everyone because he has always something good to give in return.

This book is also in the best Cerwin tradition—amusing, anecdotal, sharply perceptive when the event he is telling you about is significant. This book "marches." If you can put it down before it is finished, you'll do something I certainly could not do with the manuscript.

Frank H. Bartholomew,
CHAIRMAN OF THE BOARD,
UNITED PRESS INTERNATIONAL

CHAPTER ONE

The Big Debate

Recently, while going through an old trunk, I found some newspapers and magazines of the late twenties. How refreshing were the stories on the front pages. There was no talk of war or the dangers of cigarette smoking or of saturated and unsaturated fats. Calvin Coolidge, one story reported, always had a hearty breakfast of pancakes and pork sausages in the White House.

No one worried how he was going to pay his income taxes nor who would reach the moon first. The only mention of traveling through space was in reference to the stock market, which was climbing higher and higher. As I went through the newspapers I read about Annie Besant and her youthful discovery in India, Krishnamurti, whom she hailed as the reincarnation of Christ. Aimee Semple McPherson, the lady evangelist from Los Angeles, was healing the sick by the thousands. Judge Ben Lindsay had come up with a unique plan to reduce the divorce rate. He called it "companionate marriage," and immediately was accused by the clergy and by newspapers of advocating free love.

I remember Judge Lindsay quite well through an exchange of telegrams. I was seventeen and working as a newspaper reporter in the city of San Jose, some 50 miles south of San Francisco, getting 35 dollars a week. At that salary I didn't

see how I was ever going to be rich and successful; yet
everyone else seemed to be making money.

Joe, the barber who cut my hair, boasted he had made a
"killing" in the stock market and Nick, the Greek waiter at
Slavich's restaurant, was also in the money. I thought of
being in the stock market, but I had no money to invest.
It was then that I considered other avenues of acquiring
wealth. I decided to become an impressario.

I awakened one morning with the idea of bringing Krishnamurti, Aimee Semple McPherson, or Judge Ben Lindsay to
San Jose. Any one of the three, I was convinced, should draw
a large audience, and I would collect a percentage of the
receipts. It appeared simple enough. I only had to make up
my mind which of the three would best serve my purpose.

That day I had to cover a story at the county jail and went
over my plans with one of the deputy sheriffs.

"I sure think you got something," he said.

"It would go over big," I pointed out with increasing enthusiasm.

"No question of it," he agreed, "but the way I figure it,
you'd be better off with the Judge. It'd be too much of a
gamble with the reincarnation fellow, and mostly sick people would go and see Aimee. But all this talk of free love—
boy! that would bring out the crowd. Get the Judge and
you'll make out all right."

I discussed my idea with several other people whose opin-
ion I valued, including Louie Oneal, the political boss of
Santa Clara County. He suggested that I talk it over with
Terry McKean.

"Get him to go in with you," he counseled. "Offer him a
share—not too much—just enough to keep him happy."

Terry McKean knew me because I often wrote about road
show companies and concerts he brought to San Jose. His last
big attraction was Madame Schumann-Heink, who had sung

at the State Teachers Auditorium to a capacity audience. I had given Madame Schumann-Heink a favorable review.

Terry McKean had a small office in a music store on the main street where he arranged for forthcoming productions and sold the tickets as well. Terry was Scotch-Irish and a nervous little man with a round, red face that resembled a balloon. He was in his middle fifties and was a bachelor. Terry wasn't very busy when I stopped by, and he asked me to sit down in one of the two chairs he had in his office. I described my plans in detail.

"Lindsay would draw," he agreed, "but even a lecture by him would not go over as much as you think. If you could arrange a debate between him and someone else—then it would be a big attraction. Why don't you work on that phase of it?"

"I'd have to get Judge Lindsay first."

"Send him a wire and see if he goes for it—that's the way to do it."

"Would you help me put it on?" I asked.

"Sure, I'll give you a hand with the arrangements and the sale of tickets." Then with his Scottish caution, he added: "But I don't want to become financially involved or be responsible for it. With these road companies and concerts I bring in, I act only as an agent and sell the tickets. I am in no position to take a loss."

"But, if we got Judge Lindsay we'd make money, wouldn't we?"

"Probably, but there's nothing sure in show business. Besides, San Jose is a conservative town and 'churchy.' It might do well and it might not."

"We'd draw from all over the county," I said, refusing to let him dampen my enthusiasm. "Everyone's talking about Judge Lindsay, and they'd want to see him and hear what he's got to say. If I put plenty of publicity in the newspapers, we couldn't miss."

Then, remembering Louis Oneal's advice, I said to Terry: "I'd be willing to share half of the profits with you."

I saw now that I had aroused his interest.

"If we fill the auditorium as we did for Madam Schumann-Heink, we'd make money," he said.

"We can't miss," I said.

That evening I sent a night letter to Judge Lindsay, inviting him to participate in a debate on "companionate marriage," and asking on what date he would be available and what would be his fee.

Within two days Judge Lindsay answered, giving the date he could be in San Jose, and stating his fee would be fifteen hundred dollars, payable three weeks in advance.

I wired Judge Lindsay:

DATE AND FEE AGREEABLE. MONEY CANNOT BE PAID UNTIL AFTER DEBATE.

To which, I received the following reply:

PREVIOUS ENGAGEMENTS MAKE IT IMPOSSIBLE TO ACCEPT OFFER.

This exchange of telegrams called for a conference with Terry McKean. He read the telegrams and threw them across his desk.

"Who does Judge Lindsay think he is?" Terry said. "Not even Madame Schumann-Heink wants to be paid in advance."

"What do we do now?" I asked.

"I still think you have a good idea," Terry went on. "We forget the Judge and try to get someone else. If we do that, we won't have to pay as much."

For the next few days we went through the newspapers trying to determine who was making news and who would be likely prospects. We came across two names: Lincoln Steffens and Major H. Sheridan Bickers.

Steffens was featured in a Sunday story in one of the San Francisco newspapers, which described him as the "great muckraker" who had broken up oil trusts and corruption rings in cities and was now living in Carmel where he was writing his autobiography. Major H. Sheridan Bickers was an English playwright who was lecturing in the United States. He was quoted as coming from a fighting family which had introduced the word "bickering" into the English language.

"They may be hams, but they have names that make them seem important," Terry McKean said. "Let's wire them and we'll offer them five hundred dollars each—no, let's make it four hundred."

After many drafts we finally decided on the following telegram to Lincoln Steffens:

WILL YOU ACCEPT ENGAGEMENT TO DEBATE WITH MAJOR H. SHERIDAN BICKERS ON IS MODERN MARRIAGE A FAILURE? FEE FOUR HUNDRED DOLLARS.

A telegram was also sent to Major Bickers.

The following day we heard from Steffens:

I ACCEPT BUT WHO IS H. SHERIDAN BICKERS AND ON WHAT SIDE DO YOU WANT ME TO DEBATE?

Major Bickers was more cautious in his reply:

WILLING TO CONSIDER OFFER. STEFFENS UNKNOWN TO ME. CAN DEBATE ON EITHER SIDE OF SUBJECT.

I next checked to determine what night the State Teachers Auditorium would be available. The best I could get was a Thursday evening four weeks away. We wired Steffens and Bickers accordingly and they both found the date acceptable. The Big Debate was on.

Terry McKean worked closely with me in preparing for the debate. Four weeks did not give us too much time. Tickets had to be printed, as well as quarter cards which we planned to place in store windows, barbershops, and about every place we could get them in. We also had to get advertisements and radio spots written and announcements sent to Terry's regular mailing list. Terry went at it in a businesslike manner, even setting up a budget.

"We'll keep the expenses down" Terry said. "If we do that and we have a full house, we'll clear at least a thousand dollars each."

Terry was as enthusiastic as I about the success of our joint venture, but he also stressed the importance of getting publicity in the newspapers. I assured him he did not have to worry, for I would see to it that stories would appear regularly in both San Jose newspapers, including the one for which I worked.

Once the quarter cards were printed, I began distributing them. I didn't miss a store or a shop, even putting them in speakeasies, and I tacked one on the bulletin board in the police station and another one in the county jail. I was proud of those cards for they had Terry's and my names as presenting *the most sensational debate of the year:* IS MODERN MARRIAGE A FAILURE?

The city editor didn't object to all the stories about Lincoln Steffens and Major H. Sheridan Bickers that passed over his desk. Often at night I'd drop into the composing room and stand around while the newspaper was being made up. If the newspaper was "tight" and space was at a premium, I'd persuade the make-up editor to kill a news story in order to get one in about the debate. By the time the tickets were put on sale, everyone in San Jose must have known about it.

Two weeks before the Big Debate, Terry reported that the advance ticket sale was brisk.

"There's a lot of interest," he said. "We should do well."

"How many tickets have you sold?" I asked.

"About fifty."

"That isn't very many."

"We still have two weeks to go. People wait until the last week to get tickets."

"You think we'll do all right, then?"

"No question about it."

On Sunday, a week before the debate, the paper for which I worked ran a feature story on Lincoln Steffens and Major H. Sheridan Bickers with photographs of the two. It was an article I had written based on material obtained from both Steffens and Bickers. I was certain this publicity would send people rushing to the box office for tickets and I spent a pleasant day thinking how, in another week, I would be on my way toward being rich and successful. But on Monday afternoon Terry McKean did not report any noticeable increase in ticket sales.

"We only sold ten," he said, "but tomorrow—you'll see—it will start picking up."

"Are you sure?" I was not feeling as confident as I had on Sunday.

"Don't worry," he said. "We're going to do all right."

But, I did worry, and on Tuesday evening, only six days before the Big Debate, my worries were real. Terry McKean admitted that so far only one hundred and fifty tickets had been sold.

"But, we need to sell over six hundred to even make expenses," I said. Then with desperation: "We're into this thing up to our necks and we better do something about it."

I left Terry McKean's office and started walking. If we didn't make expenses how would we pay the printers for the tickets and quarter cards, and then there were the advertisements in the newspapers and on the radio? And how would we pay Steffens and Bickers and the rent for the auditorium?

In the morning it came to me that the way to create interest in the debate was to start a controversy. Whenever a book or a movie was banned or censored, people rushed to buy the book or to see the movie.

At eight o'clock, after breakfast, I was in the office of Fred Thomas, the district attorney for Santa Clara county.

"I'd like to get your opinion," I said, approaching him as a newspaper reporter.

"What about?" he asked.

"About that debate. Do you think it should be held here in San Jose, in a community that is conservative and church-going?"

"Do you see anything wrong in it?" he asked.

"There are many people," I went on, "who question the propriety of holding a debate which treats marriage lightly. And then there is this talk of 'free love' before marriage."

"Are they going to talk about that in the debate?"

"They're bound to—it's very much in the news."

"Such wanton talk about 'free love' would destroy our civilization," he said. "I can say that, as district attorney of this county," and now he was beginning to understand what sort of statement I wanted, "I am irrevocably opposed to such rash ideas as advocated by Judge Lindsay. Men like Steffens and—who is this other man—yes, thank you—Major Bickers, have no right to come into this community to incite our young people. There is no good reason to have such a debate. The very concept of it is degrading and demoralizing."

"Would you ban such a debate?"

"You can quote me as saying that I am considering the legal aspects of getting out an injunction against having this debate here."

"That's fine," I said. "That will do it. Thanks very much."

I left his office and then telephoned four of the leading ministers in San Jose who concurred with the district attorney and gave statements of their views about the debate. I passed the story on to the San Francisco newspapers and next morning it was on the front pages. I also had written the story for the San Jose paper and it, too, made the front page.

I brought copies of the newspapers to Terry McKean. But

he had already seen them and his red face was glowing with satisfaction.

"With all this publicity," he said, "we'll have a sellout for sure."

When I went to work that noon there was a call for me from Dr. McQuarrie, the president of the San Jose State Teachers College.

"Did you see the papers?" he said.

"Yes," I said.

"I am not at all certain it would be in the community's best interest to permit the use of our auditorium for this debate," he said.

"You can't be serious!"

"But, I am. I have already received a number of telephone calls from people who want to know why we are allowing this debate to be held in a school auditorium."

"Suppose I quote you as saying you are opposed to the debate, but that freedom of speech is inherent to our American rights—or something along those lines."

"Perhaps that might do it—I am not certain. The pressures may mount and we might have to cancel the use of the auditorium."

"You can't," I protested, holding my breath. "Where else could we hold it? Besides, wouldn't you be subject to criticism for not allowing men of the stature of Lincoln Steffens and Major Bickers to talk in the auditorium?"

I was in a panic. If he cancelled the use of the auditorium, we would be in trouble. He was hesitating, wavering on the telephone.

"All right," he finally said. "We'll go through with it, but you had better make my position clear. I am definitely opposed to the debate."

"I don't understand it," Terry McKean said.

"Understand what?" I wanted to know.

"All this publicity hasn't helped. Instead people are staying away. I haven't sold ten tickets in the last two days."

"But why Terry? What have we done wrong?"

"We haven't done anything wrong. It's the people. It's this town. They're afraid to come to this thing—they're afraid of being criticized by attending, by being seen. We have a turkey on our hands."

"A turkey?"

"A flop. Unless—unless, yes, it's possible. I've seen it happen. The tide could turn. People at the very last might change their minds and there could be a rush at the box office."

But there wasn't and on the day of the debate we had sold exactly two hundred and ten tickets. In the afternoon, around four o'clock, I met Lincoln Steffens and his wife, Ella Winters, in the lobby of the Sainte Claire Hotel. Shortly afterwards, Major Sheridan Bickers appeared and took one look at me.

"Good Lord—you're not the one putting on the debate, are you?" he asked. "It can't be, you're only a boy."

"I have a partner," I said. "Terry McKean."

"Where is he?" Bickers wanted to know.

"He's busy selling tickets," I explained.

Lincoln Steffens suggested we have tea and discuss the debate. Steffens led the way into the coffee shop adjoining the lobby.

"How is the ticket sale going?" he asked as we sat down.

"Fine," I said. "Just fine."

He was too wise not to see I was troubled. There was an understanding look to his eyes and a softness to his voice that made me like him right away. His short-cropped Van Dyke beard gave him dignity, or perhaps it merely helped to conceal his cynical outlook. In height Steffens was a little over five feet, but his personality was forceful and dominant.

"People don't like the idea of the debate too well," he said. "It doesn't surprise me. People never want to hear the truth."

"Mr. McKean says we might have a last minute rush at the box office." I tried to be reassuring.

"I think, Major Bickers, we should discuss what we are going to talk about tonight," Steffens said as the tea was brought to the table.

Major Bickers said he would prefer to take the affirmative, as he had been married three times. Lincoln Steffens said he didn't care on which side he debated.

"Why don't we flip a coin," Steffens said.

Major Bickers agreed. Bickers got the affirmative, as he wanted.

"I'm going to my room and take a nap," Steffens said. "I'll see you all later."

Terry McKean had opened the box office before six-thirty but so far there had been no customers. At seven-fifteen, three people showed up and bought tickets and went inside. By seven-thirty, those who had previously purchased tickets began to arrive. Just before eight o'clock about ten more persons picked up tickets.

At eight-fifteen I went into the auditorium which wasn't even a third full. Nothing is as depressing or as forlorn looking as empty seats in a theater or an auditorium. Each of the seats seemed to cry out: "You have failed! You have failed!" I wanted to run away and hide.

Then I saw the terrible-tempered Mr. Clarke, the editor of the paper where I worked. He had on a blue suit, a white checkered vest and he was walking down the aisle, using a cane with each step he took. Before he sat down he glanced around at the auditorium; there was a disgusted look on his face. The debate was going to be a fiasco; I was now certain I would be fired in the morning.

Finally the curtain went up and on the stage, with a table between them, were Lincoln Steffens and Sheridan Bickers. There was scattered applause. Steffens got up and began to

talk, but I didn't hear what he said or what later Major
Bickers said in rebuttal. During the debate I was in the box
office with Terry McKean going over the receipts. Including
the advance ticket sale, all we had taken in totaled less than
four hundred dollars. How, I kept asking Terry McKean, were
we going to pay off Steffens and Bickers and the other bills we
had run up.

The Big Debate, however, was not on the stage of the State
Teachers College Auditorium. It was to take place after the
few people who had heard Steffens and Bickers had gone
home. Now the four of us, Steffens, Bickers, McKean and I
sat in the empty auditorium.

Terry McKean made his position clear. The debate, he said,
and he pointed at me, "is this young man's responsibility. I
was only helping him and acting as the ticket agent."

"Just a moment," Steffens broke in. "The announcements
and quarter cards also carry your name."

"There is no contract and I am not legally responsible,"
McKean protested.

"I guess he's right," I said. "The whole thing was my idea.
I merely asked Mr. McKean to help me."

Then I began to tell Steffens and Bickers of how and why
I had become involved. I must have talked for a long time
and as I finished there was a friendly smile on Steffens' face
and he did not appear angry.

"I have never heard such a sad story," Steffens said, and
he began to laugh.

But Major Bickers was acting very British. He did not consider it a laughing matter. He said he had only accepted the
offer to come and debate in San Jose because he needed the
money. "How much was taken in?" he asked.

"Less than four hundred," I said.

"We'll give the boy a break," Steffens said. "We'll each
take a hundred and let him use the rest to pay part of the
bills."

"I cannot agree to this at all," Major Bickers spoke up.

As we sat there in the empty auditorium the two began to argue over the disposition of the money. Bickers was eloquent, forceful, and angry. Steffens was calm, patient and every so often he would look over at me with a twinkle in his eyes. In the end, Major Bickers agreed to accept two hundred dollars while Steffens refused his share.

"You know, I've had a pleasant evening," Steffens said. He put his arm around me. "Come and visit me in Carmel. We should get better acquainted."

The way I was feeling, he couldn't have said a nicer thing to me.

Dr. McQuarrie of the State Teachers College was also understanding. He volunteered to forego the rent on the auditorium. But the printers and others had to be paid. I went to see Louie Oneal and he loaned me the balance of the money I needed, and which I agreed to pay back at the rate of five dollars a week.

"I wanted to come to the debate but my wife wouldn't let me," he said.

CHAPTER TWO

Little Journeys to the Homes
of the Great

The walls of the office were covered with signed photographs of Sarah Bernhardt, Pola Negri, Isadora Duncan, Charles Chaplin, Theodore Roosevelt, Woodrow Wilson, General John J. Pershing, and many others. There was a big desk at one end of the office, two leather chairs, a couch, a worn blue carpet. Behind the desk sat Mr. Clarke and to his right was a large brass spittoon.

Everyone in the editorial department of the daily newspaper where I worked was afraid of Mr. Clarke. To be summoned by him meant either a reprimand or that you better start looking for another job. And now, a week after the debate between Lincoln Steffens and Sheridan Bickers, I had been called into Mr. Clarke's office. I stood there anticipating the worst. Mr. Clarke looked at me, chewed at his cigar and then spat into the spittoon.

"Don't just stand there. Sit down!" he said in that sharp voice of his.

I sat down. During the next thirty seconds I recalled everything I had heard about Mr. Clarke. He once had been a distinguished New York newspaper editor, but ill health and advancing years had forced him to resign. No one knew why he had accepted the position of editing a newspaper in San Jose, except that he needed the money.

I had never met him, but all of us in the editorial department were aware of his quick temper. It must have bothered him to be editing a small town daily and working with an inexperienced staff of reporters such as myself. Occasionally, too, I'd see him walking down the main street of San Jose in his well-tailored clothes, homburg hat and cane. He looked out of place, for San Jose was then largely an agricultural community. Yet in the two years he had been with the newspaper, he had done much to improve it and he had added many new features. The circulation was up and it was said that the owners had given him a free hand.

Mr. Clarke, as I was later to learn, preferred to conceal that he was a kindly, generous man. Instead he assumed a brusque manner and he made everyone think he had a bad temper.

"A man came to see me this morning who was making inquiries about you," Mr. Clarke said. "He was a truant officer. He wanted to know why you didn't finish school."

I didn't answer, partly from fear and partly because I did not know what to say.

"Why did you quit school?"

"Am I going to lose my job?"

"No. Why should you?"

Suddenly I found it easy to talk to Mr. Clarke. I was no longer afraid and I told him of my father's death and of my need to go to work. I said that I had first obtained a job as a reporter in Stockton and after six months there, had heard of an opening in San Jose and the city editor had hired me.

"How long were you in high school?"

"Six months."

"That's not very long."

"I know I'm not a very good writer."

"I didn't say that, but you need some education."

"I'll pick it up. I read a lot."

"What do you read?"

"Any book I can get my hands on. Last night I was reading James Oliver Curwood."

"He writes adventure stories. You need good, solid background stuff."

Mr. Clarke got up from his desk and walked over to a bookcase and brought out a book that was leather-bound. "Have you ever heard of Elbert Hubbard and his *Little Journeys to the Homes of the Great?*"

"No, sir."

"Many people don't care for Elbert Hubbard because he was something of a show-off. He called himself a philistine. Do you know what that is?"

"No, sir."

"I used to know Hubbard and perhaps his *Little Journeys* is not great literature. But they give glimpses into history, into philosophy, into science. He manages to make people think."

He handed the volume to me.

"This is volume one," he said. "Read it and then come and get the others. After you have finished the entire set I want to see you again."

"Yes, sir." I got up. "What about the truant officer? What's he going to do?"

"Nothing. I told him you were getting a better education on this newspaper than in any high school. He'll leave you alone."

"Thank you, sir."

I started to go but Mr. Clarke wasn't finished with me.

"Do you know that I am a friend of Lincoln Steffens?"

"No, I didn't know that, sir."

"I prefer to be called Mr. Clarke."

"Yes, sir."

"He wrote me about you. He said you were very young, but had the makings of a good reporter."

"Mr. Steffens is a very nice man."

"He's not just a nice man. He is a great man. Remember that. All right, you can go now."

During the next month I went through the ten volumes of Hubbard's *Little Journeys*. I read about Dante and Beatrice, Robert Browning, Byron, Shelley and Burns; then about Kant, Socrates, Spencer and Hegel; and on to von Humboldt and John Wannamaker. There must have been over a hundred essays, in which Elbert Hubbard tried to sum up the career and work of each person.

When I finished the last volume and returned it to Mr. Clarke, he began to question me on my opinions of the men Hubbard had selected for his *Little Journeys*. He listened patiently and then said: "I gave these books to you to read for a purpose. I want you to do something very much as Elbert Hubbard did. There are famous people living around this area or passing through. I want you to visit with them and write an interview with each one. We will then run it as a weekly feature in the paper."

As he talked he kept chewing on his cigar.

"You will arrange for the interview and write it in your own way. I have a hunch it may result in a good feature and create reader interest. Now one more thing—do you know how to take pictures?"

"No, sir."

"All right, then. Go and see our photographer and have him teach you how to use a camera. With each interview you are to take your own photographs. This feature is to start in three weeks, so don't waste any time. Understand?"

"Yes, Mr. Clarke."

He spit into the spittoon. "This assignment will give you the opportunity to know and write about people of importance. A little of what they say may rub off on you and you might get a better education than you would have had in high school. Now let's see what you can do."

I was provided with a camera, a tripod and a flashgun and tried, in three lessons, to learn how to take photographs. One of my first interviews was with Edwin Markham, who had become famous with his poem, *The Man with the Hoe*. Mr. Markham, then in his seventies, looked older than I thought he would. His white hair was long and bushy and so was his beard. He wore a black windsor tie and when he spoke, his voice had a deep resonance.

"I never wrote *The Man with the Hoe*," he said during the interview. "It came from an inner force. I awakened one morning, the poem clearly written in my mind. I had only to put it on paper. After it was published, it was quoted and hailed everywhere for its powerful message in defense of the common man."

Markham was staying as a guest at the villa of James D. Phelan, who had once been a United States Senator. The interview with Edwin Markham was at four o'clock and when I finished at five-thirty, Senator Phelan came and joined us.

"Why don't you stay and have dinner," he said to me. "I am having a few people in."

The small group he had invited consisted of thirty persons. There were butlers serving and there were high silver candelabras on the long dining table. As each course was brought in, I watched the person next to me to see what fork or spoon he used while he, probably, was keeping his eye on the guest sitting alongside him. Senator Phelan sat at the head of the table with Gertrude Atherton to his right and Edwin Markham to his left.

Most of the interviews I did were amateurishly written and yet, because I quoted verbatim the people I interviewed, they had a certain quality of truth to them. People, I found, liked to talk about themselves and often they made interesting copy. Even Will Rogers, busy and famous as he was, managed to spend two hours in a hotel room telling me, a youngster of seventeen, all about his life and his ambitions.

"People think I can come up with a 'smart crack' on the spur of the moment," he said, "but no, sir, that's not possible. I plan and rehearse everything I am going to say and how I say it. Trying to make people laugh is mighty hard work."

In the beginning, there were enough well-known people living around San Jose or passing through to provide material for the interviews. But later when I had to go further afield, I purchased a second-hand Chevrolet and one of the first long trips I made was to Monterey and to Carmel, where I stopped in to renew my acquaintance with Lincoln Steffens. He lived on San Antonio street, just off Ocean Avenue, and there was a small sign on his gate: Not at Home Until After Four O'clock. He was then working on his autobiography.

I waited until a few minutes after four, went through the gate and knocked. Steffens opened the door. He was obviously surprised to see me.

"So, it's you," he said with that impish smile of his. "How's the impressario? You seem to have survived the crisis. What are you doing these days?"

As he motioned me to come in, I began telling him about the interviews and the people I had met. I had some copies of the articles I had been writing and he read them with interest. Then I asked him if he could suggest people living in Carmel whom I might interview.

"You should see Robinson Jeffers," Steffens said. "He's the most important poet we have in the country today."

Jeffers had no telephone, no electricity, and he lived, Steffens told me, at the edge of the sea in a house constructed of ocean boulders. The following morning I found Jeffers in the secluded grove of cypress trees behind his house. As I approached, Jeffers, who was extremely shy, looked suspiciously at me.

"No visitors or trespassers are allowed here," he said.

"I've come at the suggestion of Lincoln Steffens," I explained and introduced myself.

Jeffers was tall and lanky and his face, with eyes closely set together, seemed to have the strength of the ocean boulders he had used to build his home. The mention of Lincoln Steffens reassured him. I told him of the type of interview I was writing.

"You better come in the house," he said, "and we can talk in there."

As we went in he introduced me to Una, his wife, and their twin boys. Then we went into a small living room that looked out on the pounding sea below.

At the time, his book, *Roan Stallion*, had just gone into a second edition, but Jeffers was not too well-known. I was probably the first newspaperman he had ever talked to and at the start, the interview went badly. But after awhile, Jeffers grew more at ease as he discussed his poetry and explained why his writing was frequently misinterpreted. I tried to follow him as best I could, but unfortunately, most of what he said went beyond me. While I was young and immature, I was a good listener. The time went fast and then it was noon.

He invited me to stay for lunch and we ate in the kitchen. Afterwards, Jeffers and I washed the dishes and later he took me to the stone tower which adjoined the house and which he had also constructed. We went up the narrow passageway and at the top of the tower was a small room where he worked. It had an expansive view of the sea, and far beyond in the distance was Point Sur and the rugged Big Sur country which Jeffers used as the setting for his long, narrative poems.

Perhaps because of Jeffers and of Steffens, I hoped that someday I too, could live in Carmel. I went there as often as possible, always stopping to see Steffens. Now he had become important to my life, and I knew and felt that he also looked

forward to these visits as I did. He was so wise, so understanding; his friendship meant much to me.

There were many other people on the Monterey Peninsula
whom I interviewed, but there was one I missed. He was then
an unknown writer. His wife, Carol, at the time, was working
as a secretary at the Monterey Chamber of Commerce, getting
sixty dollars a month and helping to support her husband who
was writing in a small rented house in nearby Pacific Grove.
Carol's husband was John Steinbeck.

In San Francisco I interviewed Otis Skinner, the actor; Jo
Davidson, the sculptor; and A. P. Giannini, the founder of the
Bank of America. Giannini always answered his own tele-
phone, had little use for secretaries or a private office. When
I telephoned for an appointment, his loud, clear voice was
instantly on the other end:

"Giannini talking—what can I do for you?"

He set a time for me to see him and when I arrived, he motioned for me to sit down in the chair by his desk. If I gave
the appearance of a high school journalism student, it did
not seem to bother him. He was courteous, patient and gave
me all the time I required.

"Tell me something about yourself, Mr. Giannini," I said.

"I haven't much to tell you," he replied, and then for the
next half-hour he went into great detail describing his arrival
from Italy, his early years selling vegetables from a cart and
his first attempt at loaning money to other people.

"I discovered," he said, "that money was similar to other
commodities, except that it was not perishable and that
everyone wanted it. I made up my mind that I was going to
'sell' money."

He started a small bank which eventually became the Bank
of Italy and finally, the Bank of America.

"But you know," he said as I was setting up to take his
photograph, "I really don't like being a banker. I would have
preferred singing in the opera."

No matter how famous a person was or how much money he acquired, I soon learned during the interviews that everyone liked to talk about himself. In this respect I always remember the "secret" that Peggy Hopkins Joyce told me about herself and which I have since passed on to many women. Peggy Hopkins Joyce was well-known for her beauty, her clothes and her many marriages to wealthy men.

"How is it, Miss Joyce," I asked, "that when so many women have trouble finding a husband, you seem to have no trouble at all?"

At first she just looked at me, then when she realized how young and naïve I was, she smiled.

"Why, it is very simple," she said. "When I am with a man, I *just listen.*"

My interviews for the San Jose paper went on for over a year. It was a wonderful year with complete freedom to go almost anywhere and to interview anyone. Mr. Clarke had given me an opportunity to prove myself and I was convinced I had not let him down. I was proud of these interviews and of the job I was doing. Furthermore, as Mr. Clarke must have known all along, being with celebrities, talking with them and visiting them in their homes, had provided me with confidence in myself and with this had come a certain amount of maturity.

During all this time I saw Mr. Clarke only when he sauntered into the editorial rooms. While I was not asked to come into his office again, everything I wrote was not so much for the readers of the newspaper as for Mr. Clarke. He was my friend. Then five days after I had reached my eighteenth birthday, Mr. Clarke sent me a memo, cold, formal, and to the point. "As of next Monday," the memo read, "the series of interviews you have been writing are to end. You will hereafter report to the city editor for future assignments."

What had gone wrong? Why hadn't Mr. Clarke called me to his office and told me why I was being taken off as a feature writer? I was convinced I had done something to arouse Mr. Clarke's ire. I made several attempts to see Mr. Clarke, but each time his secretary put me off, telling me he was too busy.

When the final interview was written and published, I began getting assignments from the city editor. Now that I was no longer under the protective wing of Mr. Clarke, the city editor took pleasure in giving me the worst assignments possible, writing the church and funeral notices and then I was put on the police beat covering routine news. Finally one day I drove to Carmel and went to see Lincoln Steffens. I told him what had been happening and as I went on talking Steffens stopped me.

"Don't you know," he said, "that everything good has to have an ending? So the bubble has burst, eh? Well, there's going to be others—many that are going to burst right in your face—and they will be worse. Clarke isn't letting you down. He's teaching you a lesson."

"Why? What have I done wrong?"

"You haven't done anything wrong," Steffens continued. "Clarke is showing you the hardest lesson people have to learn—not to become dependent—only depend on yourself."

Sitting there with Steffens and listening to him talk seemed to make all the difference. I no longer felt disappointed. My confidence in the world and Mr. Clarke was restored. I drove back to San Jose that night and next day when the city editor gave an assignment to cover a convention of the Native Sons of the Golden West, I was quite cheerful about it. The city editor was taken aback.

"You don't mind covering that convention?"

"Of course not," I said. "It's my job, isn't it?"

From then on as the city editor realized I did not resent or argue about the assignments he was giving me, he put me on better stories. For the next six months I covered murders, suicides, accidents, divorce cases, and court trials.

Then one day I was summoned to Mr. Clarke's office. He was sitting behind his desk, chewing as always on his cigar. He was wearing a black and white checkered vest under his dark alpaca coat and his blue polka-dot tie, hand-tied, was crooked, one end lower than the other. He looked at me for a full minute.

"Ever heard of Milio Vekuvich?" he asked.

"He was convicted of killing a shopkeeper," I said.

"Was he guilty?"

"I don't know, sir. At least the jury thought so."

"He's going to hang tomorrow," he said, and waited for his words to sink in.

I remained standing in front of his desk for he had not asked me to sit down as he had on previous occasions. He reached into the papers on his desk and held up a card in his hand.

"This is a press pass," he said as he handed me the card, "to the death chambers at San Quentin Penitentiary. You will go there early tomorrow morning to witness the hanging of Milio Vekuvich."

He went on chewing his cigar and watching me for what impression his words might have made on me.

"For over a year you have seen the pleasant side of life," Mr. Clarke continued. "You have covered a few sordid stories. Now you are going to see the State put a man to death. It will not be easy for you, but it will help, I hope, to make you a better newspaperman." His eyes were still on me. "You can go now."

As I started to leave, Mr. Clarke called me back.

"You are to write the story of this hanging as you see and feel it," he said. "But I don't want a lot of sentimental, sob-sister stuff. I want accurate, straight reporting. You understand?"

"Yes, sir," I said, and walked out of his office.

In the morning I was up at five, drove to San Quentin and went through the prison gates. As I approached the prison buildings I was stopped and told where to park and then was led to the warden's office. There were half a dozen reporters already there and the assistant warden was serving them coffee. Several pulled out flasks and put whiskey into their coffee. It was nine o'clock. The execution was to take place at ten.

The newspapermen present were veteran reporters and most of them had covered previous executions. Yet no one looked forward to watching the hanging of Milio Vekuvich. They all seemed to know each other and as I walked into the room, they glanced at me and went on with their conversation which was mostly about yesterday's ball game. I was given a cup of coffee and tried to join the group. At first they ignored me; then one of them made an effort to be friendly.

"Where you from?" he asked.

I told him.

"Your first hanging?"

"Yes."

"You're just a kid."

"I'm a reporter," I said almost defiantly.

"It's not pretty, what you are going to see," he said, "but don't let it get you down."

At nine-thirty we left the warden's office and went through the prison. We walked toward an anteroom leading to the death chamber. We now joined a group of about 20 persons who were also waiting to witness the execution. Several were police officers involved in the case and among them was a deputy sheriff who must have weighed over 250 pounds.

At nine forty-five the door of the anteroom was opened and we marched into the eggshell-colored death chamber. Before us stood the scaffold with the thick rope and a noose hanging down from the upper structure. We now took our places forming a semicircle around the scaffold.

"I don't know why," whispered the newspaperman who had been friendly, "but there are always thirteen steps to the platform and all executions take place on Fridays." Then almost sarcastically, "They got it down to a science. They'll rush this poor bastard in and string him up so fast, it will be over before you know it."

The worst part was the waiting and watching the big electric clock on the wall of the death chamber. The minute hand seemed to move slowly, as if it were dragging, giving Milio Vekuvich that much more time to live. At first there had been a wave of whispering among the group gathered in the death chamber. Then there was solemn silence and I looked around at the people, trying to make mental notes of their appearance and their expressions.

I glanced at the clock. It was now five minutes to ten. Then—four, three, two, finally the minute and the hour hand were at ten o'clock. A door to the right of the death chamber opened and two prison guards with the convicted man between them dashed into the room. The guards were holding Milio Vekuvich firmly by each arm and pulling him along as fast as they could. They passed in front of us and then up the thirteen steps. The man about to die had his hands tied behind his back and he was wearing a white shirt, open at the throat.

One of the guards slipped the noose over Milio Vekuvich's head and the convicted man stood there on the platform looking down at us. His lips quivered.

"I am innocent!" he suddenly cried out. "You dirty bunch of murderers!"

Then the trap was sprung and the body of Milio Vekuvich

swung in midair, dangling at the end of the rope like a sack of potatoes. The prison doctor stopped the body from swinging and placed a stethoscope over Milio Vekuvich's heart. Once more I looked at the clock. It was one minute after ten. The execution had taken less than sixty seconds. We all stood there silently, then there was a heavy thud as the 250 pound deputy sheriff fell to the floor.

"It's nothing," the newspaperman next to me whispered. "He's probably only fainted. The bigger they are, the harder they fall."

As I continued watching the minute hand on the clock, I tried not to think of what I was seeing, but of the story I would write. How could I describe and put into words this thing I was witnessing? One moment Milio Vekuvich was alive and screaming out at us, and now he was a lifeless dead weight at the end of a rope. What were the thoughts of Milio Vekuvich in those final seconds as the rope broke his neck?

I wanted to shout out in protest. It was wrong, morally wrong, to put people to death like this—no matter whether they were guilty or not. What a horrible, terrible way to die.

The prison doctor who had been holding onto the body of Milio Vekuvich with one hand and with the other, the stethoscope, released his grip and started walking down the steps. The deputy sheriff who had fainted was being helped to his feet and we quietly began marching out of the death chamber. The doctor now officially pronounced Milio Vekuvich dead. The time was now eight minutes after ten.

"He died quicker than most of them," the newspaperman next to me said. "Some of them take a lot longer."

CHAPTER THREE

Selling News by the Inch

Mr. Clarke invited me for dinner at his home and after that I went there every Thursday. Often I'd sit in his study until midnight listening to him reminisce about his newspaper days in Chicago and New York. Frequently he'd go over news stories I had written, pointing out mistakes and making suggestions. He always selected a book for me to read.

Through him I became acquainted with the works of Sherwood Anderson, Carl Van Vechten, Ernest Hemingway and James Joyce.

"You won't understand Joyce at first," Mr. Clarke said. "But read him anyway and in time you'll get something out of it."

Night after night I made an effort to struggle through *Ulysses*, which had recently been published, but it went far beyond me. I did not realize either how difficult it was to get *Ulysses* and that Mr. Clarke trusted me with his copy which a friend had smuggled in from France.

Then, one evening when I was in Mr. Clarke's study he said: "Tomorrow you are through at the paper. I want you to quit."

"But, Mr. Clarke," I protested, "I like working here."

"I know that and it won't be easy for you to leave. Yet, that's exactly what you are going to do. There's a job open on the *Post Enquirer* in Oakland. It's a Hearst paper and it's on its last legs. But, the rough, hard school of Hearst journalism is what you need."

I tried to argue but he had made up his mind. A week later I was working for Hearst. I went to work at six in the morning and did not finish until late in the afternoon. I was given every type of assignment. I also learned that when I was sent out to get a story or to dig up a photograph, I didn't dare return without it, even if it meant climbing into a second story window. It was cold, impersonal journalism, rough and hard. Within six months I was toughened up. Nothing bothered me and I temporarily lost my respect for the truth and for the privacy of other people. I became skeptical of everything and everybody.

There was another man being toughened up at the same time. He was a young district attorney and his job was to convict three city councilmen, a deputy sheriff and a sheriff of accepting graft. One of the politicians indicted by the Grand Jury had filed a libel suit against Hearst and the instructions came from San Simeon that all five men had to be convicted and quick. I was assigned to cover the trial. The young district attorney was Earl Warren and it was rumored that Hearst had offered to support him for the governorship of California if he got a conviction.

Day after day at the press table in the crowded courtroom I listened to witnesses testify. I heard testimony introduced that shouldn't have been permitted. Earl Warren's examination of witnesses was piercing and damaging. He had little regard, I thought, for understanding the motives that brought about political graft and corruption. These men on trial were guilty and should be convicted. Yet, my sympathy was for them and I had a growing distaste for Earl Warren and his methods.

"Earl Warren would convict his own grandmother if he thought it might help him politically," I heard a newspaperman at the press table say.

And yet one had to admire the way he hammered in his points and how he tore down the arguments of the defense counsel. Earl Warren was advancing his career and he made every effort to get the press on his side. Occasionally after a day in court, he would ask us into his office where he would brief us on what tactics he would use the next day and provide us with "behind the scenes" information. It was prohibition time, and it was illegal to possess alcoholic beverages. But in the district attorney's office there was invariably whiskey, seized in raids, for the press.

"Don't worry, boys," Earl Warren would say. "These men are going to the 'pen.' We got the goods on them."

Warren had a pleasant personality and a warm smile, but in the courtroom he turned into another person, ruthless and merciless. He appeared to enjoy watching the defense witnesses squirm under the onslaught of his questions and the evidence he managed to draw from them. Perhaps he was a good district attorney, only doing his duty. In my remaining youthful idealism, I began to doubt the value of this court trial. Then I realized why I felt as I did.

Lincoln Steffens had made his reputation as a muckraker, and in city after city, he had exposed political corruption and graft. Many people had gone to prison as the result of his investigations and magazine articles.

"It did not take me long to find out that sending these men to prison was not the answer," Steffens had said to me in his home in Carmel. "They were guilty all right, but the real guilt lay in our political system that allowed and encouraged graft. The men who received graft went to prison, but those who corrupted them, those men almost always went free."

Nowhere in the trial did Earl Warren or the defense counsel blame the system, or the companies and the men who had brought about the political corruption. It was the defendants who had to be convicted and punished.

"There is not a drop of the milk of human kindness in me

for these corrupt officials who violated their public trust," Warren said in his closing argument. "Nor should there be in you, the jury. These men must go to prison and it is your duty to send them there."

The jury was out only a short time. Earl Warren had won and so had the Hearst newspapers. Not too many years were to pass before Earl Warren was elected Governor of California and later named Chief Justice of the Supreme Court.

After the stock market crash in 1929, few foresaw the economic crisis and the depression which was to follow, I least of all. I had never been so rich. *The Reader's Digest* had paid me three hundred dollars for an article I had written. Just about this time, too, another important event took place in my life.

I had never thought of getting married until I met Dagmar. She was born in the United States but she spoke and read Norwegian fluently. Her auburn hair was shortly cropped and her eyes were hazel, though at times they had a greenish tinge. Her facial features, I thought, were as delicately carved as a cameo. People, no matter how important, seldom impressed her and neither was she interested in social position. She preferred to be a nonconformist and, as a Mexican painter once said of her, *"Ella es muy rebelde,"* she is very much of a rebel.

"But you can't be a newspaperman," she said after we first met. "All newspapermen wear raincoats and you don't wear one."

She loaned me books by Knut Hamsun, Selma Lagerlof and Sigrid Undset. I told her about Jeffers and Steffens and about James Joyce.

Within a few months, Dagmar and I were married and living in a small apartment we had rented in Berkeley. Her father, a Lutheran minister, who had a wonderful red Van

Dyke beard, performed the ceremony and he must have put in an extra prayer for us.

But two weeks later Hearst fired me.

We were young and in love, and we had two hundred and fifty dollars in the bank.

"We are going to Carmel," I said. "I don't know what we'll do, but we'll find something."

The next day with our few possessions and our books in the back of our car, we started out. When we came over the Carmel Hill, the blue water of the sea was as beautiful as I was ever to see it. There was a fragrance of pine trees in the air and of wood fires burning.

We found a room over a candy store. The room was old fashioned with a brass bed, red wallpaper and a light that hung down from a green wire. There was no running water, but there was a wooden stand with wash bowl and pitcher.

"It ain't much of a room," Delos Curtis, who owned the candy store and rooms above it, said. "But it isn't going to cost you much either. Two bucks, the night."

I took Dagmar for a drive around Carmel, pointing out the homes of Steffens and Jeffers. We parked the car on the edge of the water and watched the pounding surf and the sun dropping into the sea. When we drove back, Delos Curtis introduced us to his wife.

"Mama is a fine cook," Delos said. "We serve dinner for fifty cents and you can't beat it."

We had homemade tomato soup with croutons that had been sautéed in butter, and we had baked ham and sweet potatoes with marshmallows. With our coffee we had chocolate cake and then Delos brought us a little bag of lemon drops.

"Take this up to your room," Delos said. "I make all the candies, but my specialty is lemon drops. I make better lemon drops than anyone else. People buy 'em faster than I can make 'em. Sometimes I wonder if it's worthwhile to make 'em at all."

Next morning we found the kind of redwood cottage we wanted. It was hidden away among the pine trees, less than a block from the beach and only a short distance from the home of Lincoln Steffens. Our cottage consisted of a small living room, two small bedrooms, and a kitchen. The living room had a rustic stone fireplace with coils of pipes in the back for heating water. The rent was thirty-five dollars a month.

In the kitchen there was an old kerosene stove. In the morning when we were preparing breakfast I tried to light it, but I couldn't get it going.

"We had a stove like that in the Middle West," Dag said. "Let me try."

She had it working in a moment. The eggs and the coffee tasted of kerosene, but it was our first breakfast in our Carmel home and we didn't mind.

We enjoyed everything about Carmel, including the thick fog that hung on day after day, the dark streets at night, the long white beach, the miles of sand dunes, Gus Englund, the town marshal patroling the streets from atop his horse and every Sunday, we saw Delos Curtis pass by in his truck. In the back of the truck was an overstuffed chair and sitting in it, enjoying her Sunday ride was fat Mrs. Curtis.

One of the first things we did was to visit Lincoln Steffens. He was surprised to learn we had moved to Carmel.

"Most of us have come here to die," he said, "but you have come here to *live*."

Then I told him how I had been fired and that I thought I would now try writing for magazines and perhaps even do a book.

Steffens was not enthusiastic about my plans.

"We are headed for trouble and a depression," he said. "There will be millions out of work. Writing for magazines

is too risky. Most of them will be going broke. You better
find something that will assure you an income, even if it is
a small one. You seem to have a nose for news. Why don't
you do something with it?"

"Like what? We want to stay here."

"There's plenty of news in Carmel and in Monterey and
Salinas. News doesn't just always happen. A good reporter
sometimes creates news. He makes things happen. Carmel
is the kind of a place where you can *make* news. Be a correspondent to a bunch of newspapers. Sell them news by
the inch. You might not make much, but at least it will keep
you both eating."

I wrote to the United Press, the Associated Press, the International News Service, and to the newspapers in San
Francisco and in Oakland. Before too long I became known
as a "stringer," providing the wire services and the newspapers with news. They paid space rates on what they used
and the more they published, the more money I made.

Because I was the only stringer in the area, I literally
cornered the news. Nothing happened in Carmel or in Monterey which I did not report. If nothing happened, I tried to
make it happen. The most commonplace story given the right
twist, would usually make news. I soon learned the knack
of doing this and sensed what editors wanted.

My method of working was simple. Once I had a story, I
gave it to one of the wire services. Then the other wire
services would query me as to this story and could I furnish
additional facts. I would in turn wire the complete story
padding it with three or four more paragraphs. Then I would
send in the story to the newspapers I represented but with a
slightly different angle. At the end of the month I got a
series of small checks, seldom over twenty dollars each. It
gave us a living.

Because Carmel was considered an artists' colony, almost
anything that I reported seemed to make news. The more

unusual, bizarre or whacky were the stories, the more they were played up by the newspapers. Editors were looking for stories on the light side, to balance the bad news coming from about everywhere else.

I tried not to disappoint these editors and soon readers across the country were reading about Perry Newberry, the detective story writer, pleading before the city council for a pine tree that had been condemned; they read about John Catlin, the blacksmith mayor who wanted to put in pink-colored sidewalks on the main streets; and about Joe Roscelli, the garbage man who refused to collect the town's garbage while he attended the opera in San Francisco.

Joe Roscelli was no ordinary garbage man. He was a philanthropist and a guardian angel, all wrapped into one. His home in Seaside was modest, but he had about ten acres of land and on it he raised chickens, vegetables, and fruit. He sold little of it; most of it he gave away.

Several days before Thanksgiving Joe Roscelli filled his truck with cartons containing freshly-killed chickens, vegetables, eggs, and fruit and these he distributed to people he knew were having a bad time.

John Catlin said there was omniscience to Roscelli, and this was true. He seemed to know everything about everybody. Once, when my wife was ill, he arrived with an armful of flowers from his garden. Joe never appeared in a hurry and from time to time he would visit with us in the kitchen, talking mostly about music and, once in a while, about himself. He often brought a gift; one day it might be a freshly caught salmon, or a gallon of red wine, or some homemade salami.

Joe had a soft voice and he spoke slowly. Unlike most Italians he rarely gestured with his hands, though he had a habit of taking off and putting on his hat every few moments. It was an old gray felt hat and he was never without it.

"I do nothing," Joe would say when questioned about his

philanthropy. "Now is bad times and in bad times some people need more help than others."

Selling news by the inch was not easy at first; there were stories around, but they had to be unearthed and the right twist given them to create sufficient interest. I did not limit myself to Carmel; my news beat included nearby Monterey, Pacific Grove and then Salinas, some twenty miles away. Each morning I would check with the police departments of these communities and the sheriff's office for possible stories. Carmel, however, remained the best source of news.

Every Wednesday evening while Dag waited for me at Delos Curtis' candy store, drinking hot chocolate, I covered the city council meetings. There were almost always arguments over the smallest issues at these meetings and they generally made news because it was Carmel and I was there to report it. When the council session was over, I would join my wife at Delos' and we would walk home through the darkened streets, using a flashlight to keep from tripping over tree roots. Except for the main street, there were no lights or sidewalks and almost everyone who went out evenings carried a flashlight.

Occasionally a big story did break in either Monterey or Pacific Grove. One afternoon we came in from the beach just as the telephone was ringing. It was Fred Moore, the police chief in Monterey.

"Better get over here," he said. "We got a hot one for you."

"What is it?" I asked, for we were in our wet bathing suits.

"A woman shot her lover and she, in turn, shot herself. He's a doctor and she's a society woman."

We dressed hurriedly and within minutes, Dag and I were in Monterey. Fred Moore was right; it was a big story. Both the doctor and the woman were prominent and for over a year they had been coming to Monterey together, spending a night each week in a cheap hotel on a side street. They had made a suicide pact; she was to shoot her lover and then herself. Dag stayed in the car while I went to the hotel room.

The bodies were on the floor and there were several police officers and a deputy from the sheriff's office waiting for the coroner. As the coroner came in, I saw that Dag had walked in behind him. The officers knew her and didn't stop her as she wandered around the room. She looked down at the corpses and then went over to the writing desk. I watched her as she picked up a small black book and glanced through it. I went over to where she was standing.

"It's very messy here," I said. "Why didn't you stay in the car?"

"I wanted to see what the man looked like for whom a woman would give up everything."

"Are you satisfied?"

"Sort of," she said.

"What's the book you picked up?"

"I think it's her diary," she said.

I went through it quickly.

"Let's get out of here," I said.

We went to the car and made notes as fast as we could from the diary. The entire story of the woman meeting the doctor, their trips to Monterey and the final entry, the suicide pact, was all written. I went back to the hotel and returned the book to the desk. There was so much confusion in the room that no one was aware of what we had done.

We started for Carmel where we put together our notes and telephoned in the story.

"You're a good reporter," I said to Dag. "Those entries in the diary will get us a lot of space in the papers. How did you happen to suspect she had a diary?"

"Just a hunch," she said. "I've read that women who have love affairs always keep diaries."

Next morning when the papers carried the story on the

front pages, and the entries from the diary, Fred Moore, the police chief phoned me. He was fuming.

"How did you get that diary?" he wanted to know. "We never released it to anyone."

I didn't tell him and he never found out.

When we first came to Carmel, Edward Weston was already recognized as one of the country's great photographers. His portraits and his still lifes of rocks, driftwood, and of sand dunes were in museum exhibits and winning top awards.

After we met Weston he invited us to his studio and later he agreed to give me lessons in photography. I often went on field trips with him and found that by just watching him work, I learned more about photography than I had ever known.

Weston had little patience for photographers with expensive cameras and special lenses. In fact most of Weston's best work was done with either an old Graflex, or a cardboard box with a tiny pinhole as a lens.

"People with expensive camera equipment are gadget fiends," he said during one of our first sessions. "They belong to a cult that believes in taking dozens of pictures, hoping that one may turn out good. Fine photography is a creative art and you think out your shots and how you are going to take them, long in advance. I think about a photograph I am going to make for weeks, and have it clearly in my mind. Shooting a picture is the easiest and final stage."

Weston taught me to take portraits outdoors in the bright sunlight and with the aperture of the shutter closed down as far as possible.

"There's no substitute for outdoor light," he maintained, "and you always want to strive for depth and detail. Remember that the camera does not take pictures—*you* are taking the picture. A painter must have brushes, paint and

a canvas. A photographer must use his camera the same way
—only as a medium for his art."

I did as Weston told me and the portraits I began taking
had a dramatic and professional appearance. I was so pleased
that for a time I thought I might do better financially as a
photographer than selling news by the inch. But the Depression was now at its worst and no one had money for photographs, or for that matter, for paying medical bills or funerals.

"You might not believe it," Mr. Freeman, the undertaker in
Monterey said when I talked to him about having his portrait
taken, "but the Depression has hit me just as bad as anyone.
People aren't dying. They can't afford to die—so they just
hold on. When things get better, I'll have plenty to do. Then
maybe we can talk about your making a picture of me."

Finally I did get an order to take a portrait of Sinclair
Lewis, who was staying at Hotel Del Monte and working on
a new book. When I showed him the prints, he paid me but
he didn't like them.

"I'm ugly," he said, "but not that ugly."

Edward Weston, however, thought they were good pictures.

"Why you have wonderful detail in those marks on his
face," he said. "I couldn't have done any better."

I went on to take pictures of Robinson Jeffers, Jo Davidson
the sculptor, and Gertrude Stein.

"I look just as I thought I would look," Gertrude Stein said
when she saw the photographs I had taken of her.

CHAPTER FOUR

Not a Nudist in Sight

Long before there were automobiles and super highways, the Monterey Peninsula, hidden away along a rugged coastline one hundred and twenty-five miles south of San Francisco, had been discovered. The Spanish padres, making the rounds of the missions at Carmel and Monterey, came by foot or muleback and later by stagecoach. Robert Louis Stevenson arrived by stagecoach and stayed in Monterey for almost a year.

Old Mr. Berwick who was over eighty when we knew him, remembered Stevenson well.

"He looked like a tramp and when he knocked at our door and asked for a place to sleep, we found room for him in the hayloft of our barn," Mr. Berwick recalled.

Stevenson was probably the first in the group of writers, artists and musicians who were drawn by the beauty of the Monterey Peninsula. Some went to live in Monterey, a few chose Pacific Grove, but the majority preferred the easygoing life of Carmel.

Each section of the peninsula developed an identity of its own. Monterey had its Italian and Portuguese fishermen and the canneries which, on a warm summer day, sent out pungent fish odors in all directions. Pacific Grove, adjoining Monterey, had started out as a religious community and continued to remain conservative and churchy. Carmel was called an artists' colony, but it was also a place for retired people and little old ladies who gave it an air of respectability. There was no jail in Carmel and Gus Englund, in his khaki police uniform and atop his horse, kept law and order.

"By Gott," Gus would say with his Swedish accent, "no one's going to violate the law vile I am here." And he would chase away anyone who wandered up the main street in a bathing suit. Yet he didn't seem to care what went on inside the rustic redwood cottages among the pines. "That is their business," he maintained, and he felt that way about the Los Angeles evangelist, Aimee Semple McPherson, who for a week remained secluded in a cottage with her lover while thousands of her parishioners prayed for her reappearance after she had mysteriously vanished.

In addition to the three towns, there was also Seaside where some of the fishermen and the cannery workers lived. Then there was Pebble Beach, with its golf course and the homes of wealthy people built along the 17 Mile Drive, and Canary Cottage, where there were roulette and crap tables catering to a small group, who somehow, despite the Depression, still had money. Finally there was Hotel Del Monte, famous as a fashionable resort area where people came from all over the world to spend a night, a week, or a month.

Carmel, of course, attracted the strangest of all characters, and in time took on a Left Bank atmosphere. There was no Le Sélect Bar, but there was Whitneys' where you could get a big milk shake for ten cents, and the Carmel post office where everyone met as they went to get their mail.

John Catlin was a prominent attorney when he first came to Carmel. A few months later when he returned, he had abandoned his law practice and opened a blacksmith shop— the Forge in the Forest, he called it. He ran for the city council, and eventually, became the blacksmith mayor. There was William P. Silva, who at the age of fifty had sold his hardware store in the southeast and had gone to Paris to study art. He also came to Carmel, started his own art gallery and sold more paintings than any of the other artists.

In the Carmel Highlands, Harry Leon Wilson turned out such best sellers as *Ruggles of Red Gap*, and *Merton of the Movies*. Then, there were Steffens and Jeffers and many others, including Stephen Allen Reynolds, who wrote adventure stories for what were then known as the pulp magazines.

We first heard about Steve from Nelson Valjean, a reporter on the Salinas paper, who came to Carmel almost about every weekend, usually to visit Steve.

"You have to know Steve and his wife," Val told me one day in the sheriff's office in Salinas. "He writes for a living, but he also makes money in other ways. He has an ingenious mind and a great imagination."

At one time, Val said, Steve had agreed to promote a restaurant in Carmel that wasn't doing well.

"Steve thought of all kinds of ideas and, sure enough, the restaurant had all the business it could handle," Val said. "They couldn't come to terms on paying Steve for his work; perhaps Steve asked too much. Anyway, they had a fight. And guess what happened? Steve began bringing in as his guests smelly fishermen from Monterey to the restaurant for dinner. In less than a week, the restaurant called it quits and paid off Steve."

"He must be quite a character," I said.

"He is that," Val agreed. "He is also the most interesting person I've ever known. I'll be in Carmel this weekend, and if you want I'll take you and Dag to meet Steve and Jean. I'll have to clear with him first. He doesn't care for strangers, but you ought to hit it off fine with him."

"All right, just let us know," I said.

"Oh, one more thing," Val said. "Steve is in his sixties and Jean—isn't even thirty, if she's that old."

On the following Sunday, Val passed by the house.

"I saw Steve and Jean last night," he said. "They want to meet you. We'll go there this afternoon after lunch."

Around three o'clock we started for Steve's cottage. We drove through the woods and over a narrow, bumpy street in an isolated part of town until we came to a small redwood cottage covered with brilliant cerise bougainvillea vines. As we left the car and walked down the path to Steve's house we heard loud, angry shouting followed by the crash of broken glass. Val appeared uneasy.

"They must be fighting," he muttered.

The door to the cottage was open and as we peered in, we saw an old man on the floor, his shoulders against the wall. He seemed unconscious and blood was trickling from his forehead. Near him a young woman, whom we assumed to be Jean, was holding a bottle in her hand and yelling: "Get up, you bastard! Get up!"

Val pulled us back. "We better leave," he said. "We've come to see them at the wrong time."

We thought so, too.

As we climbed back into the car and drove away, Val tried to apologize for them. "Whenever they drink, they usually end up fighting," he said. "But it's not often that it happens. I'm sorry you had to see them that way. They'll be all right, next time we call on them."

We were in no hurry to meet Steve and Jean and it must have been a month later that, on Val's insistence, we made a second attempt to visit them. This time they were sober and as Steve and Jean greeted us, they were friendly and relaxed.

"Come in, by all means, come in," Steve said and led us into the living room.

Steve was now well groomed, his thinning white hair combed back and the ends of his mustache carefully waxed. He was wall-eyed and he wore gold-rimmed glasses with thick lenses. He did not look at one—he stared. There was an ugliness to Steve, and yet at the same time he had an air of dignity to him. One wondered what Jean saw in this old man, for she was young and attractive. She was thin with well shaped features and her hair was a light brown worn in a chignon.

"The place is a mess," she said and her voice was soft and rhythmic. "You just can't keep up a house when you have two airedales around."

The dogs were by her side and she put an arm around each one. "This is Pooch and this is Rummy," she said.

"They're old and as decrepit as I am," Steve added and then invited us to sit while he took his favorite chair in a corner. He kept on staring at us from behind his thick lenses.

The cottage was simply furnished, but done in good taste. There was a fireplace in the center and the walls were covered with shelves of books. On the floor were expensive Persian rugs that somehow did not belong in a redwood cottage and of course, they didn't. Steve had obtained them through one of his devious methods with which we were to familiarize ourselves later as we got to know him better. Steve never paid for anything, if he could help it.

Dag maintained throughout the period we knew Steve that he had a warped mind, and possibly he had. Nevertheless, there was a streak of brilliancy in Steve and as a writer, he was an excellent craftsman. He sold virtually every story he ever wrote. The trouble with Steve was that he did not allow his writing to interfere with his drinking. He wrote only when it became absolutely necessary to take care of his mounting debts.

One never knew when Steve lied or told the truth. Most of the time he lived in a world of fantasy fed by an inexhaustible imagination. Once he told us he sold short story plots to Sinclair Lewis and other writers, and naturally we did not believe him. When I happened to mention this to Lewis, he admitted that it was true. "I did buy several plots from him," he said, "and I paid him well for them. As a human being, Steve is no good, but he certainly can come up with the ideas."

At one time, Steve and Jean left Carmel for a year and told everyone they knew that they were going around the world. Every so often their friends received postal cards from Steve and Jean from Singapore, Cairo, Shanghai, Berlin, Paris, Rio de Janiero and other parts. While their friends received these cards, Steve and Jean were living in a dingy hotel room in New York. Steve had arranged with a sailor he knew, who was traveling on an around-the-world ship, to mail out the cards.

Yet when Steve wrote about a foreign country, he had so thoroughly researched it, that he knew as much about it as if he had lived and spent years there. He was a detailist, working everything out in his mind, before acting on it. He could be delightfully charming, amusing, and entertaining, then there was that perverse side to him that made him vicious, vulgar, and diabolical.

The first afternoon when we met him he was on his best behavior; he was kind and affectionate toward Jean and he went out of his way to be pleasant to us. We forgot the bad things we had heard about him and, as we fell under the spell he wove, we found ourselves liking Steve and especially Jean. He was a born storyteller, and the hours quickly passed and soon it was dark outside. He and Jean invited us for dinner and it was nearly midnight when we left.

"He's no good," Dag said, "but at least he's not dull or boring." It was that side of him, we decided, that intrigued Jean and kept her from leaving him when he was drunk and objectionable.

During the next few months we saw them many times. Steve was a gourmet and a fine cook and he taught us about French sauces and the differences between ordinary cooking and *haute cuisine*. He gave us recipes and loaned us books. When he was drunk and troublesome, we left him alone and while we worried about Jean, we also felt she could take care of herself.

We were enjoying ourselves in Carmel visiting with Jeffers, Steffens and Steve, and occasionally we drove up to the highlands to spend an evening with Harry Leon Wilson. During the day I made the rounds, trying to dig up news, but it was Steve and that fertile imagination of his that most often gave me ideas for stories.

Steffens, in the beginning, had said to dramatize and create news. "Be like Hearst," he had said. "Invent news when necessary and get excited about it."

There were days when nothing happened in Carmel, Monterey, Pacific Grove or Salinas, and I had little to write about. Yet I always knew that if I'd go over to visit Steve and he was in the right mood, he would come up with something that would make a story. It would delight Steve to see these stories in print and it would amuse him, if he could start a controversy through a story I had sent to the papers. He liked best of all to spoof and poke fun at Carmel.

One afternoon Steve telephoned me. "You want to be sure to attend tonight's meeting of the Carmel city council," he said.

"What's going on?" I asked.

"I don't know," Steve said, for he enjoyed being mysterious, "but there might be a front-page story."

I tried to question him further and I even checked with various members of the city council and Saidee van Brower, the city clerk, but they did not know of anything unusual that was coming up. That evening at the council meeting they only went over routine matters, none of which could possibly make news. The session was almost over and I was getting ready to leave when John Catlin, the mayor, asked if there was any other matter up for action.

It was then that Saidee van Brower spoke up: "Just before the start of the meeting," she said, "I was handed a letter by a messenger that should perhaps be read." She handed the communication to John Catlin. He glanced at it, looked around at the small group attending the meeting and then at the members of the city council.

"I suppose I better read it," he said, and then looked at it again. "It is addressed to the council and it comes from a Madame Mathilde Baumgardner, president of the Society of the Sun—whatever that might be."

Then he read the following letter:

Society of the Sun
P.O. Box 345
Carmel, California,

To the Carmel City Council
Gentlemen:

We are followers and worshippers of the Sun. We believe that only the Sun provides the necessary health-giving qualities that everyone requires. We believe that God never intended human beings to wear clothes.

While we are not a religious sect, we are clean in mind, body and spirit. As the ancient Aztecs worshipped the Sun so do the members of our society.

For some time now, we have been living in a home located just outside the city limits of Carmel. It has only a small garden, but has a nice, high wall where, from morning to evening, we work and live in the Sun. As our membership has grown, the house and garden have proved inadequate.

We have been fortunate, however, in locating a home that will suit our needs and which has a large patio and also a high wall. It is located within the city limits of Carmel. We are ready to sign a lease, but we have been advised that before we proceed any further, we should seek the Council's permission so that the police and other authorities will not disturb us.

While we are worshippers of the Sun and believe that health and clean living come only from nudism, we are people of high morals who wish to be left alone. We know that Carmel is a sophisticated community where the rights of the individual and of groups such as ours are respected.

We, therefore, request approval to move within the city limits of Carmel so that we may sign the lease that is before us.

> Respectfully,
> Madame Mathilde Baumgardner,
> President, Chapter Ten of the
> Society of the Sun

For a moment after John Catlin finished reading no one said a word. Then one of the councilmen spoke up: "We can't permit nudists in Carmel! Society of the Sun—they call themselves—but they are nudists, nothing but nudists!"

Clara Kellogg, a spinster in her sixties and a long-time member of the city council, quite unexpectedly came to the defense of the Society of the Sun.

"What is wrong with nudism?" she wanted to know. "Since when have we set up ourselves to judge what other people should wear or not wear? I hope we have not become a narrow-minded community. By all means, grant them permission."

Long and heated arguments followed, one group in favor of granting the request, and another opposing it. Finally it was decided to postpone action until the next meeting of the city council.

I had my story, though I did not realize how big it was to become even after I had telephoned it in to the wire services and the newspapers. By the time I was home, the wire services and the newspapers were on the phone again. They wanted more details—everything I could give them. What kind of a reporter was I, anyway? Why wasn't I aware of the existence of a nudist colony in Carmel? Find the location. Get an interview with Madame Baumgardner. Get interviews from other members of the colony. Try for photographs.

"You're on a big story," one of the city editors said to me. "Get on it!"

I couldn't give them any more information than I had and I could not tell them what I suspected.

"Steve's behind this whole thing," I said to Dag. "He's dreamed it up and he must have even had that stationery printed on which the letter to the city council was written."

"Of course this is Steve's doing," she agreed.

We didn't get much sleep. At six o'clock in the morning the telephone began ringing. Once again it was the wire services and the newspapers. When was I going to get them more facts about the nudist colony? What about the interview with Madame Baumgardner?

I went uptown and got the morning newspapers that were just in from San Francisco. They had eight-column streamers on the front pages. NUDIST COLONY IN CARMEL, one of the headlines read.

While I was convinced Steve had all the answers, I purposely kept away from him. Instead I began working on the premise that the colony did exist and that Madame Baumgardner was a real person. I also knew that the more information I gathered and telephoned in, the bigger my checks for that month would be. So, I interviewed Mayor Catlin, Gus Englund, and a number of real estate agents. Next day their comments on the nudist colony were on the front pages.

The newspapers and the wire services were impatient and becoming more demanding. Why couldn't I locate the nudist colony? Where was the interview with Madame Baumgardner? Didn't I realize, they asked, that this story was being played all over the country? If I couldn't get the information they wanted, they would have to send reporters who could get the story I was missing.

"Send them down," I said. "I am doing the best I can."

The next telephone call was from New York. The stately New York *Times* said: "If you do talk with Madame Baumgardner, call us collect by all means, and say 'hello' to her from those of us who are sun worshippers."

The story broke Thursday morning and on Saturday and Sunday, thousands of curiosity seekers invaded Carmel looking for the nudist colony. The only building with a high wall outside the city limits was the Carmel Hospital. Everyone seemed to be convinced that behind those walls, they would find the nudists. In desperation, the Carmel Hospital had to ask the sheriff's office for special protection to keep out the intruding hordes of people.

The United Press was so intrigued by the story that Frank Bartholomew, its West Coast vice-president, came to interview Madame Baumgardner. But he had no more luck than did Stan Delaplane and other reporters who came to Carmel in search of the Society of the Sun.

On Monday evening we drove to Steve's cottage. He and Jean were just finishing dinner.

"You started this, Steve," I said, "and you've got to finish it fast, or you are going to be in trouble."

Steve looked at us from behind his thick lenses and he appeared quite serious.

"If I were not an honest man," he said, "I could make a lot of money." Then he pointed to the table in the living room. On it were hundreds of letters from people from all parts of the country, either asking to join the Society of the Sun or seeking information about it.

Steve had obtained a post office box under the name of the Society of the Sun and from the time the story broke, every night he went to the post office and picked up the letters addressed to the Society of the Sun or to Madame Baumgardner.

"We could charge from ten to twenty-five dollars to join the society," Steve said. "Almost everyone who writes in wants to become a member."

"You can't keep it up," I said. "You're going to be found out."

"You could also end up in jail," Dag protested. "You have to stop it, Steve. You have to find a way out."

Steve was enjoying it, but he also knew that the story was getting out of hand.

"Leave it to me," he finally said. "I'll take care of it."

On Wednesday when the city council held its weekly meeting it received another communication, printed on Society of the Sun stationery. The letter read:

Society of the Sun
P.O. Box 345
Carmel, California

To the Carmel City Council
Gentlemen:

For a long time we have looked forward to living quietly and unmolested and worshipping the Sun. We believed that in coming to Carmel we would be left undisturbed. Instead, we have been held up to ridicule and we have received such notoriety that we can no longer remain in this area.

It is with deep regret that we find it necessary to leave immediately and to go somewhere else where we shall be treated with respect and understanding. By the time this letter reaches you, we shall already be on our way. It has become a most unpleasant experience for us. We know that in some other location, we shall find the freedom and the peace we seek to worship the Sun.

Yours very truly,
Madame Mathilda Baumgardner

Once more, the Society of the Sun was on the front pages, as the newspapers reported that Madame Baumgardner and her followers had fled from Carmel and were searching elsewhere for refuge. For several months after that, reports appeared in the newspapers that the Society of the Sun, late of Carmel, California, had located its headquarters in Sante Fe and in Taos, New Mexico; in Tucson, Arizona; in Palm Springs, California; and Lake Chapala, Mexico.

The Society of the Sun, like flying discs from outer space, existed only in the imaginations of people and especially within the walls of the cranium of Steve Reynolds.

Lincoln Steffens watched the goings on of the Society of the Sun with great interest.

"You see," he said, "there are stories everywhere, but you have to either create or search for them. People do not want realism—they want fantasy. At night we sleep; it is in the daytime that we dream. We dream that there never will be wars again and that the right person in the White House will look after us. We know this isn't true, but we want to believe it is so. A little spoofing is good for us. We have been spoofing each other since the world began."

CHAPTER FIVE

The Saga of an Old Horse
and an Old Soldier

Lincoln Steffens had long ago finished his autobiography and now that he had more time, I saw him working almost every afternoon in his garden. Sometimes I would stop and chat and on other occasions, he asked me in. I valued his friendship and the advice he gave me.

On this particular afternoon when he saw me, he motioned me to come in. I went through the little wooden gate and Steffie put down his trowel.

"I have something to show you," he said and I followed him into his study. He had a stack of books on his desk.

"The book is finally out," he said and he handed me his two volume autobiography. There was a photograph of him on the jacket by Edward Weston. I glanced through the first volume and the chapter headings, and then I read the publisher's comment on the flyleaf of the jacket: "The remarkable feature of Steffens' autobiography is that, though he takes one to the bottom of the world and records one disillusionment after another, the author comes out at the top an optimist."

"I never thought you were an optimist," I said.

"But I am," he replied, "And so are the publishers getting out a two-volume edition to sell for seven dollars and fifty cents in the midst of a Depression—isn't that optimism?

Who's going to buy it? Who will want to read about Lincoln Steffens? I am a nobody—a has been."

He sat down at his desk, opened the first volume and in his small, precise handwriting, he wrote in my name and then added: "to my colleague and neighbor."

No newspaper reporter at the age of twenty could have received a greater compliment than to be called "a colleague" by one of the greatest reporters of the century.

"Here is your copy," he said. Shortly afterwards I left, proudly carrying the two-volume edition under my arm.

Steffens was wrong. Despite the Depression and the seven-fifty price, the two-volume edition soon was a bestseller. Steffie was not forgotten. At the age of sixty-five, Lincoln Steffens became better known, more famous than he had ever been.

He enjoyed his sudden fame and it also amused him.

"Remember the big debate," he chuckled. "No one was interested in hearing what I had to say. Now everyone wants me to lecture and to give my views on any subject."

Steffens turned down all offers, preferring to work in his garden and to visit with old friends as they passed through. Only he and his doctor knew that his stout heart was giving out.

No two persons could be as different from each other as Lincoln Steffens and Steve Reynolds. Steffens was wise, kind and worldly; Steve was mischievous, perverse, and cunning. Yet, they respected one another; both, too, had a definite influence on my life. Steve was capable of great charm, the bewitching charm of a bunko artist.

Steve enjoyed matching wits and then seeing how far he could go and how much he could get away with. For a long time he had a running feud with the utility company. He had discovered a way to jam the electric meter and keep it from registering beyond a certain point; the utility company tried to catch him, but never did. He had the mind of a fine chess player and he could map out the strategy of moves far ahead. He plotted his stories and developed his characters so thoroughly that, when he sat down at the typewriter, he seldom had to change a line or a word. He followed a similar pattern in everything else he did; there was nothing impulsive about Steve. He thought it all out first before he acted. When he wanted to, he could be so convincing, he could disarm almost anyone.

Steve had been in the Spanish American War and each month he received a disabled veteran's check. No matter how many bills he had, or who was dunning him, he always used this check in paying off his butcher and his grocer and with them he had unlimited credit. Once when he invited Sinclair Lewis, who was staying at Hotel Del Monte, for cocktails at his cottage, Steve found himself without liquor and money. But this did not stop him—he went to his grocer, bought thirty quarts of milk on credit and then he made the rounds of his neighbors and gave them the milk free as long as they had containers into which it could be poured. When the milk bottles were empty, he returned to the grocer, obtained in cash the deposit on the empties and, with this money, bought the liquor he needed to entertain Sinclair Lewis.

Steve thoroughly enjoyed doing warped things of this kind; somehow it satisfied his ego. His agile mind was always working, planning and scheming. We never met anyone like Steve before or since, which is probably just as well.

At that time, and as a young reporter, I could not have found a more resourceful person than Steve to assist me in the manufacturing of news. Steve knew how to make news and big news. If he used and manipulated me, it was done openly and above board; I accepted and went along with his ideas. It was Dag, conservative and a balancing wheel in the erratic and precarious way we were making a living, who feared we would eventually get into trouble because of Steve.

She and Jean became good friends, but she was always wary of Steve.

"It is not beyond him," she used to say, "to put a skunk in our house if we do something he doesn't like."

Steve was usually amusing and entertaining but when we would go with him and Jean, we were never sure what might happen or what he had in mind. Often he and Jean would stop by the house and we would go shopping together in Monterey or in Pacific Grove, or we would go to Dr. Underwood's, the veterinarian. Steve was very fond of his two airedales, Pooch and Rummy, and every month he would take them to Dr. Underwood's to have them sheared and groomed.

One afternoon, when they came to pick us up, Steve had the airedales in the car and said he would leave them at the veterinarian's. We drove over the Carmel Hill and we stayed in the car while Steve took in the two dogs. He was gone for a long time and when he returned he seemed preoccupied. He climbed into the front seat and lit a cigarette. "Doc Underwood has to operate on a horse and get this," he said, "the only operating table available is at the Monterey Presidio and those bureaucrats won't let him use it because it's a civilian horse." Steve turned on the ignition and started driving, the cigarette hanging from the corner of his mouth. "It would be a damn shame to let that horse die just on account of red tape," he went on. "There must be a way to help Doc Underwood and that horse."

We drove on to Pacific Grove where Jean and Dag did some shopping. By the time they returned, Steve already had thought of a plan to save the life of the aging horse and he now proceeded to tell us about it.

"That horse Doc Underwood has for a patient is no ordinary horse," Steve pointed out. "His name is Flying Cloud and he ran at the leading race tracks in the country until he got too old. Then they sold him and put him out to pasture in Carmel Valley. He's got a tumor, Doc Underwood says and unless he gets operated on he's going to die. We need some fast action and I think I know how to get it. We'll talk about it when we get back to the house."

When we reached Steve's cottage, he poured us a drink and then he took out a pad and began writing. After a short time, he said, "The only way to get action is to appeal directly to the White House. Here's a telegram which I thought we might send." He read aloud:

"FLYING CLOUD THE FAMOUS RACE HORSE WHO HAS RACED AT BENNINGTON TRACK WITHIN A FEW MILES OF THE NATION'S CAPITOL IS ABOUT TO DIE HERE IN MONTEREY BECAUSE GOVERNMENT RED TAPE WILL NOT PERMIT THE USE OF THE ONLY OPERATING TABLE AVAILABLE AT THE MONTEREY PRESIDIO. IN THE NAME OF HUMAN KINDNESS TO ANIMALS WE URGENTLY ASK YOU TO INSTRUCT THE SECRETARY OF WAR TO INTERCEDE TO SAVE THE LIFE OF FLYING CLOUD."

"Are you really serious Steve," I broke in, "about sending that telegram to the White House?"

Jean and Dag were silent. They wanted no part of it.

"Of course I am," he said. "Why not send it to the President? That's the way to get action."

"But who's going to sign the telegram, Steve?"

"That's what we have to consider," he said and poured us another drink.

"John Catlin, the mayor, probably wouldn't mind signing it," I said.

"But we need more names than Catlin—important names."

"How about Steffens?" I said, by now carried away by the drinks and by Steve's enthusiasm. "Then there's Jeffers, Weston and Harry Leon Wilson. They won't object if it would save the life of a horse—or would they? I could go and ask them, but that would take too long and a lot of explaining. No," I added after further thought, "let's use their names."

While Jean and Dag prepared dinner, Steve and I drove downtown and gave Western Union the telegram. I didn't think Steve's idea would work and I was asleep early the following morning when the telephone rang. It was John Catlin, the mayor.

"Hey, what's all this about Flying Cloud?" he was shouting into the telephone. "I suppose you're back of it. You better fill me in. Just got a call from the Monterey Presidio. They have orders from the Secretary of War to put every facility at the disposal of Flying Cloud. What's this Flying Cloud business? If you're in on this—you better get over here."

"Who's that on the phone?" Dag asked.

"Oh, it's nothing," I yawned and stretched. "Only the White House wants to save Flying Cloud."

While Steve went to the Monterey Presidio, I phoned the wire services and the newspapers. The story of how the War Department had cut red tape and had interceded to save the life of Flying Cloud was soon in the headlines and on the front pages. As the story gained momentum, the newspapers and the wire services kept telephoning. When was the operation to be performed? What was the condition of Flying Cloud? When would it be known if the operation was successful? Did Flying Cloud have a chance?

I remained by the phone waiting for Steve to call. At three o'clock I received a report from Steve.

"I'm just out of the operating room," he said. "Flying Cloud is doing fine. He's a brave, wonderful horse. They removed a tumor as big as a football."

"What does Doc Underwood say? Is he going to live?"

"Of course, Flying Cloud's going to live. But why don't you put some suspense into it? Say that his life is hanging on a thread and not until sometime tomorrow will his fate be known. Tell the papers the operation took more than two hours and that everyone at the Presidio did everything possible to help Flying Cloud."

Flying Cloud recovered fully and remained in the limelight for a few more days. Then he was brought back to Betty Green's stables where he eventually assumed his former place as a dollar-an-hour riding horse. Betty began calling him Flying Cloud, but he always responded better to Jupiter, which had been his true name before he was befriended by Steve.

Steve saved the life of Flying Cloud, but he was having trouble saving his marriage. The periods when he was sober were brief and fewer. He was drunk more often now, and disgustingly so, picking at Jean and quarreling with her. She, in turn, and perhaps in self-defense, was also drinking and it seemed that every time we went to their cottage they were fighting and throwing everything that was movable at each other.

One afternoon Jean came to our house. Her hair was disarranged, she had a black eye and her arms and shoulders were cut and bruised. There was a beaten, defeated look to her face.

"I've had it!" she cried out. "I'm finished with him. I can't take it any longer. He'll either kill me or I'll kill him."

Dag tried to quiet her and after awhile, Jean began to talk. She said she was leaving Steve and going to her brother's home in Washington, D.C.

"And I need your help," she added.

She wanted us to go to the cottage, distract Steve and keep him occupied while she would sneak in through the back door, pack a suitcase with her clothes and take a train that night for the east.

It turned out to be easier than we had thought. Steve was still drunk when we arrived at his cottage and he was sitting in his chair in a daze.

"Where ish she?" he muttered more to himself than to us. I went into the kitchen and poured out a drink and brought it to him. He finished the drink and then he was out cold. Jean was already in the house and in the bedroom and we could hear her packing. Dag went in to help her, while I kept guard, fearful that at any moment he might come out of his drunken stupor.

It took Jean less than fifteen minutes to get her things together. As she came out of the bedroom Jean gave Steve one last glance and then she embraced the two airedales and kissed them.

Once we were out of the cottage, I closed the door softly and followed Jean and Dag to the car. We drove over the Carmel Hill to Monterey and then on to Salinas where we put Jean on the train.

Steve must have stayed drunk for days. And at least a week passed before we saw him again. He was sober then, well-groomed and on his best behavior. He also wanted sympathy. He said that Jean had left him, "and with not even a line of where she has gone."

"I'm a lonely old man," he added. "Where am I going to find someone like Jean again?"

For more than an hour he kept on talking about Jean and the many things he had done for her and how much she had meant to him.

"I guess she's gone for good," he said, shaking his head.

I almost felt sorry for Steve as I walked out to the car with him. The two airedales were in the front seat. He climbed into the car next to them and started off.

Steve passed by our house almost every other day during the next few weeks. He always asked if we had heard from Jean, for he was convinced that eventually she would write to us. We did get a brief note from her thanking us for our help, but we never told him.

Steve was not drinking, and for a change he was writing, primarily because he needed money. When I saw him again it was in the post office. He looked much better now that he was on the wagon and he said that he had written three stories and had sent them off.

A week later, very pleased and satisfied with himself, he dropped by the house. He wanted us to go out and have dinner at Del Monte Lodge in Pebble Beach.

"Two of the stories sold," he said, "and I think I have a take on the third. Merely need to make some changes on it."

Prohibition was over and drinks were available at the Lodge, but Steve ordered only tomato juice for himself while we had martinis.

"That stuff was killing me," he said. "I'm never going to drink again."

Steve was in a good mood and he kept us amused throughout the evening. When we were finished with dinner and the coffee was served, Steve ordered an expensive cigar for himself and brandy for us. As he lit his cigar, he said: "I finally located Jean. She's with her brother in Washington."

We said nothing.

"She's not coming back," he went on. "But I have to have someone to look after me, to take care of the house and type my stories." He reached into his pocket and brought out a piece of paper. "I am running this advertisement in the want ad section of the San Francisco papers." Then he read:

"Aging writer with failing eyesight needs young secretary to help him with his manuscripts as well as with light household duties. Small salary and will teach applicant how to write fiction."

"You're really running that ad, Steve?" Dag asked.

"I thought I'd try it," he said. "I'll probably get some answers and perhaps I might find one who might do."

Steve must have mulled over that advertisement for days before writing it. He also must have weighed each word for

impact and effectiveness. Steve was no fool; he knew how
to arouse interest. But he did not (nor did we) imagine the
response that would come from this small, unassuming want
ad. The clincher, of course, was the line about teaching the
applicant how to write fiction. Everybody wants to write and
it seemed that every young girl in or around San Francisco
wanted to work for Steve.

By the end of the fourth day, Steve had between three
and four hundred replies. Some were graduates from Vassar
or Wellesley; others from Stanford and the University of
California. There were secretaries that were employed in
banks, in wholesale houses, in the oil companies—they all
wrote to Steve, fascinated by the thought of living in Carmel and working for a writer.

Steve was so pleased with himself that he telephoned us
to come and look over the letters. We couldn't resist going,
and we found him sitting in the kitchen with the letters
carefully sorted and stacked up high on the table.

"I like this one," he would say and he would read parts
of it then he would go to another. "Now, this one might be
just right, but her name is June. I never cared for the name
June. But listen to what she says." In that soft drawl of his,
he would read excerpts from it, putting emphasis on some
words and dramatizing the whole thing.

To Steve, the people who wrote him might well be characters in one of his stories. He was thoroughly enjoying the
situation he had created and the part he was playing in it.

"Now, this one I like," he said. "Besides her name is Jean.
She might just do. And then there are Phyllis and Gloria,
and Ellen. They are the best in the whole lot. I think I'll
talk to these four. And I'll tell them the truth—that I am
a sick, old man, who spills on himself when he eats and that
I am all alone in the world."

"And if one accepts are you going to bring her here?"
Dag, not at all amused, wanted to know.

"Give me one good reason why I shouldn't?" he stared at her and then at me through his thick lenses. "Jean left me and I haven't anyone to look after me. I'm lonely—a lonely old man."

"But, these are all young girls, Steve," Dag went on. "Get someone more your age. Not just out of college. You'll be deceiving them."

"But I'm not at all," he said. "I made it clear in the ad that I was an old man. And when I interview them, they can see, can't they? And they can ask questions, can't they? Why, for the right girl who wants to write, I can, in time, make a fine writer of her." He rose from the table and momentarily he appeared angry but then a relaxed expression came over his face. "You see, I have no intention of going to bed with her," he was now smiling, "at least not at first, anyway."

"He is like a spider," Dag said as we started for home, "spinning a web in which to catch her. I feel sorry for the girl he brings here."

Steve went to San Francisco to interview the four girls in which he was interested. He was on his best behavior, not drinking and even taking time to have his hair cut and his mustache brushed and waxed. We did not see him, but he must have looked distinguished and impressive, as he well could when it served his purpose.

As he told us later, he took a suite at the Clift Hotel and then he talked to each of the four girls separately after having set up appointments with them. He doubtless had a fine time, questioning them and expounding his views on writing and on life. In the four girls he had a captive audience, and they must have listened to him attentively while he charmed them with his persuasive, soft voice.

For three of the girls it was a waste of time. He had set his mind on the one named Jean. "The moment I saw her," he told us, "I knew it had to be her. She reminded me so much of my own Jean."

He brought her back to Carmel in his old brown Chevrolet, with the two airedales in the back seat. She was very young, barely 18, with light, reddish hair, a small upturned nose and with big dimples when she smiled. She acted nervous and uneasy, and she was extremely shy.

Steve had tried to reassure her that he was a person of standing and worthy of respect. One of the first things he did was to take her to the Carmel Mission where he introduced her to Father O'Connell. The parish priest, benevolent and friendly, was not aware of the reason for the visit, and took Jean for a tour of the Mission. He spoke well of Steve, especially after he had seen him put a few dollar bills in the collection box.

Then Steve had called on us to show her off, and also to let her see that he counted us among his friends.

"Isn't she just like my Jean?" he said after he introduced her. "She will soon be accustomed to my ways," he added, giving her a slight squeeze.

He invited us for dinner, and I was surprised when Dag quickly accepted. I had thought she wanted no part of this involvement. But there was a good reason why she was willing to go; she, too, was scheming, planning how to keep this young, inexperienced girl away from Steve. She had her first opportunity when she said to Jean, "Would you like to freshen up a bit?" and then Dag followed her into the bathroom.

Steve sat in the living room, and while he waited impatiently, he described his visit to San Francisco and the other girls he had interviewed.

"But the moment I saw Jean I knew it would be her," he said. "She's young, very young," he added. "I plan to be like a father to her. I have it all arranged. She will have the bedroom and I will sleep in the studio."

Whatever Dag said to Jean in the bathroom, it was convincing enough and had the proper effect. Jean was no longer nervous and there was a look of relief on her face. During dinner Steve put on all of his charm. If we had not known him better, we too would have been taken in. He was playing well the role of a kindly and considerate old man with the highest moral standards.

"My weakness has been liquor," he said, now seeking sympathy, "but I shall never drink again. I have reformed, and you, Jean, shall bear witness to my rebirth. I shall work and work and work."

But Steve's spell over Jean was broken. When we had finished dinner and were getting ready to leave, Jean suddenly announced:

"I'm not going to stay in your house, Steve," she said. "I'm sorry, but it was a mistake coming with you. I am imposing on your friends for the night and in the morning I'm returning to San Francisco."

He tried to argue, to be as persuasive as only he could be, but after a time he knew it was useless. "Perhaps you are right," he finally admitted. "You are very, very young."

Jean stayed the night with us, sleeping on the davenport in the living room. She had telephoned her boy friend in San Francisco, and the next morning he arrived on his motorcycle for her. We prepared breakfast for them and saw them go off, Jean riding on the back of the motorcycle and holding on to her boy friend.

Steve, however, was not at all discouraged. A few days later he brought Gloria, one of the other girls he had interviewed, to Carmel. Gloria was older, in her late thirties, and now Dag did not interfere.

"She's old enough to know what she's doing," she said.

Gloria was efficient, an experienced secretary who was not swayed or impressed by Steve. She took over the bedroom and the running of the house and Steve had to be content

to stay in his studio. During the first few weeks she kept
Steve from drinking and he put eight and ten hours in at
the typewriter. For a time we were convinced that Steve
had reformed and that Gloria, never letting him out of her
sight, had brought about a miracle. But Steve was too resourceful and too clever for her. Somehow he managed to
get liquor into his studio and he resumed his heavy drinking.

Gloria stood ten days of it and then she packed her suitcase and was gone.

For a month Steve stayed drunk and we did not see him.
We heard about his plans to leave Carmel from Val, his
newspaper friend from Salinas, who had first introduced us
to him.

"Steve is sick," Val said. "He looks terrible. He's selling
everything he has and he's going to Washington. He wants
to be buried in Arlington Cemetery."

Val asked us to go and visit Steve. We finally went on
Val's insistence—I wish we hadn't. He was drunk, but he
also looked ill. He had lost weight, his cheeks were sunken
and he had not bothered to shave for days.

We put him in the Carmel hospital and Steve had so much
stamina left that within a week, he was well enough to
return to his cottage.

"He's like an old bull," Kay Brownell, a nurse we knew
at the Carmel hospital said about Steve. "He'll go on living
for years."

No matter what Kay Brownell thought of him professionally, Steve was failing. He lost weight and he looked old.
Nevertheless, he was still determined to get to Washington
and in order to raise money for the trip, he sold all his
books, his furniture, and his typewriter.

Yet he would not part with his two airedales. They were
now his only company and he felt that they were his only
friends. They climbed into the back seat of his brown Chevrolet as he started out for the nation's capital. Enroute he

made one important stop that we know of. After he left Carmel he must have decided to have one last fling. On his way out of Monterey he drove into the grounds of Hotel Del Monte, parked his car and went into the main dining room.

William Parker, the maitre'd, described Steve's visit.

"It was two o'clock when he came into the dining room," he was to tell me after he learned that I had known Steve. "We were closing the door as the lunch hour was over when he walked in. In the business I am in, I am good at sizing up people. This man looked like an important guest, accustomed to getting what he wanted and willing to pay for it. He introduced himself as Mr. Reynolds and said he'd like to have lunch. I explained that he had come too late. But he was very insistent. I said that to serve him lunch he would have to pay the waiter and the chef overtime. 'That's perfectly satisfactory with me,' he said, 'and by the way, I want a table by the window overlooking the gardens.' I gave him the table he asked for and handed him the menu. He studied it carefully and I still remember what he ordered. He started off with *Potage Parmentier* and as an entrée, he had Steak *Béarnaise*. Then he called for a bottle of Richebourg, 1926, which I opened and poured a little into a glass. He rolled the wine in the glass, looked at the color approvingly, gently sniffed at the bouquet, and then slowly sipped it. 'Not a bad wine at all,' he said as I filled his glass.

"He ate leisurely, as if he had all the time in the world. When he was finished with the entrée, he asked for some ripe Camembert cheese and water biscuits. With it he drank the last of the wine and with his coffee, he had a glass of brandy. By now it was almost four o'clock and he had run up a good-sized bill. I handed him the bill and he glanced at the charges. The amount did not seem to bother him. He signed it and put in a generous tip for the waiter, the chef and for me. He complimented us highly on the food and the service and we were very pleased. You don't often get a connoisseur like him. He was a fine, old gentleman. He completely fooled me. The hotel was never able to collect on the bill he signed."

The last we heard about Steve was from his former wife, Jean. First she wrote us saying that he had arrived in Washington and that, as a war veteran, she had arranged to put him in Walter Reed Hospital, "where he is being very well taken care of."

Two weeks later we received another letter from her in which she wrote: "Steve died two days ago and yesterday he was buried at Arlington Cemetery with military honors. That must have pleased him, but you cannot imagine what a relief it is to know he's dead."

CHAPTER SIX

The Strange Disappearance of Carmel's Romantic Police Judge

Judge Richard Hoagland was an ordinary little man with a wrinkled face, washed-out blue eyes and deep creases around the sides and back of his neck. His flat nose was tomato red with thin, purplish streaks. His hair was almost gone and his clothes never seemed to fit him. There was always a licorice odor about him to conceal the liquor on his breath. Judge Hoagland was certainly not the romantic type; yet he had captured the attention and the hearts of three different women, one of them at least half his age.

The first to fall, and to remain in love with Richard Hoagland was Saidee van Brower, the Carmel city clerk. Her love for Hoagland began in the days when Carmel was but a small and isolated town. Saidee and young Richard often used to walk together on the Carmel beach, the sand dunes, and occasionally they had a Sunday picnic at Point Lobos. Everyone in Carmel assumed they were engaged and would soon be married. Then Saidee made a fatal mistake. Her younger sister, who was going to school in San Francisco, came to Carmel for the summer and Saidee invited her to join them at one of the Sunday picnics at Point Lobos.

Young Richard began seeing Saidee's sister surreptitiously at first and then quite openly, and before anyone realized it, they were married. When Saidee found out about the marriage, she left her house, telling her mother she was going for a walk. When she failed to return, a searching party was organized and they combed the beach, the sanddunes, and the woods without a trace of Saidee.

Eventually they turned to Point Lobos and there, perched high in a tree and almost hidden by the foliage, was Saidee. She was suffering from hunger and fatigue, but she was still well enough to protest.

"Can't I go off and think without everyone looking for me?" she demanded.

They carried her to one of the cars and drove her home. Saidee had been rejected and her pride hurt. For awhile she stayed at home, preferring not to see any of her former friends. Everyone felt sorry for Saidee, and when the city council decided Carmel needed a city clerk, she was named to the job.

Hoagland had gone to work as a construction foreman and there the episode would have ended. Three years after he married Saidee's sister, she caught cold and within the week was dead of pneumonia.

People in Carmel said God was balancing things and had freed Hoagland so he could now marry Saidee. Hoagland did begin taking her out again, but the young widower apparently had no intention of marriage. The two nevertheless seemed inseparable; they went together to the concerts, the movies, and to the plays given at the Forest Theatre. The years passed and when Saidee's mother died, Hoagland continued to live alone, but he became a star boarder at Saidee's, taking most of his meals at her home. It was through Saidee's influence with the city council that Hoagland was appointed police judge which at the time was mostly an honorary position. Occasionally a motorist cited for a traffic or a speeding violation by the state police was brought up to his court, a small office adjoining the city council chambers. There were times, too, when Gus Englund had a drunk or someone for disturbing the peace brought up before Hoagland. Perhaps, with the exception of Saidee and Gus, few knew that Hoagland was hitting the bottle hard. No one took too seriously his red nose and the smell of licorice on his breath.

His salary as police judge was modest, but Hoagland, through wise real estate investments when property had little value, had done well for himself. He owned five houses, and the rent from them gave him a good income. He was close with his money and he spent very little on himself or on anyone else. He did pay Saidee for the meals he took at her home and for doing his laundry, but according to Gus, who never liked Hoagland, Saidee charged him a nominal sum.

"She's a fool," Gus often would say. "Why, after all these years, she's still in love with him."

By the time we came to live in Carmel, Judge Hoagland was nearly sixty and Saidee, with her white hair and pinched face, looked older than her years. She treated him with great respect and always referred to him as "Judge." He was drinking more than ever and he now kept a bottle in his desk, from which he would take frequent sips. Out of respect and sympathy for Saidee, nothing was done about Hoagland. He was tolerated and left alone and if a serious case came up before him, it was usually transferred to the justice court in Monterey.

Despite his drinking, no one suspected that he had fallen in love, was courting another woman and that he was secretly planning to marry her. She was in her early thirties, almost half his age; they had applied for a marriage license and were now only waiting for the three day legal period to pass before they were to be married.

Gus was the first to discover Judge Hoagland's plans and he came to our house in the late afternoon. He could no longer keep it to himself.

"Something happen?" I asked, when I saw him at the door.

"Not yet," he said, "but it's going to happen soon unless we stop it. You mind if I come in?"

He was already in the house, but he seemed too perturbed to take a chair. As always, he was wearing his police uniform with its high, military collar. Dag, who had been reading by the fireplace, got up.

"How about some coffee, Gus?"

"Ya," Gus said, "and I'll even take some gin if you have some."

I poured him a glass of gin while my wife warmed up the coffee. He took a big swig of the gin.

"My Gott," he said, "it is terrible what goes on. You will not believe it possible. The goddamn fool—he's going to get married. And I tell you one thing sure—she only wants his money. Ya, vy else would she marry the Yudge?"

Gus was getting more excited and his Swedish accent was getting stronger.

"He's got the license and tomorrow he'll marry her unless it's stopped. I can't arrest him or put him in jail. But we got to do something."

"Come on, Gus, what's it all about?"

"Vhat's wrong with you?" he said. "Don't you know that the Yudge wants to get married? And poor Saidee—yust think what will happen to her when she finds out. Ya—she will die from the shock. So, I come to you. We put our heads together and we think what we do with the Yudge."

Dag brought the coffee and then in more detail he told us about Judge Hoagland and Ann Martin, the woman he planned to marry.

"He's been courting her on the sly and none of us catching on until I hear today about them getting a license. The Yudge —he's drunk—and that woman, she yust after his money. We yust got to think up a way to stop it."

"What about putting him in the hospital, Gus?" I said.

Gus shook his head. "No, that will not work. We gotta hide him somewhere so she can't get at him."

Then it came to me.

"I have it, Gus! I know exactly where to take him. To Tassajara Springs. No one would ever think of looking for him there."

"Ya—Ya. That sounds goot."

"We'll send him with a registered nurse and keep him there until he sobers up."

If Kay Brownell, the nurse at the Carmel Hospital who had taken care of Steve was free, she would know how to handle Hoagland. I went to the telephone and called Kay.

"We need you," I said. "Can you get away? We have an emergency."

"What kind of an emergency?"

"A patient who's been drinking."

"Another one like Steve?"

"No, but just as difficult."

"What's his problem?"

"He wants to get married."

"Why don't you let him then?"

"He's too drunk to know what he's doing. Can you get away and handle the case?"

"I suppose so. I need work. We haven't too many patients at the hospital."

"Then come along. You better pack a suitcase. You're going to Tassajara Springs for two or three days."

"I'll be there in an hour," she said.

It was getting dark when Gus, Kay, and I drove to Judge Hoagland's cottage. The door was unlocked and we went in. Hoagland was lying fully dressed on top of the bed.

"Be careful, Gus," I cautioned. "You're liable to awaken him and we might have trouble."

"He's drunk," Gus said, and he leaned over and picked him up and carried him out as if he were a baby. He put him on the back seat of the car and Kay brought out blankets and a pillow covering him carefully. The Judge gave a few groans and then was out again.

"He's plastered now," Kay said. "But what do I tell him when he sobers up?"

"Use your charm and keep him entertained," I said. "We'll be in touch with you and tell you what else to do."

Kay climbed into the front seat and waved at us as she started out for Tassajara Springs, a two-hours drive in a remote part of the Carmel Valley.

In the morning I went to Gus' office and waited for developments. Then, at two in the afternoon, Ann Martin, Judge Hoagland's bride-to-be, came in.

"Where is the Judge?" she demanded in an angry voice. "He was to meet me at nine o'clock this morning, and he has disappeared, vanished into thin air. I have just come from his home, and he's not there!"

"I'm sure he's all right," Gus tried to quiet her, hoping Saidee van Brower, working in an adjacent office, would not hear the conversation.

"Well, he can't get away with it," she went on, her voice getting louder. "Why, we were going to be married today. If he walked out on me, I'll sue him for plenty."

"Do you wish to report him missing, Madam?" Gus looked and acted innocent.

"You're the police chief, aren't you?"

"Ya."

"Well, you better find him or I'll sue him for breach of promise."

She turned and stamped out of the office. But Saidee had heard and now as she faced Gus, there was a wild look in her eyes.

"It isn't true—it can't be true!" she cried out.

"The Judge wouldn't do that—not to me. Tell me, Gus," she was pleading. "This woman was lying, wasn't she?"

"The Yudge's been drinking," Gus tried to explain and to let Saidee down as easily as possible. "He's not going to marry no one. Just calm down Saidee. Everything will be all right."

Gus walked out of the office leaving Saidee alone. I followed a moment later and found him waiting for me on the sidewalk.

"Vel, ain't it funny—two women fighting for that drunken fool," Gus said.

"If you don't mind, Gus," I said, "I'm going to phone the story to the newspaper."

"Vhy not? It's going to be known anyway. Yust never let on how we got him out of town."

Most of the afternoon I was on the telephone. The newspapers and the wire services were asking for all the details I could get. How old was Hoagland? How old was the girl friend? Where had they met? How long had they gone together? Where was the Judge now? Why had he walked out on her? I answered as many questions as I could, discreetly.

"Having sent that nurse with him was a stroke of genius," I said to my wife.

"You still might be charged with kidnapping," she said. "For you did kidnap him, you know."

"He was ill," I said, "and we just sent him away with a nurse."

That evening I telephoned Tassajara Springs and asked for Kay Brownell.

"How is he, Kay?"

"He's beginning to feel fine. Got him into one of the steam baths and that sobered him up fast."

"Is he angry at getting him out of town?"

"No, he seems happy as a lark. Thinks it all a big joke. He's playing checkers right now with Warden Houllihan."

"Who's Warden Houllihan, Kay?"

"He's the Warden at San Quentin Penitentiary," Kay said. "His wife owns Tassajara Springs, and he's up here on vacation."

That's all we need, I thought, having the Warden of San Quentin and Judge Hoagland under one roof.

"The story will be in all the papers tomorrow," I said. "Hoagland might feel differently then."

"Don't worry," Kay reassured. "He likes me and I can handle him. Just let me know when you want him back."

On the radio that night, and in the newspapers in the morning, the story was out. Some of the headlines read: Carmel Judge Vanishes on Wedding Day; Romeo Judge Disappears; Hunt On For Missing Police Judge.

The story was growing and it had all the elements of a front page mystery. And, of course, it made bigger news that the police judge was from Carmel.

How long did we dare keep the Judge hidden? How would we bring him back and what would be his story of why he had disappeared? By now, I wished I had Steve to help me. He would have had it all worked out and with the right ending.

I talked it over with Gus. He was of no help. "Let him stay there," was his only comment.

Once again I telephoned Kay at Tassajara Springs.

"How's the Judge?"

"You'd never recognize him. Those steam baths do wonders. Besides I'm a good nurse."

"Is the Warden still there?"

"Yep."

"What does he think of the stories in the papers?"

"He says it's just newspaper talk. Thinks the Judge is all right."

"We'd better think of a statement for Hoagland to make. The papers are getting anxious about him. They want him found."

"He's not capable of making a statement. You better make one up for him. Why not say he's been ill and has gone to Tassajara Springs for a rest cure? Besides, what's all the fuss about anyway? Can't a man take a rest cure?"

"Sure, but not on his wedding day."

"Well, make up something. The Judge won't mind."

"I'll write out a statement."

I made up a half-dozen statements, yet none of them sounded good. I was beginning to feel sorry for Hoagland. I wanted to write a story that might put him in a better light. But what excuse can a man give who walks out on the woman he's going to marry?

Finally, I had an idea and it didn't sound too bad. I phoned Kay at Tassajara Springs again.

"Let me read you this and see if he'll go for it."

Then I read what I had written:

"Police Judge Richard Hoagland was found today at Tassajara Springs under the care of a registered nurse. He said he had been ill and issued the following statement: 'For several months I have not been well and when I first met Mrs. Ann Martin, she was very kind and good to me. Because I am a widower, I felt that marriage to a fine woman was a logical step to take. But then I decided I was too ill and too old for such a marriage to be consummated. I have been under extreme nervous tension and upon professional advice decided to go to Tassajara Springs for a short rest cure. I am now feeling much better, and I apologize to anyone I might have caused embarrassment. I am returning to Carmel to assume my duties and responsibilities.'"

"That sounds good," Kay said. "Read it to me slowly and I'll write it down and then take it up with him and see what he says."

A half hour later she called back. "It's all right with him," she said. "When shall I bring him back?"

"The sooner the better," I replied.

Judge Hoagland and Kay Brownell returned that evening and I went over to his cottage to meet them. He was sober and the few days at Tassajara Springs had done wonders for him and he was enjoying all the attention he had been getting. He didn't even mind the front page publicity. For the first time in his life he felt important. He wasn't worried about Saidee. "She's angry now," he said, "but she'll forgive me."

The Carmel city council was not as considerate or as forgiving. The next day at an executive session, he was fired as police judge and a week later Mrs. Ann Martin filed in the Superior Court in Salinas a breach of promise suit and asked for fifty thousand dollars in damages.

The suit was finally settled out of court and Judge Hoagland continued to remain Saidee van Brower's star boarder. Occasionally and in the early evening we'd see him and Saidee walking down the street, holding hands.

CHAPTER SEVEN

Lickety-split Went Cynthia the Seal

During the first few years we lived in Carmel, we had no refrigerator and if we needed ice we bought a block of it for ten cents and placed it in the kitchen sink. Margarine came snow-white and to make it look like butter we had to mash it and mix into it the yellow coloring that was in the package. We did our cooking on top of two burners, though it seemed we were always running out of kerosene or the wicks had to be trimmed or changed. Everyone, especially the artists and writers, rolled their own cigarettes and doing it expertly became something of a status symbol.

Food was available at rock-bottom prices, but people were either hoarding their money or they just didn't have it. For five dollars we came out of a grocery store with bagsfull of food that lasted all week with some careful management. I was doing well with the newspapers and the wire services, but the checks were small and there were not too many.

At Pebble Beach, some of the homes built in the twenties by free-wheeling millionaires were up for sale or the government had seized them for back taxes. S. F. B. Morse, who headed the company which owned Pebble Beach and Hotel Del Monte, had sold his yacht and discharged his two butlers. In Monterey, during the worst part of the Depression, the sardine canneries shut down and the fishermen were not putting out to sea because, as one of them said, "the fish are biting, but no one's buying."

While it was a difficult period, the Monterey Peninsula did not get the full impact of the Depression as did many industrial and agricultural areas. It was bad enough, but somehow we all managed to get by. The people who worried the most were those who still had money.

Mrs. Olga Fish, reputed to be the wealthiest woman on the peninsula, put her limousines in storage and drove around in a Ford. "In times like these," she said, "one must not be ostentatious."

The hardest hit was not S. F. B. Morse, deprived of his yacht, or Mrs. Fish, unable to use her fine cars; it was instead, Gus Englund. Atop his horse, Gus, for years had been a majestic figure, as much a part of the local scenery as the wind-swept cypresses and the sand dunes.

The Carmel city council, quite unexpectedly, had also become economy minded. Once each year, Gus put in his annual feed bill for his horse. This time, when his claim came up for payment, the city council balked. The horse belonged to Gus, the council said, and feeding it from now on was his responsibility. Why should the city pay for its hay? John Catlin, as the mayor, tried to influence the other members of the council in behalf of Gus, but he failed to win them over. Then Saidee van Brower rose to her feet and in her squeaky voice made a last minute effort to help Gus. But the council would not budge from its position; it refused to honor Gus' claim.

Gus was indignant and his pride hurt; he left the council chambers swearing under his breath. The following day he rode out of Carmel on his horse and headed for Monterey; in the afternoon he returned on the bus. He wouldn't tell anyone what he had done with the horse.

Without it, Gus was never the same picturesque figure that had kept law and order for so long. He looked rather pathetic in his riding trousers and leather leggins, and he appeared more bowlegged than ever as he walked through the streets of Carmel carrying out his police duties on foot.

"The city council's decision in taking away Gus' horse clearly shows that this town and the world is going fast to hell," Perry Newberry wrote in his weekly Carmel paper.

Perry Newberry was no soothsayer, nor did he foresee what was going to happen in China, in Spain, and in Germany, but he knew intuitively that when Carmel could no longer keep Gus on his horse, something was wrong. He knew that Carmel and the world was changing and that it would never be the same again.

It was to change for me, too and it came about through a telephone call. I had been out trying to gather news and when I returned in the late afternoon, I asked if there had been any calls.

"Only one," Dag said.

"From whom?" I said, tired and not interested.

"You would never guess," she said. "From S. F. B. Morse."

"What in the world would S. F. B. Morse want to see me for?"

Dag's intuition was as good as Perry Newberry's.

"I don't know why, but I have an idea that he wants to offer you a job," she said.

"I don't want a job," I said. "I'm doing fine."

"Of course you are," she said. "So, don't take it—no matter what he offers you—don't take it."

S. F. B. Morse was big in size and in girth, but he was not fat; he was mostly muscle and bone and he kept himself trim. He had a flattened nose that looked as if it had taken some rough treatment and he also had a powerful, protruding jaw. He had once been captain of the Yale football team and he had never forgotten it—or allowed anyone else to forget it. He hailed from Boston, a true Yankee aristocrat, who could be snobbishly friendly when it served his purpose.

He had been named after his great uncle, who had invented the telegraph, and from him he had inherited a talent and an appreciation of art. But he was at the same time a tough and a hard business man with that canny New England touch for making and holding on to money.

People bowed and scraped to him because the company of which he was president owned great portions of the land that made up the Monterey Peninsula, including one hundred miles of paved highway in the Del Monte forest; Pebble Beach, and Hotel Del Monte. To S. F. B. Morse his twenty-thousand acre estate was a monarchy and he king and ruler. He loved land and though the main business of his company was to promote and to sell it, he created Pebble Beach and Cypress Point as golf courses so that great parts of the ocean front property would remain unspoiled.

At ten o'clock in the morning his secretary ushered me into his large, blue-carpeted office. He looked at me, his eyes taking in my cheap sports jacket, my dollar-ninety-five white shirt and my baggy linen trousers.

"Why you're just a youngster," he said sizing me up. "But from what I hear, you've been creating quite a bit of excitement in Carmel for the past year or so. Every time I pick up a newspaper there's something in it about Carmel."

"Carmel just happens to make news," I said.

"But you do something to make it news—fluff it up, or whatever you do, you manage to do it. And that's what I'm looking for—someone to make news, not about Carmel, but about Del Monte and Pebble Beach."

He rose from behind his desk and I saw how big and overpowering he was. "By the way, how old are you?" he asked.

"Twenty-one."

"Well!"

He left his desk and went to the window and drew back

the draperies. The bright morning sun swept into the office. He looked out across at the gardens of Del Monte and at the oak trees in the distance. He seemed more relaxed, and more friendly as he went back to his desk.

"We've had some bad years since the Depression," he said. "But things are going to get better. The cycle is turning. I am going to put this company and Del Monte back on its feet. We'll be needing publicity. I need someone to create excitement—to make this whole area talked about. You might be just the person to do it."

"I'm just a reporter," I said. "I'm not a publicity man. Besides you wouldn't approve of the things I might dream up. Anyway, you wouldn't pay me what I would want."

"How much do you want?"

"It would be too much."

"I'll be the judge of that."

Now, I didn't know what to say next. I wanted to come up with some ridiculously high figure that would immediately stop him. The manager of the Bank of Carmel, I had heard, was making four hundred dollars a month. That was a high salary to be getting during the Depression.

"I would want at least four hundred dollars a month to start with," I said.

"That's exactly what I was planning to offer you," S. F. B. Morse said.

I couldn't believe it. With all those little checks I received, if we averaged two hundred a month, we thought we were lucky and doing well.

"I want you to start next Monday," he said.

"But I can't accept just yet," I stalled. "I want to think it over and I have to talk it over with my wife."

"Fair enough," he said, getting up from his desk again. "Talk it over and call me."

I felt his big hand gripping mine and then I was out of the office and walking through the grounds toward my car.

With that kind of a salary, I thought, we could move into a better house—one that had a gas stove with an oven. And Dag had talked of someday renting a piano. If I went to work for S. F. B. Morse and Del Monte, we could well afford a piano. Did I want to work for him? Dag had cautioned me against it. But what a challenge it would be, I thought, to be thinking up stories about Del Monte. I didn't have Steve to help me yet I knew I could do it.

I drove back from Monterey and as I came up the hill, there before me was Carmel and the sea, a turquoise blue under the morning sun. I continued driving slowly down the hill, through the main street, past the post office, past Gus standing on the corner of Ocean and Dolores and down to San Antonio street where I turned left and stopped in front of the cottage with green vines. At the gate there was a small sign which read: Not at Home Until After Four O'clock.

I knew that Lincoln Steffens wouldn't mind my breaking in on him.

As he listened to me, his face had that impish, whimsical look that was so much a part of him whenever he was amused.

"You didn't come for advice," he said. "You made up your mind before you ever got here. You just want to be reassured. Of course, take this job. Why not?"

"But I want to write magazine articles and books."

"Anybody can be a writer," Steffens said, "but not everyone can live. Enjoy life while you can—take everything it offers and never have regrets. Remember one thing, and that is that the best years are the young years. It is then, when you are in search of something that is not there, and yet it is there all the time. The tragedy and the irony is that when you find what you are searching for and get it, you suddenly don't want it and don't care. Now, let me tell you about people like Sam Morse."

He sat back in his chair, puffed on the cigarette he had been smoking and flung it into the fireplace.

"I've known people like him most of my life. Don't ever expect too much from him. If he's offered you a job with a good salary, it is because he needs you. He's buying you for what you can produce. He's not doing you a favor—you're doing him a favor. Learn all you can from Sam Morse and the people around him that you are going to meet. Then when you are saturated with them, get out! And, if there's a war going on somewhere—and there'll be many—go and cover it."

I left Steffens' home. A week later I was working for S. F. B. Morse and Del Monte with an office, a secretary and with so many things to do I did not know where to begin.

Sam Morse turned out to be different than I had expected. He shouted and his voice bellowed like a bull's, but he was also kind and considerate and when I was impatient, he was patient. He liked my boyish enthusiasm and my immaturity. He gave me a free hand and allowed me to do about everything I wanted to do. When others in the company tried to stop me, Sam Morse was there to provide encouragement and support.

"Del Monte is like a morgue," I said. "It needs life, excitement and things happening."

"Then do them," he said.

I knew that people draw more people and that an empty hotel with only a handful of guests is cold and unfriendly. We began offering free dancing to certain groups in Carmel if they came in dinner clothes; polo matches, which had been abandoned during the first few years of the Depression, were resumed; we had the huge swimming pool emptied and the bottom waxed, and hired an orchestra—we gave a party in the pool that was talked about for days, and which brought us newspaper coverage everywhere. The same kind of stories that I had been doing in Carmel, I now tried at Del Monte and soon found that the wire services and newspapers wanted anything unusual or the least bit amusing.

There was no television, but there were newsreels that were seen by millions in the thousands of movie theaters. The newsreel men began coming to Del Monte and we thought up stories that they could film. That's how I first met Cynthia, Alice, and Murial.

The newsreel men, always searching for different approaches that provided human interest and dramatic value, came up with the idea of getting some seals on the golf course and letting them try their skill at putting on the sixteenth green at Cypress Point, which was on the very edge of the ocean. It sounded like an easy thing to do.

We thought we would have to get the seals from Hollywood, but we learned that not too far from Monterey was a man whose business was training seals to perform for the movies and for circuses. We told him what we wanted and he agreed next day to take three of his best trained seals to the golf course.

"Here are the three I'll bring along," he said. As he called each by name they came plunging out of the pool he had in his backyard. "This is Cynthia," he said. "She'll do about anything I tell her. And, here are Alice and Murial. All three are magnificent performers."

We arranged to have him meet us the following day. The newsreel men had their cameras and equipment set up around the sixteenth hole and I also had Spike Graham, the publicity photographer there, to shoot stills for the photo services and newspapers.

Our man arrived in a truck with the three seals in cages. The newsreel men explained how and where they wanted the seals to perform.

"We'll start off with one seal," Jack McHenry of Universal Newsreel said. "We'll have a golf ball on the green and see how well the seal can putt it."

"It'll be easy for Cynthia to sink a ball," the seal trainer said.

"Probably, but let's rehearse it first," Eric Mayell of Fox Movietone said, "and then we'll shoot the scene."

The seal trainer went to his truck, opened one of the cages and let Cynthia out.

Cynthia came along on her flippers, and as she approached the edge of the sixteenth green, she raised her head high, looked around and whiffed the fresh sea air. Her trainer began telling her what to do, but Cynthia wasn't paying any attention. Only the beach and the sea below interested her. Her long mustache began quivering and she gave a series of barks and suddenly started out across the green and toward the ocean.

"Cynthia! Cynthia, stop!" her trainer called but Cynthia was now moving along at a fast clip and heading toward the ocean. The trainer began chasing her and he yelled at us, "don't let her get away! Stop her!"

We all started after Cynthia, trying to head her off from reaching the water. One of the newsreel men managed to reach her, and like a football player, he leaped upon her and tackled her. But Cynthia had heard the call of the sea and she was tasting freedom again. The newsreel man could not hold her. She slipped easily from his grasp, and lickety-split went Cynthia, across the beach and into the water. In another moment we saw her swimming out in the sea and playfully diving in and out of the water. Then in the distance we saw only her head and finally she disappeared from sight.

Her trainer was broken up. He said in great dismay, "I've lost her—I've lost Cynthia!"

We went back to the sixteenth green and now we could hear the loud mournful barking of the other two seals trying to get out of their cages. The trainer went to comfort them, giving them fish to eat and he finally managed to quiet them.

He was an angry and unhappy man, swearing and whimpering to himself. "I'll never have another Cynthia again. She was so devoted to me. I should have known better. I never should have brought them out here. It was the sea—the smell of the sea that got her! Poor Cynthia. I'm going to miss her."

He was in no mood to go on with the story, but the newsreel men were persistent. They talked and argued with the trainer and finally he agreed to take his remaining seals to the Del Monte golf course, where there were only oak trees and sand traps and no water for miles around. Later that day the newsreel men filmed their story, Alice and Murial performing admirably, pushing the golf balls with their snouts and expertly sinking the putts. The following week, Alice and Murial were on thousands of theater screens, billed as Del Monte's newest golf champions.

Hotel Del Monte was snooty and Del Monte Lodge at Pebble Beach was even more so. Each morning the guest list was checked against *The Social Register, Burke's Peerage, Who's Who* and other books. The list was sent on to Spike Graham, the Del Monte photographer who took pictures of those marked. The photographs were then distributed to the society sections of newspapers and magazines. There were, however, two persons who came to Del Monte who did not need to be looked up.

As I was going through the lobby, John Powers, one of the hotel clerks, called me over. "I thought you should know about the two women who have just checked in," he said. "One of them is quite famous though she sure is mighty strange looking and wears the funniest clothes you ever saw. But you never can tell how far a frog will jump by its looks, can you?"

The two were Gertrude Stein and Alice B. Toklas. Both had stayed at Del Monte when they were young girls and now that they were touring the United States for the first time in many years, they had returned for a brief visit.

I invited them to join Dag and me for lunch at Del Monte Lodge. We met them at twelve-thirty in the lobby. We didn't have any trouble identifying them. Gertrude Stein had a long, tweed skirt and a tweed jacket with a velvet collar. Her grey hair was shortly cropped and over it she wore a small cap. Miss Toklas, smaller in stature and delicate in appearance, was similarly attired.

"Look at them," Dag whispered. "They look like two characters out of an old novel."

Stein and Toklas were both pleasant and said it was thoughtful of us to invite them for lunch. They climbed into my old car and we drove through part of the 17 Mile Drive on the way to Del Monte Lodge.

"Things do not change very much," Miss Stein said as we drove along the ocean. "It is very much like it was so many years ago. It is all very beautiful, even more so than the Riviera."

They referred to each other as Lovey and Puss. Gertrude Stein did most of the talking while Miss Toklas was more reserved. At the Lodge we were given a table overlooking the eighteenth hole at Pebble Beach and Stillwater Cove. Gertrude Stein liked the view but she seemed more impressed by the modern and colorful murals on one of the walls of the dining room painted by Gene McComas.

We were given menus by the dining room captain and as we went over them, Alice Toklas reached for the large handbag she was carrying and extracted two packages of Rye-Krisp and handed one to Gertrude Stein. Both began munching on the Rye-Krisp as they discussed what to order. They finally decided on abalone chowder, a specialty of the Lodge, and Chicken Tarragon. While we waited for the food to be prepared and served, Gertrude Stein talked about the days she and Alice B. Toklas lived in Oakland, California.

After a while, Miss Toklas joined in the conversation, but most of the time, it was Miss Stein who did the talking.

I asked them whom they might like to meet while they were on the Monterey Peninsula. I suggested Robinson Jeffers, Lincoln Steffens and John Steinbeck.

Gertrude Stein wasn't interested.

"There's only one person I want to meet," she said.

"I always liked his stories so well I consider him the greatest exponent of American humor. I understand he lives here. Do you happen to know Harry Leon Wilson?"

"We know him well," I said. "He lives in the Carmel Highlands. If you like, we can call on him after lunch."

"Yes, that would be very nice," she said, still munching on the Rye-Krisp.

The abalone chowder was prepared in a heavy cream and they appeared to enjoy it thoroughly, as they did the Chicken Tarragon. Miss Toklas said she did most of the cooking at home and that if we ever came to Paris she would prepare some of her favorite dishes.

"Puss is a superb cook," Gertrude Stein said, "but no one, not even the finest chef in France, can make apple pie as they make it in America."

"They have excellent apple pie here at the Lodge," Dag said. "Wouldn't you like to try it?"

We had finished with the Chicken Tarragon and all the Rye-Krisp was gone.

"Apple pie? Yes, we must have some," Gertrude Stein said. "Don't you think so, Puss?"

"By all means," Miss Toklas said.

I ordered the apple pie. It was brought warm to the table and it had a faint cinnamon flavor to it.

"It is wonderful," Gertrude Stein said, an expression of great satisfaction coming over her face. "It is the best apple pie I have ever eaten."

"The crust is done with butter, Lovey," Miss Toklas said.

"You cannot make a good crust without using lots and lots of butter."

While they were finishing the apple pie and coffee, I went to the telephone and called Harry Leon Wilson. He was not in good health and for some years had been perturbed that his fame as a writer had waned. I also knew he didn't like to meet strangers, and perhaps that was the reason that, when I finally got him on the phone, I said: "Harry, I'm with two old ladies who want to meet you. They are long-time fans of yours."

Harry Leon Wilson could be cranky and temperamental. "I don't want to see 'em." he said.

"But, these are two unusual old ladies and they think you are a great writer."

"I don't give a damn what they think. Don't you dare bring them up."

"Not even if their names are Gertrude Stein and Alice Toklas?"

There was a long silence on the other end of the phone.

"Why didn't you tell me that before. Of course I will see them."

We took them up to Harry Leon Wilson's home in the highlands. He was flattered and impressed that they should want to meet him and the visit which was to be only a brief one, went on for hours. The sun had gone down and it was dark when we finally took Gertrude Stein and Alice B. Toklas back to Hotel Del Monte.

Several months after the visit and after they both had returned to Paris, Miss Toklas sent Dag a recipe which she said was her favorite. It was a *Pâté à Beignets* using acacia flowers. Then she put a postscript to her note: "We shall never forget the apple pie. Do you think you could ask the chef to send us the recipe?"

Soon after their visit, came Lincoln Steffens' death. It was unexpected for only the previous day I had stopped by and chatted briefly with him. The next day he was gone.

About twenty came for the funeral services which were held in the living room of his home. Dag described it as being impressive though very simple. Una Jeffers spoke and then excerpts were read from the *Bhagavad Gita*. I just didn't want to go. Instead I sat on the beach and watched and listened to the pounding surf. Then in the late afternoon, as a bank of fog formed in the distance, I started walking back. I passed by Lincoln Steffens' house. There was the familiar sign: Not at Home Until After Four O'clock. He was not there, and yet he was there and would always be there.

CHAPTER EIGHT

The Fleet Suddenly Came to a Stop

They were fighting in Spain, the Japanese were getting ready to move into China, and the man with the little mustache was talking big in Germany. In the United States people who had been hoarding money were beginning to spend it, and those who didn't have any were going on WPA and other projects. The Depression was leveling out and business was picking up. The canneries in Monterey were working again and the fishing fleet was putting out to sea. There was still no prosperity, but there was no longer fear, either.

Hotel Del Monte was beginning to do better and on some weekends it was even full. S. F. B. Morse was pleased, and thought the publicity we had obtained had helped; perhaps it had. When my salary was increased we bought land in Carmel Valley and began building a home.

Movie people, celebrities and others in the news now often came to Del Monte. One of them had a little mustache, but there was nothing cruel about him. Everybody thought he was the funniest man in the world; but I always thought there was great sadness to him. His name was Charlie Chaplin. He liked Del Monte, because he was left alone and no one bothered him. We met on the tennis courts and conversation turned to Robinson Jeffers.

"I admire him," Chaplin said. "That man can write and has something to say and he says it with a wallop."

"Most people don't care for his poetry," I said. "They maintain it is too sordid and that he has a dirty mind."

"It startles them that's why. He digs in too deeply. I'd like to know him. He interests me."

"I'm sure you would interest him. When would you like to meet him?"

"Any time. I'll be here all week."

Several days later, in the early afternoon, we drove out to Carmel Point and to Jeffers' home. Una Jeffers brought out a bottle of sherry and some crackers, and after awhile Chaplin talked about the character he had created and which had appealed to so many millions. He spoke about him in the third person.

"Sometimes I don't know him at all," Chaplin said. "He gets completely away from me and he acts impulsively. He's a funny little fellow, and naturally I have often wondered what there was about him that people like. His make up, his attire, his behavior is beyond reality—he is a caricature of man at his best and at his worst. The little fellow is penniless and his clothes and shoes are too big for him. Yet he wears a bowler and he carries a cane, and he tries hard to be dignified—and to be what he isn't. In doing this he is pathetic and we feel sorry and our hearts go out to him, because he is so ridiculous. He isn't you know. When we see him we say to ourselves, 'thank God, we're not like him.' But we are just like him, though we refuse to admit it. And so our sympathy goes out to him and we laugh and we cry at the things he does and the messes he gets into.

"The mustache is the final touch. I remember him standing in front of the mirror before he appeared for the first time. He looked just as I wanted him to look. Yet I felt there was something missing. The cane, the bowler were symbols of wealth. They helped to make him ludicrous, but not enough.

Then it came to me—the mustache. I don't know why, but there is something about a small mustache on an otherwise clean-shaven face, that is startlingly funny. The moment I put the mustache on him, he was complete."

"When you are making a movie, do you follow a set script?" Jeffers asked him.

"Yes, but only to a point," Chaplin said. "I give him a free hand sometimes, I am unable to control him. He runs away from me and he does things I do not expect."

Chaplin went on talking and finally the conversation turned to poetry and Jeffers told him of how he worked and how sometimes he sat at his desk all morning without writing a line.

"I'm now on a narrative poem, one which I think I am going to call 'The Women of Point Sur,'" Jeffers said. "If you have the time, I'd like to read you parts from it."

Una poured some more sherry and Jeffers took out a handwritten manuscript and he began to read, his voice pitched low and yet it had a piercing quality. Charlie Chaplin sat there fascinated as he listened. As I watched Chaplin I thought of how strange it was that this man with his hair already growing white and the sad look in his eyes was a comedian who had amused and had brought laughter to so many people.

Later in the afternoon, Jeffers took Chaplin through his house and then up the narrow stairway to the stone tower. Jeffers pointed out the nearby Carmelite convent.

"All day long the nuns in there pray," he said. "I sometimes wonder if poetry isn't also a type of prayer to reach inside of people."

We checked in early in the evening at the Waldorf-Astoria. It was the largest hotel we had ever been in and we didn't know what we should do and where we should go. We were frightened by New York and everything we had heard about it. We didn't feel like venturing from our room; there was security in those four walls, but out beyond we did not know what to expect. Finally, we called room service and ordered dinner. The waiter rolled in the table with our food and on it was a vase with a rose. On seeing the rose we didn't feel so lonely and afraid.

In the morning as we walked down Fifth Avenue, the sky was clear, the sun was shining and New York no longer seemed overpowering. The people on the streets were just like the people in San Francisco, except that they walked faster and their faces had a more determined look. We took a ride on a bus, went to the end of the line and rode back again. In the evening we had dinner at Schraft's, and it reminded us of a deluxe version of Delos Curtis' candy store. Then we walked with the crowds on Broadway and stood on the corner of Times Square.

New Yorkers were cold, indifferent, and hard-boiled, we had been told. S. F. B. Morse had given me a list of people I should meet on newspapers and on magazines. Among the first I called in the morning was Frank Crowninshield, editor of the then influential *Vanity Fair* magazine.

"Sam Morse wrote me about you" he said. "Can you meet me at twelve-thirty at '21'?"

I had no idea what '21' was, but I told him I'd be there. He was a tall, thin man with white hair, and the captain and the waiters made a fuss about him. Later he took me to his office and listened patiently to a few ideas I had about possible articles for *Vanity Fair*. He gave me advice on ways we could get publicity about Del Monte into the magazines, including his own. Then as I was about to leave, he said and I know he meant it: "If you need any additional help while you are in New York, be sure to call me."

A few days later, we went to lunch at the old Ritz-Carlton with Edna Woolman Chase, editor of *Vogue*. We ordered salads and Mrs. Chase tucked a napkin on the front of her dress, and afterwards Dag said that only *the* Mrs. Chase could do that at the Ritz-Carlton without waiters raising their eyebrows. Mrs. Chase had all kinds of suggestions about Del Monte and she thought of sending fashion models and photographing them with cypress trees and sand dunes as backgrounds.

"We're always looking for the unusual," she said. "I think we might just do that next Spring and ask Edward Steichen to go out. He's the best photographer we have in the east. He could do some perfectly marvelous things with all that magnificent scenery you have."

Perhaps because we were young and inexperienced Mrs. Chase took a liking to us. She told us what plays to see and where to eat.

"And be careful," she cautioned, "of restaurants that serve salads in large wooden bowls and have their menus written on small blackboards with no prices. They are expensive. Never be afraid to ask prices and always be demanding— the waiters respect you for it."

Harry Bull, then the editor of *Town & Country*, took us to dinner and introduced us to Ludwig Bemelmans who wrote articles and did drawings and covers for the *New Yorker*. Bemelmans invited us for cocktails at a brownstone where he lived. His little daughter had been to a party and as she came into the house, Mrs. Bemelmans asked her if she had enjoyed the party.

"Why, Mamma," she said, "it was all peaches."

It was all peaches for us, too, that first visit to New York. We took the Bemelmans to dinner and he chose the restaurant. They had large wooden salad bowls and the menu was written on a small blackboard and there were no prices on the entrées. When the bill came—Mrs. Chase had been right—it was expensive.

I asked Bemelmans if he would do a color drawing for a Christmas mailing piece for Del Monte. I described what I

had in mind and he liked the idea and said he would do it
and send it out. I inquired what it would cost.

"Oh, between two and three hundred dollars," he said.

"Could you do it for less—say, a hundred?" I asked.

"I suppose so," he said, and laughed.

I never thought we would hear from him again, but after
we were back at Del Monte the drawing came. It was amusing and colorful, but S. F. B. Morse didn't care for it.

"He paints like a child in kindergarten," he said.

"It has a certain charm," I protested, "and it's very sophisticated."

"But not worth a hundred dollars," he said.

Another person I called on during the first visit to New
York was E. G. Coblentz, publisher of the *Journal American*.
He had been with Hearst for years and he was known as
a tough New York editor. The building where the *Journal
American* was published was in Brooklyn; it was old and
antiquated and Mr. Coblentz's office was small with a worn-
out and discolored green carpet.

"So, Sam Morse sent you," he said. "How is he? Still showing off his strength? What can I do for you?"

I told him I wanted to meet Cholly Knickerbocker, the
society columnist, and anyone else he thought I should know
and to whom we could send items and photographs about
people at Del Monte.

"I guess that can be arranged," he said and he took me
to the editorial room and introduced me to Maury Paul, who
did the Knickerbocker column, and to several other colum-
nists. Then I went back to the office with Mr. Coblentz.

"Where are you staying?" he asked.

"At the Waldorf-Astoria," I said.

"How are you going to get back?"

"I'll pick up a cab."

"That's almost a three dollar fare. You can go in the subway and you'll be there in no time."

"I've never been in a subway, Mr. Coblentz," I admitted. "I wouldn't know how to go about it or where to get off."

"You mean you are scared of them?"

"I guess so."

He got up from his desk, went to the clothes hanger that was in the corner of his office, put on his coat and hat. "Come on," he said, "I'm going to put you on the subway."

He led me out of his office and we walked two blocks to the subway entrance. We went down the stairway and stood on the platform until the right train came.

"That's it," he said. "Get in there and when you see a station that says Lexington and Fiftieth, you get off and the Waldorf is right there. Got it?"

"Yes, sir," I said and walked into the subway and saw the doors close. I looked out the window and there was Mr. Coblentz still on the platform as the subway started moving.

I suppose they were all friendly and kind, Frank Crowninshield, Mrs. Chase, Harry Bull, Mr. Coblentz—and others, because they knew Sam Morse and he had written to them about me. Or, perhaps they felt sorry for me—young and inexperienced as I was or it could be, and I think this is so, that New Yorkers aren't cold, indifferent, and hard; there is a soft spot in their hearts for a youngster, searching, trying to get somewhere.

Mrs. Chase kept her word and the fashion models came to Del Monte and then models from I. Magnin's followed. Sometime later, Edward Steichen arrived. He and Spike Graham, the photographer from Del Monte, and I tramped all over the peninsula showing him areas he might want to photograph. Steichen didn't use his camera until he knew exactly what he wanted to photograph. Unlike the photographers of today, the great Steichen only took a limited number of pictures, but those he did make had depth, power and beauty.

The trip to New York was bringing results. Soon Del Monte was in *Vogue, Harper's Bazaar, Town & Country, Life, Fortune,* and other magazines. I had given up gathering news for the wire services and the newspapers I had once represented. But if an important story broke, they still called me and I would cover for them.

One afternoon early in February, as I was getting ready to leave, the most dramatic story of the year was taking place in our own backyard. The *Macon,* the giant dirigible of the U.S. Navy, and the Pacific Fleet were coming up the coast after two days of maneuvers. The *Macon* was the pride of the Navy and it was huge—as long as three football fields and as high as an eleven-story building. Twelve great balloons containing over six million cubic feet of noninflammable helium gas held her aloft.

As the *Macon* and the Pacific Fleet moved up the coast, the dirigible was an hour and a half away from its base at Sunnyvale. Most of the afternoon there had been rain and wind, and as Commander Wiley of the *Macon* sighted the Point Sur Lighthouse, there were wisps of heavy fog and orders were given to change course. The *Macon* was then at 1200 feet altitude doing sixty knots an hour. Directly below it was the fleet of battleships, cruisers and submarines. Aboard the *Macon* was a crew of 83 men and officers.

A few minutes after five o'clock, the men on the dirigible felt a jar, and the *Macon* swerved wildly. As it began to lose altitude, orders were given to drop ballast.

At the Point Sur Lighthouse, Thomas Henderson, the lighthouse keeper, was watching through binoculars the fleet and the *Macon* pass by. Henderson saw a flash of light on the *Macon,* then it began to gain altitude and disappear into the clouds. Henderson glanced at his watch and then started out for the barn to milk his cows. While Henderson headed toward his barn, the *Macon* found itself in serious trouble. As one of the officers described those fateful moments . . . "now the over-heated engines gave out for good. The *Macon* teetered at 4600 feet, a giant slanting obelisk, a great panatella cigar, buoyed in space by a bubble of gas . . ."

The *Macon* was breaking up and Commander Wiley sent out an S.O.S. and then gave orders for his men and officers to prepare to abandon ship.

At five-fifteen, the wire services picked up the *Macon's* distress signal, and because I happened to be the closest to the scene, they phoned and asked me to rush down to the Big Sur area.

"Hurry!" they said. "We'll take everything you can get on it."

I ran downstairs and found Spike Graham in his studio.

"Get your camera, Spike," I shouted. "The *Macon* is sinking in the Big Sur, and we're going to cover it."

Spike Graham was from the South, brilliant but slow moving and nothing very much ever bothered him. As a photographer, I always thought, he was as good as Weston or Steichen. But he never pushed himself and had little interest in fame. He was tall, gaunt and his hair was almost white. He had once been a baseball player, a court reporter and then he had turned to photography. He interchanged between smoking cigars and a pipe and now, sitting next to me in the car, he was calmly filling his Dunhill.

"Don't you realize this is a big story, Spike?" I said.

"It's also a long drive down the coast and by the time we get there, it will be getting dark and there won't be a damn thing," Spike said cynically.

"But, if the *Macon* is down and you get any pictures, every photo service and newspaper will want them and you'll make yourself a mint of money."

"That'll be the day," Spike said, and lit his pipe with the kitchen matches that he always used. "You better watch your driving," he added, drawing leisurely on his pipe. "You're going over seventy."

Spike Graham was a taciturn person, sometimes going for days without talking unless it was absolutely necessary, and then it might be a mere "yes" or a "no" in response to a question. He could be stubborn, but he also had a fine sense of humor and he enjoyed listening to or telling a good story. But when he was moody, it was hard to get him out of it. He wasn't especially moody that late afternoon driving to Big Sur. He was, as he might say, "thinking." However, excitement, like yawning, can be contagious, and Spike soon began to feel the excitement I felt.

"If the wire services are right and the *Macon* has plunged into the drink, it would be a big story," he finally admitted.

"It is a big story," I reiterated as we approached the Point Sur lighthouse.

There was still plenty of light, for the sun had just gone down and the sky was a reddish-brown.

The lighthouse was on a high mound several miles away, and there was a dirt road leading to it. There was an eight-foot wire mesh fence and a wooden gate with a large sign reading:

Trespassing Forbidden

U.S. Government Property

The gate had a heavy chain and a lock. As I stopped the car, Spike jumped out and went to examine the chain.

"They've got it locked," he reported as he walked back and got into the car. "There's only one way to get in."

"How?"

"Just back up, give it gas, and we'll break through."

"But, it's U.S. Government property."

"So what? Isn't this an emergency?"

I backed up the car several hundred yards, put my foot on the gas and we plunged head-on toward the gate. The chain snapped and the gate swung open.

When we reached the lighthouse, we could see in the distance a long line of ships that made up the Pacific Fleet. Flares were still burning and small boats from the fleet were picking up and searching for survivors of the *Macon*. We knocked at the door of the lighthouse, but there was no answer. When I heard the telephone ringing, I opened the door and picked up the receiver.

"Hello, there—Point Sur lighthouse?" a British voice was on the line.

"This is the lighthouse," I said.

"I'm calling from London—from the *Daily Herald*. What goes out there with the *Macon*? She's down, we hear. Any survivors?"

"I wouldn't know," I said. "The lighthouse keeper is not around."

"Who are you?"

"A reporter."

"Jolly fast on the scene, aren't you? Can you tell me anything?"

"Not a thing. Just got here."

"The *Macon's* down in the drink. That's all we heard. If you find out any more, will you give us a jingle collect? Cheerio, old boy."

"Cheerio," I said and hung up.

Just then Spike Graham and I saw a man approaching with a pail in each hand. He came into the house and put the pails down.

"What goes on here?" he asked. "Who are you?"

"Newspapermen—don't you know the *Macon* is down?"

"So, that's what them ships are hanging around for—sort of figured something was wrong," he said. "My name's Henderson. I'm the lighthouse keeper."

"Didn't you see anything?"

"About half-hour ago I was watching the Fleet through the glasses and caught a flash of light. The *Macon* was kind of wavering. I figured something was wrong, and I even thought of getting my movie camera and taking some shots."

"You mean you had a camera and could have filmed it?"

"I reckon I could—my camera was loaded and everything. But it was getting past milking time, and I always milk my cows about around five-thirty."

"You could have made yourself a fortune," I said.

The telephone began ringing again. I reached for it. It was the United Press and the moment I hung up it was the Associated Press and then the San Francisco newspapers. They were frantic. The *Macon* was down and the survivors were being picked up from rubber rafts by ships from the Fleet, they said.

"Spare no expense," I was told. "Hire a boat and get on the Fleet. Interview the survivors. Find out what happened. It's the biggest story of the year!"

"But, where am I going to get a boat?"

"Hasn't the lighthouse keeper got one? Just find a boat and get aboard one of the ships."

I relayed the information to Spike and to Henderson.

"I've got no boat," the lighthouse keeper said. "Besides they must be crazy. Don't they realize there are just rocks and a pounding sea below us? There is no way to reach any of the ships from here. You're close, but you might as well be a million miles away."

"What are we going to do, Spike?" I asked.

Spike filled his pipe, lit it and began puffing on it.

"We could go back to Monterey," he said after awhile, "and try to rent a fishing boat. If we could get a boat, we might manage to board one of the ships."

"Let's go," I said, and we left behind a puzzled lighthouse keeper as we rushed to the car and started back on the road again. It was now past six o'clock. The fog was beginning to get thick and it was cold.

When we reached Monterey, we went on the wharf and

began searching for boats. The sardine fishing season was on, and the large purse seiners had put out hours before. There was only one boat left, and it was at the end of the pier; there were lights in the cabin, and it was getting ready to go out. We could see a member of the crew untying the ropes.

"Hey!" I yelled from the car.

The man in rubber fishing boots looked over at us and then went right on untying the ropes.

I jumped out of the car. "Where's your captain?" I asked.

"Below."

"Call him."

"He busy. We gonna fishin'," he said.

"You tell him I want to see him."

"Okay—okay."

Spike had joined me and we both looked at the boat and then at each other.

"That thing's not much larger than a rowboat," Spike said. "We can't go out into the sea in that tub."

"We have to," I said, "or find another."

The pier was dark and deserted; we stood there in the cold. The captain finally came out of the cabin.

"Hey, watcha you want?" he asked, standing on the edge of the deck.

"You going fishing?"

"Sure. Watcha you think we gonna do?"

"How much are you going to get for the fish you catch tonight?"

"I not know that. No fisherman know how much fish he catch."

"Two hundred dollars?"

"Maybe. Maybe four hundred."

"We'll give you two hundred dollars if you take us out."

"Where you want to go?" he asked, showing a little interest.

"Way out beyond the bay," I said, and then explained

about the *Macon* and the men aboard the Navy ships. "Just take us to the ships—that's all we want."

The captain, whose name we learned later, was Salvador, called together the two other members of his crew. They began talking in Portuguese and they appeared to be arguing among themselves. Finally the captain spoke out.

"Three hundred dollars, and we take you out."

"Two hundred."

"Three hundred."

"Two hundred and fifty—that's all we can pay."

Once again there was another conference in Portuguese, but it didn't go on for long.

"Okay," the captain said. "We take you."

The two crew members helped us on board, Spike holding on to his camera. We went on below. The cabin was tiny and it stank of fish and of engine oil. We sat down on one of the two wooden benches and in a few more minutes we slowly began moving away from the pier. We were out in the bay only a short distance when the engine backfired and died. The men began yelling at each other in Portuguese and one of them started working on the engine. After awhile he had it going again.

Salvador, the captain, came into the cabin.

"You think the engine no go, hey? It go. We make good time soon we get out of bay. You want glass of wine?"

"Sure," I said. "Have you anything to eat?"

"No, we all have big dinner before we start out, but we got lots of wine."

He brought out a gallon jug of red wine and filled two coffee mugs. He gave one to Spike and one to me. Then he filled a mug for himself.

"The wine will keep us warm," he said.

Neither Spike nor I had eaten since lunch. The wine was strong and we began to feel it right away.

"You have no bread or salami?"

"No food. You hungry?" he seemed concerned.

"We sure are."

"Too bad, we no carry food. Maybe on the other ship you go on board, they feed you."

He left us and went up on deck. The fishing boat, now that it was in the middle of the bay, began gaining speed as it headed toward the open sea. It also began to roll and pitch, but rather gently at first. Then when we were no longer in the bay, but out to sea, the boat rocked from side to side. I glanced over at Spike. His eyes were closed and one moment his face was white and then it was green; he was getting seasick.

"Spike," I called to him.

There was no answer.

"Spike."

Still no answer.

I managed to open one of the windows of the cabin. A piercing cold gust of wind came blowing in. That seemed to help. Spike opened his eyes.

"You all right?"

"Guess so," he said, and closed his eyes again.

The fishing boat went on rocking back and forth and leaping through the waves for what seemed hours. I looked at my watch. It was barely nine o'clock. Salvador, the captain, had said it would take three hours before we reached the channel the Navy ships would use on their way north to San Francisco. There were no charts, and no radio on the boat; it didn't need them. Salvador seemed to know exactly in which direction to go.

"If the Fleet, she going north, I find 'em," he had said when we first started out.

The Portuguese are great navigators and Salvador lived up to this reputation. At exactly eleven o'clock, he yelled into the cabin.

"The Fleet—she here!"

I looked out the window and in the distance and only a few miles away, was the Pacific Fleet, a long string of ships sailing in a straight line. I left the cabin and went up on deck. "Head for the first ship," I said. "That must be the flagship." "Okay, we go there," Salvador replied.

It was cold and windy on deck. I had only a light jacket and I turned the collar up and tried to keep it closed around my throat. There was no fog now and the night was clear. At first the ships looked like toy ships, and then as we got closer and closer they seemed huge.

We were getting near to the flagship and would soon be in its path.

"Blow your whistle—make some noise!" I shouted at Salvador. "Do anything to attract attention."

"Okay," Salvador said.

He began blasting away. It sounded loud to me, but I wondered if the officers on the bridge of the flagship could hear it. Spike apparently had, for he left the cabin and was standing by me.

"What's going on?" he yelled.

"Look—the whole Fleet's there," I said, then over to Salvador who appeared to be enjoying thoroughly this new experience, "Make more noise. Blast it louder!"

"Giving it all I can give," he shouted back.

"Got any flares?"

"Yep."

"Shoot some flares out."

"We get in trouble. Flares only good when boat is in trouble. We violate maritime law."

"Give them to me," Spike said, now no longer seasick. "I'll send them out."

"Okay," Salvador agreed, and in another few moments Spike was lighting and throwing the burning red flares into the water.

Each minute the Fleet was coming closer toward us. The

flagship was less than half a mile away. Unless it stopped or changed course it would run us down. But Salvador held his course.

In another few seconds floodlights began beaming on us. They had seen the flares from the bridge of the flagship. The Fleet, as we learned later, had picked up eighty-one survivors from the *Macon,* and two were still missing. Did the admiral in command assume we had those survivors? I don't know. But now, from the tower of the flagship, an urgent Morse code signal went flashing to the second ship, which picked it up and relayed it on to the third, and so it went all the way down to the last ship. The Fleet suddenly came to a stop.

"Jeeeeeesus H. Christ!" Spike shouted out. "You've done it! Christ, you've done it! You've stopped the whole goddamn Pacific Fleet."

As we approached the flagship, we heard an officer calling out through a megaphone. "Aye, out there! What is it? Can you hear me?"

I cupped my hands and yelled loudly:

"We hear you. We're newspapermen. We want permission to come on board."

"Hold on there!" came the officer's voice.

We waited. A full minute. Another minute. Our small boat was pitching back and forth in the choppy water. Salvador had cut off the engine and it was strangely quiet out there in the open sea. Finally we heard the officer's voice calling us again.

"Can you hear me?"

"We hear you."

"No one's allowed on board. Admiral's orders."

I yelled back, trying to argue. It was no use. I saw the lights on the tower of the flagship signaling again in Morse code to the other ships. Salvador, standing next to us on the deck, waved his fist at the flagship.

"Hey, you, Admiral," he shouted out. "Why you not let my friends on board?" Then he spat out at the flagship.

In a few more minutes the Fleet began moving, and from a distance we saw the other ships, including the *Richmond*, the *Concord* and the *Cincinnati*, pass by us. We were so close and yet, as the lighthouse keeper had said, we might as well have been a million miles away.

It was after one o'clock when our fishing boat made its way across the dark waters of the bay and tied up at the pier. We were cold, hungry and, more than anything, we were frustrated. Even Salvador was depressed. "He no good, that Admiral," we could hear him saying as we climbed out from his boat and started walking toward the car we had left on the wharf.

CHAPTER NINE

The Mysterious East Gets More
Mysterious

After that trip on Salvador's fishing boat, it wasn't likely that Spike Graham would be eager to put to sea again. Although he was many years older than I—he was approaching fifty while I was still in my twenties—he, too, was searching for excitement and adventure.

It began one afternoon when I was in his studio. The radio was on and most of the news was about the invasion of China by the Japanese.

"Wouldn't it be great to be a foreign correspondent in China covering the war," I said.

"There you go, dreaming," he said.

"I wish somehow we could get there," I, nevertheless, went on.

"China's a long ways off," Spike said. "You and I just wouldn't have a chance going there."

"Why not?"

"We're stuck here, that's why. Besides how would we go?"

"That's simple," I said. "On a ship."

"That would take a lot of money and time."

"I know Ed White and Mr. Takahashi of the NYK line. Perhaps they'd give us a special rate."

"Well, talk to 'em next time you see 'em. But the closest

we'll ever get to China will be Kin Fat Ho's restaurant," Spike said, and started for his darkroom.

I left Del Monte, got into my car to go on the Carmel Valley road toward the ranch house where we lived, a good thirty-minute drive. I turned the radio to the *Time Marches On* program. This was sponsored by *Time* magazine, dramatizing important events of the week with realistic sound effects and it also had a commentator with a deep, pontifical voice. "In Germany and in Italy," he was saying, "millions of soldiers are getting ready for war and in Japan, now the third member of the Axis, troops and ships are invading the coast of peace-loving China. Generalissimo Chiang Kai-shek is fully prepared and waiting for the enemy—his highly trained army will repulse the little men from the Rising Sun . . ."

How wrong were the commentators and how wrong and misinformed were most people. There were not many who really knew or cared what was gonig on in the world, and as far as China was concerned, it was too far away and too remote to worry about.

As I listened to the radio that afternoon I began to hear the voice of Lincoln Steffens. *"Find a war and cover it. It will give you maturity and the type of experience you need."*

By the time I reached home I had made up my mind I was going to China. It was now only a question of when and how I'd do it. I was making good money, but we were in debt over the property we had bought and the house we had built. A trip to China was expensive. If I could persuade a magazine or a newspaper to send Spike and me to cover the war . . .

I wrote to editors, but they said they had their own correspondents in the Orient and they were not looking for additional coverage. Only *Life* magazine and Lester Markell of the New York *Times* seemed interested in any material we might gather.

I talked to Ed White and Mr. Takahashi of the NYK line, whose Japanese ships went to Japan from San Francisco twice a month. The ships were loaded with cargo, but the passenger cabins were virtually empty. "If you will do some articles about Japan that will bring tourists there, perhaps we can arrange something," Mr. Takahashi said.

Mr. Takahashi not only arranged something, he managed to get free round trip passages to Yokahama for Spike and me. In return we agreed to do a series of articles with photographs on tourist attractions in Japan. The plans were to leave in November and we would be gone for three to four months. We did not hide from Mr. Takahashi our intentions of going to China; he merely closed his eyes to it.

By now Japan had invaded large parts of China and the little men from the Rising Sun were not being repulsed; the front pages were full of stories of bombings and atrocities. China had become a testing ground for the Japanese Army and Navy.

Dag recognized that our going to China involved a certain danger and risk and she faced up to it. But not Alice Graham, Spike's wife was opposed to the trip from the start.

"Why, they are just going away to have fun," she remonstrated to Dag. "Don't think they're not. Besides I wouldn't put it past them if they never came back."

Nothing could convince her otherwise. She was bitter and emotionally upset about Spike leaving with me.

Getting ready for the trip had taken time. The State Department, as the invasion of China by the Japanese took a critical turn, restricted travel into China. The United Press, however, assigned us as special correspondents and arranged for our passports. There was also a fashion story at Pebble Beach which had been planned long ago and which had to be finished for *Vogue* magazine before our departure.

Half a dozen models had come from I. Magnin's in San Francisco for the story on which Spike was doing the photographs. The models had been to Del Monte in the past and included Peggy, Doris, Beverly, and Leah. Leah was a brunette, tall, thin and with long, beautiful legs. She was married to an automobile salesman and they had a seven-year-old child.

To the models, our going to China to cover the war seemed dramatic and we thoroughly enjoyed our new roles. Late in the afternoon, when we were finished and just before the girls started back for San Francisco, we stopped at Del Monte Lodge for a drink.

"Say, Spike," Leah said while we were sitting at the bar, "want to do me a favor?"

"Of course, Leah—if I can," he said, expecting her to ask for prints of the pictures he had taken.

"It isn't much," Leah's long eyelashes fluttered. "My son, Timmy—he's collecting matchbook covers. Would you pick some up for him in the Orient?"

"Glad to, Leah," Spike answered.

"But you'll forget about it."

"I won't. I promise."

"I know you, Spike. I'll write you a reminder," she said, and opened a Del Monte Lodge matchbook cover she had been holding in her hand. With a pencil she printed inside: DON'T FORGET LEAH.

She gave it to Spike and he slipped the matches into the pocket of his sports jacket. We drove the girls back to the hotel where they had left their car and they returned to San Francisco while we went on home. The incident was forgotten and within a week we were on the *Chichibu Maru* headed for Japan.

Because there were few passengers on the ship, Spike and I shared one of the larger cabins in first class; but we spent most of our time in second class where there were students, two university professors and an American wrestler going to Japan. All the way to Hawaii the trip was calm and pleasant. In Hawaii the ship docked early and we had time to take a

tour of the island and to swim and sunbathe at Waikiki before
the *Chichibu Maru* set sail again.

We were two days out of Hawaii when news came over the
ship's wireless that the Japanese had taken Nanking, the then
capital of China, and that Chiang Kai-shek, the members of
his cabinet and other Chinese officials had escaped. The occasion called for a full-scale celebration by the captain, the
officers, and the members of the crew. They kept on toasting
each other and shouting "Banzai! Banzai!" after each drink of
saki.

Three days later we learned that the *Panay*, a United States
gunboat, had been bombed and sunk by the Japanese with
only a few survivors. We stayed down in second class with our
friends, the university professors and the American wrestler,
most of that day and evening wondering whether or not the
United States would declare war on Japan and if so, what
would happen to us, traveling aboard a Japanese ship. By
then, the weather had turned cold and during the night we
sailed straight into a hurricane. The ship began tossing and
for a time it seemed as if we were on Salvador's fishing boat.

By morning the storm had not let up and out on deck it
was windy and cold. Spike wasn't feeling well and I suggested
we go for a walk and get some fresh air. We had both brought
overcoats, but had not worn them during the trip. We slipped
on our coats, left the cabin and as we started around the deck,
Spike's hands went into the pockets of his coat. He stopped
abruptly, and the strangest expression came over his face.

"What in the hell is this?" he said. In his hand he was holding a Del Monte Lodge matchbook cover and on it was tied
a gold wedding band. Spike opened the match cover. It was
the one on which Leah had scribbled: DON'T FORGET
LEAH. There was no other note or explanation—only the
wedding ring Spike's wife had worn for twenty-five years.
Spike looked at it for several moments and then his hand
closed tightly around the matchbook cover and the ring. With

a powerful swing, he threw them over the railing and into the sea.

When we finally arrived in Yokohama we took the night train to Kobe and picked up a French ship that, five days later, landed us in Shanghai which for years had been China's largest and busiest seaport. But now the docks were deserted and as we drove in a taxi through the International Settlement, there were, however, no signs of destruction by bombings. The Japanese had been careful to avoid shelling the French, American, British, Russian, and their own sectors.

The Japanese Army had surrounded the city and thousands of Chinese refugees had sought safety inside the International Settlement. We stopped in front of the Cathay Hotel, registered and went up to our room. While we were unpacking Spike noticed that by the bedside table there was a square black box with five buttons, each one a different color.

"I wonder what they are for," he said, "and do they work."

"Try them," I said, and Spike did. He pushed all five buttons at one time.

The response was immediate. There was a knock at the door and five Chinese appeared, wearing long, blue-colored housecoats.

"You call, master?" said Number One Boy, and the rest stood in line alongside him waiting for instructions from us.

"We've rubbed Aladdin's lamp," Spike said. "What do we do with them now?"

"We're in the mysterious East," I said. "Tell them what you want and your wish will be granted."

"Ask them if they got any girls," Spike said, not really meaning it.

But, not Number One Boy, who seemed to be the spokesman. "Yes, master," he said. "Can do. Master want White Russian, Chinese, French—what kind of girl, master want?"

"No girls," I spoke up. "We make fun, savvy? No girls."

"No girls?" Number One Boy appeared disappointed.

"No girls," I repeated. "Perhaps press clothes, yes?"

"Yes, master, pless clothes."

We turned over some suits to Number One Boy. But the rest still stood waiting. I pointed to the door.

"Go away, now. Savvy? Go away."

Finally they left the room and we went on with our unpacking. We had just barely finished putting things away when there was a knock. I didn't want to open the door for I was certain that Number One Boy had not fully understood and that a Chinese, a White Russian or a French girl would be standing there.

I called to Spike. "It's your turn to open the door."

It was no girl. It was Joe Rucker of Paramount Newsreels, who had covered many stories at Hotel Del Monte and had helped in trying to stop Cynthia, the seal, from escaping into the ocean.

"They just told me at the desk you were here," he said as he came into the room. "If you'd like to see something of Shanghai, I have a car outside and I'll take you around."

Joe Rucker knew China and Shanghai, for he had been there many times. We couldn't have had a better guide. He took us outside of the International Settlement and into the outskirts of the city. Now the little men of the Rising Sun were everywhere, fully armed. There was a determined look in their faces, and disdain in their eyes when they saw the American flag on Joe Rucker's car. The Japanese had done a thorough job of shelling and bombing the city; thousands of Chinese had been killed and only a few buildings and houses were still standing. We left the car and walked along some of the streets; the smell of filth was horrifying. In some sections the stench was so strong that we tied handkerchiefs across our mouths and noses.

Eventually, we returned to the International Settlement; here there was practically no sign of war, except for the feeling of anxiety that was evident everywhere. Those who lived in the International Settlement knew that it was only a matter of time, perhaps months before the Japanese took over. There was no assurance either in the French and American destroyers that were anchored outside of Shanghai in the Whangpoo River.

"When we passed off the sinking of the *Panay* as only an 'unfortunate incident,' the Japs became convinced they could get away with almost anything they might want to do," Joe Rucker said. "From now on, no one's going to stop them."

Later that evening we met Joe Rucker at the bar of the Cathay and he introduced us to some of the foreign correspondents, including Art Mencken of Pathé Newsreels. Over gimlets and gin and bitters, they talked about the war. Most of them had recently returned from Nanking. "There's no loyalty or will to fight," one of the correspondents said. "There's just confusion."

Night life in Shanghai did not start until late. It was after ten o'clock when Joe Rucker took us to a Russian restaurant where we ate caviar, Chicken Kiev and drank champagne. The restaurant was luxurious and there were dimly lit antique chandeliers hanging from the high ceiling. A group of four violinists playing Russian music, went from table to table.

"What a way to cover a war," Spike said as he dug into the huge dish of iced caviar.

"It's a war without any fronts," Joe Rucker said. "The Japs are jumping all over the place and moving so fast you can't catch up with them. They took Nanking in just a short time."

"Aren't we ever going to get near any fighting?" I asked.

"Not around here," Joe said. "We'll have to go south—in and around Canton. Perhaps there, we might see some."

When we were finished with dinner it was close to midnight.

"It's still early," Joe said, "but we might start picking up some night life. You're going to get homesick," he went on. "I'm going to take you to the Del Monte Nightclub."

And there was a Del Monte in Shanghai. From Joe's car

we could see the big electric sign: DEL MONTE flashing on and off. The Del Monte was no ordinary night club; it had an orchestra and a dance floor, and it also had girls and more girls—almost all white Russians, young and attractively dressed in low-cut dinner gowns. They were sitting at half a dozen tables and they looked us over. Then one of the girls walked up to us.

"You like to buy a nice box of American candies?" she asked, and held out a box of chocolates.

"No candies," Joe spoke up, sending her on her way. Then he said: "Demon Hyde, who owns and runs the place, once told me that one box of candy lasts a year or more. It is resold hundreds of times, as no customer who buys it ever bothers to open it. So the same box is used over and over again."

The night club was almost empty, but Joe said it was still early. "Things don't begin to happen around here until after two or three in the morning," he explained.

We ordered another drink and then Demon Hyde saw Joe Rucker. He came over to our table and Joe introduced us.

"So you're from Del Monte," Demon Hyde said. "Small world, isn't it? You know, I was once a bellboy there. When I came to Shanghai and Al Israel and I opened this spot—I thought, What shall we call it? Then I remembered the Hotel Del Monte and we decided to call it Del Monte, and it's been that way ever since. Glad you fellows are here."

Demon Hyde was tough and hard, and he looked the part of a night club owner. He was wearing a diamond ring on his right hand and he turned it back and forth with his other hand as he talked.

"You've come here at the worst possible time," he went on. "Up to a year ago, this place was jumping. But now it's dead. No tourists. Only some of our old customers drop in, and a few sailors and officers from ships. Not too many ships anymore, either." He spoke in a loud, sharp voice using short sentences. "Can't really tell how long we'll be operating. Liable

to close down any time. We're just holding on. Maybe a
month. Two months. Perhaps a year. Nobody knows. When
the Japs take over—they will, you know—all of us old Chinese
hands are finished. Correct, Joe? Joe knows."

Joe nodded and Demon Hyde kept on.

"The U.S. and the French, and about everyone else, are
ostriches. Put their heads in sand. Don't want to see what's
happening. Even worse. They don't care. Don't give a damn.
Chiang's not much better either. Or those around him. The
Japs are not always winning by bombing or shelling a place.
They're buying off Chinese generals with silver bullets. No
use telling you all this. You'll find out in no time."

He clapped his hands and hailed a waiter.

"Bring some champagne," he said. "You fellows don't seem
to be having fun. Better have some fun." He motioned to
three of the girls sitting at a table not too far away and they
were over instantly. "Entertain the boys," he said. "And be
nice to them. They're friends. From back home. Boys, meet
Anna. And Sonia and this is Olga." He got up from the table.
"Have a good time while you can. See you boys later."

Anna took a seat next to me. She had blonde hair cropped
short, and her blue eyes sparkled. She was wearing a black
dress with thin straps and a pearl necklace. She was young—
in her early twenties—and she laughed and tried to be gay
and entertaining, yet she was forcing it and could not conceal it.

"You're sad," I said.

"All Russians are sad," she said. "We have nothing—we
White Russians are nothing. We are lost here in China."

"You are young and very beautiful."

"You are sweet to say this to me," she said, and she gently
squeezed my hand.

The waiter appeared with the champagne that Demon
Hyde had ordered. He served it in crystal glasses that had
been properly chilled.

"Banzai!" Spike said as he raised his glass.

"Please, don't say that," Sonia, who was sitting next to him spoke up. "Say son-of-a-bitch—say anything, but not bonzai. They are dogs—traitorous dogs—the Japs. I hate them. We all hate them."

The music began playing.

"Come on, Anna," I said. "Let's dance."

I held Anna close to me.

"You are nice American man," she whispered in my ear. "I wish to see you again. Not here. Somewhere else. Could we not have lunch? Tomorrow? Yes, please," she was almost pleading. "We have lunch tomorrow. Yes?"

"I don't know what our plans are for tomorrow, Anna."

"But you will have lunch with me?"

"Sure—why not? We'll have lunch tomorrow."

"Good," she was smiling now and the disappointment was gone from her face and from her voice. "Where are you staying?"

"Cathay."

"Tomorrow I will meet you there. At one o'clock."

When the music stopped we went back to the table. We finished the bottle of champagne and ordered another. It was after four o'clock when we finally left the Del Monte and returned to our hotel. I was exhausted and a little drunk.

"Tomorrow we're having lunch with Anna," I said as I climbed into bed.

"What do you mean, *we?*" Spike said.

"WE," I shouted and in another moment I was asleep.

There was a knock at the door. The drapes over the windows had been drawn and it was dark in the room. Could it be one o'clock already? I heard a key in the door. The door opened and there was a streak of bright light. I sat up in bed. Spike had also awakened. In the middle of the room and coming toward us was Number One Boy, and he was carrying a tray.

"Good morning, master," he said and politely bowed.

Spike stretched, yawned and looked at his watch. Then to Number One Boy: "What's the idea of waking us up?"

"Your tiffin, master."

"Tiffin! Tiffin, hell!" he shouted at Number One Boy. "You get out of here and leave us alone."

"Velly solly, master," Number One Boy said, but made no effort to move.

"Didn't you hear me?" Spike went on. "Get out! Leave us alone. We don't want tiffin."

"I savvy, master, but we always bring tiffin at eight o'clock."

Number One Boy had been well trained and disciplined. He wouldn't leave until we had our tea. When he was gone we fell asleep again.

When I awakened it was twelve o'clock. Spike had drawn the drapes and he was already dressed and getting ready to leave the room.

"Where are you going, Spike?" I asked, still half asleep.

"I'm going to look for a place where I can get films developed," Spike said, and started toward the door carrying two film magazines of pictures he had taken the previous day.

"Don't forget we have a luncheon date with Anna at one," I said.

"Better have lunch with her alone."

"No, sir," I said. "See you at one."

"You're sure you want me?"

"Sure."

I knew now that it was a mistake to agree to have lunch with Anna. Perhaps she wouldn't show up. Well, if she did, we'd take her to a restaurant, have some lunch and by three o'clock we'd have her out of our hair.

I climbed out of bed, went into the bathroom, took two

aspirins, shaved and showered. While I was in the bathroom, Number Two and Three Boys had come into the room and were making up the beds. I still wasn't dressed.

"Come back later," I said. "Make up room while we are at lunch, savvy?"

"We savvy, master," Number Two Boy said, and they both went on cleaning the room.

As I dressed I watched how expertly and quickly they worked. I wasn't angry with them, or at Number One Boy who had awakened us with tea. It was just amazingly funny, I thought. They were set in their ways and that was that. The mysterious East. You couldn't fight all of China.

I still had a headache, so I took two more aspirin. It was now a quarter to one. The two Chinese boys had finished cleaning the bathroom, had brought in fresh towels and were gone. When I next looked at my watch it was one o'clock. I slipped on my coat and thought I'd go down to the lobby and wait for Anna and Spike; just then I heard the key in the door and the door opened. It was Number One Boy. There was a pleased expression on his face.

"Young lady outside, master," he said. "Very nice lady."

"All right. Tell her I meet her in the lobby."

"Not in lobby, master. In hall."

Suddenly and right behind him was Anna. Number One Boy turned to her and bowed slightly.

"Master says, please come in."

Anna was in the room, Number One Boy was gone and the door was closed. Anna walked toward the window. She was wearing a dark blue tailored suit, an embroidered white blouse, and a silver fox fur.

"You think perhaps I do not keep luncheon date?" she said. "I am punctual. It is exactly one o'clock, no?"

"I was just leaving to meet you in the lobby," I said. "Where would you like to eat?"

"Food here in hotel is very good. We eat here, yes?" She

walked over to the table by the bed and pressed one of the buttons.

"You mean you want to eat here in the room?"

"Why not? You have nice room and it is quiet. Here we can talk better."

The door opened and it was Number One Boy.

"Bring bottle of champagne," Anna said, "some caviar and a menu, chop, chop."

"Chop, chop, Missy," he said and was gone.

"Look here, Anna," I said, "we're not going to eat here. Besides, Spike's going to join us for lunch."

"Your friend from last night?"

"Yes. He's traveling with me and he should be back in a few minutes."

I thought she wouldn't take to the idea of Spike having lunch with us, but it didn't appear to make any difference to her.

"If he's your friend, I do not mind. It is all right. He's a nice man, too."

Our room at the Cathay Hotel was spacious. In one corner there was a dining table, a sofa, and three comfortable lounging chairs. Anna sat on the sofa, took out a long cigarette holder and a package of cigarettes from her purse, and I lit the cigarette for her.

"It is nice to be here where it is peaceful and one can talk —the noise and the music at Del Monte—one can never talk there," Anna said. "Mr. Hyde has been very good to me—to all of us—but, soon there will be no Del Monte—no Shanghai."

Number One Boy was back in the room with the champagne in a silver ice bucket. He took out the bottle from the ice and showed me the label.

"Very good champagne. I open, master?"

"You open."

He filled two glasses and brought them to us. He placed a menu on the table.

"Caviar being made ready. I bring soon," he said, and once more he disappeared.

Anna and I sipped the champagne. I glanced at my watch. What was holding up Spike? Now, as I watched Anna sitting in front of me, her shapely legs crossed, I wasn't so sure I cared if Spike ever returned. Anna drained her glass.

"More champagne, please," she said. I refilled her glass and mine. A feeling came over me that I wanted to get drunk —that both of us should get very drunk.

Anna put another cigarette into the long holder. As I reached over to light it, I became aware of her perfume. It was very subtle. I felt far away from everything and everybody. I was weightless, rising high into the air and into a euphoria where nothing mattered.

"I wish to have a little talk," Anna said. "I wish to make a proposition to you."

The bubble burst and I came crashing down to reality. Now it comes, I thought. She is about to set a price for coming up to the room.

"Yes," I said.

"All of us White Russians in Shanghai, in Harbin and in other parts of China, we have no passports. We are people without a country. When the Del Monte closes—what will I do? So, I think. I think hard. You are a nice American man. You will help me, no? I wish you to marry me, yes?"

"What? Marry you!" I wasn't sure I had heard right.

"Yes, marry me. I have money saved, and I have jewels my family brought from Russia. I ask only you marry me."

"But Anna, I can't possibly marry you."

"No?" She got up from the sofa and stood before me. "Look at me. Am I not attractive and pretty?"

"You are all of that, Anna."

"I have good legs, yes?" she walked around the room and

pirouetted several times as models do. "I have much to offer a man. I will make a good wife. I also know how to cook. And I sew and make my own clothes. I am not afraid of work. I will work hard."

"I am sure you will make someone a good wife."

"Then, you will marry me?"

"I can't, Anna," I said. "You see, I already have a wife."

That stopped her, but only momentarily. "You have a wife number one. I will be wife number two."

"I'm not a Mormon," I said.

"A Mor-Mon? What is that? I do not understand, please."

"Forget it," I said. "I couldn't marry you under any circumstances. Besides, why would you want to marry me? We hardly know each other."

"You are American. If I marry you I can come into United States. I leave China. I come to America with you."

"It would never work out."

"You do not like me. I do not please you?"

"You are beautiful, Anna. Very beautiful. But no marriage."

"No marriage?"

"Yes, no marriage."

I gulped the champagne and as I put the glass down I heard an angry voice outside the door of the room. It was Spike. I went to the door and opened it. Spike was arguing with Number One Boy, who was standing, his arms widespread, guarding the entrance to the room.

"Get out of my way," Spike was shouting at him.

"No one come in," Number One Boy was saying. Then, as he saw me at the door. "I explain, master. I say, 'Master busy with girl. Cannot be disturbed.' He no savvy. Master busy with girl."

"He's my friend. Let him come in," I said.

Number One Boy stood aside, but there was a puzzled expression on his face.

Demon Hyde came to see us off on the boat we were taking to Hong Kong. Joe Rucker and Art Mencken were making the trip with us. Demon Hyde was carrying two bottles of champagne. He placed them on the bureau of the cabin.

"Here's a little Christmas cheer for you," he said.

We thanked him and then, turning to Spike and me, he said, "You didn't see Shanghai at its best, but you'll be back again some day. Shanghai is the kind of a place you don't easily forget."

CHAPTER TEN

Everything Available at All Times

We had traveled thousands of miles to cover a war that we were still trying to find. The Japanese had preferred to call this war an *incident*, but their armies nevertheless had seized the principal cities of northern and central China. While some Chinese war lords remained in control of certain areas, the fighting that did take place was sporadic and in remote sections difficult to reach. There was consequently no well established military lines or battle fronts; almost everywhere the Chinese had failed to resist or had retreated.

These were the conditions in China at that time. Neither Spike nor I knew too much about it, but the experienced correspondents and men such as Joe Rucker and Art Mencken did, and they made a point of telling us. If there was to be any fighting in the future, they said, it might be in Southern China and in Canton. The south was strong, aggressive and would put up a battle. They were going there and they suggested we go along.

So we left Shanghai and took the ship to Hong Kong. Five days later the four of us registered at the Peninsular Hotel in Hong Kong and that first night sat in the bar drinking Scotch and soda with no ice, while an orchestra played very British dinner music. It was also at the bar that Joe Rucker said he was going to send a telegram to General Cohen about our traveling to Canton.

"General Cohen? A Jewish general in the Chinese army? You're kidding," I said.

"No, I'm not," Joe Rucker replied. "General Cohen is not exactly in the Chinese army, but he's one of the most influential men in Southern China. Getting into Canton right now might not be easy, but if anyone can arrange it, he can."

Then, Joe Rucker and Art Mencken began describing General Morris Cohen, who though born in England, had come to China from Canada while still in his twenties.

" 'Two Gun' Cohen, as they sometimes refer to him," Rucker said, "became a bodyguard to Dr. Sun Yat-sen. Dr. Sun was China's great revolutionary leader, and he came close to uniting China. There was a price of a million dollars on his head and that's where Cohen came in. He watched and protected Dr. Sun and he also became his friend and in time something of a legendary figure. Cohen was honest and dedicated his life to Dr. Sun and to China. Before the old man died, he made 'Two Gun' Cohen a general. He's in his sixties now, I guess, but General Cohen is about the only foreigner the Chinese will listen to. Even the war lords pay attention to him. What he says in Southern China still goes. That's why I am wiring him and I'm not going to move from here until he answers."

"That's straight what Joe has been telling you," Mencken added. "Old 'Two-Gun' Cohen still calls the shots, and it's strange, all right, that in China where there's so much graft and corruption, that Cohen made his reputation by being honest. The Chinese know this, and they don't understand Cohen—but they respect him."

While we sat at the bar, Rucker called for a telegraph blank and ten minutes later the wire he prepared was on its way to General Cohen. The following afternoon, Joe Rucker received the answer, and it read:

TRAIN BOMBED DAILY BETTER TAKE BOAT
WILL MEET YOU   COHEN

Early next morning, we were on the Pearl River on our way
to Canton. There were two Englishmen and four Germans
traveling with us. In steerage there were at least a hundred
Chinese men and women headed for Canton. The Germans
posed as doctors, but Joe Rucker said he was sure they were
machine gunners brought in by the Chinese government.

The trip on the Pearl River to Canton does not take long
and we were due in by late afternoon. We started drinking
Scotch in the galley around eleven o'clock and both Rucker
and Mencken tried to engage the Germans in conversation,
but they were not communicating. Shortly after twelve
o'clock, two Chinese boys began serving lunch, and we were
just finishing our soup when we heard the faint roar of planes.
We rushed out on deck and saw in the distance a squadron
of Jap planes coming in our direction.

At first they were just pinpoints in the sky, but in a matter
of minutes they looked huge and threatening.

"They might pass us up," Rucker said, and as he was saying it, two of the planes from the squadron nose-dived. In a
matter of seconds we were back in the galley and lying face-
down on the floor under the table. The two planes pelted the
river boat with machine gun bullets; then there was quiet
and we did not move from where we were hiding. One of the
Englishmen got up first and looked out from the windows of
the galley.

"They're gone," he announced. "Don't think they did much
damage—the bloody bastards."

We crawled from under the table and the Chinese boys
were back. They brought us Scotch and we drank it straight
and after awhile we went on with our lunch as if nothing had
happened. No one said anything as we ate.

In the late afternoon the water of the Pearl River seemed
more muddy and the river itself widened. We began to see

Chinese junks and sampans and then around four o'clock, we slowed down and made our way toward the docks. Everywhere along the Bund were houseboats—thousands of them with Chinese families living on them. Spike, Joe Rucker, and Art Mencken gathered their camera equipment and placed it on deck. Just as we were going to disembark, a group of Chinese officers came aboard and proceeded to examine passports and to ask questions. It was then that a man, short and rather stout, with broad shoulders and a flattened nose appeared. He was wearing a dark suit and a hat with the brim over his eyes. He looked over at us and saw Joe Rucker.

"Hello, Joe," he called, and with something of a cockney accent, he added, "Just hold on. I'll take care of things."

He joined the Chinese officers and began talking with them. The conversation went on for about ten minutes. Finally he came over.

"Everybody is giving orders and no one knows exactly what to do," he said. "The way things are going, newspapermen and photographers are not especially welcome. But I have it fixed for you now."

The man in the dark suit was, of course, General Cohen, and Joe introduced him to us. In a few more minutes, Chinese coolies began taking the camera equipment from the boat and transporting it to a waiting car. General Cohen took us to the Victoria Hotel and then asked us to join him later for dinner.

Except for the shoulder gun holster that bulged from inside his coat, there was nothing unusual about General Cohen. He was bald, his complexion dark and his eyes a yellowish brown. In height he was a little over five feet, but solidly built. He didn't smile very much but when he did there was a warmth to him. He sounded discouraged as he talked to us that night.

"China has had it," he said. "Every day we are losing ground. We haven't the arms or the military equipment to fight. None of the countries are willing to sell to China; what we get is contraband—leftovers. It seems as if it has always been that way."

Then he spoke of his years with Dr. Sun.

"Yes, I started out as his bodyguard," he said. "After a time my job was to bring guns and ammunition into China. I bought them from wherever I could—from England, from Germany, from Russia, from America—but always it was deals. China has never had any real help. Now it's almost too late. It's only a question of time before Canton and all of Southern China is in the hands of the Japanese. You've come here to cover a war? Well, there is no war. Only one defeat after another. Someday," and his eyes brightened, "China will be united and it will have power and strength." He got to his feet. "It's time to go and eat."

We stayed in Canton for a week. Every day the air raid sirens and the Japanese bombs that fell in the outskirts of Canton brought the war closer. After each bombing, we would go out with Joe Rucker and Art Mencken and they and Spike would photograph the destruction. There were no air raid shelters, no emergency hospitals, no organized civilian defense—just hundreds of maimed bodies lying on the streets and on the roads. Occasionally some were carried away by relatives; always there were the stark faces of the Chinese who did not know or seem to understand what was happening.

On the sidewalk in front of the hotel, there were youngsters in threadbare clothing crying out, "No papa, no mama, no whiskey soda—cumshaw, please, Mister Charlie," and they would put out their small hands begging for anything we might give them.

Yet, during all the bombing raids, there existed a fatalistic attitude among the Chinese. There were no outbursts of emotion, or of hatred. They seemed to accept the Japanese bombings as they had accepted everything that had happened to them through centuries of privation and suffering. If there were any signs of emotion, it was seen only momentarily on the faces of mothers as their grasps tightened on children held in their arms. I never heard a child cry out.

"The children are born old," General Cohen said. "They have learned not to cry."

Despite the air raid sirens and the bombings, life went on in Canton. There seemed to be enough Scotch and gin in the bars, and even the night clubs remained open. The sing-song girls sang and there was Chinese music that sounded loud and noisy to us. In restaurants there were always rich Chinese who ordered shark fins, bird-nest soup, and other delicacies, seemingly unperturbed that their way of life was disappearing.

In the United States, we had gone through a depression, unemployment, and bread lines. In Canton a bread line would have been a luxury. Millions existed on a bowl of rice a day, if they were fortunate enough to get it. Would there ever be a solution to the problems of China? No one, including General Cohen, had an answer. Cohen could have gone to Hong Kong or back to England or Canada. But he was staying. "When the time comes," he said, "and if I have any bullets left, I'll peg a Jap or two." He did not know then that he would end up in a Japanese prison camp, brutally beaten and punished, but refusing to reveal information that was wanted from him.

Spike and I had seen enough. He had taken many pictures and I had made many notes. We had material for half a dozen articles. Through our photographs and by what I planned to write, we would describe what was happening in China and perhaps America would become aware and send help. We did not know the thinking of our diplomats abroad and the mysterious ways of the State Department, or of the politicians in Washington, D.C. When China was finally helped, it was too late.

Back in Hong Kong, we booked passage for Japan on a German ship, the *Scharnhorst*. While we waited for its departure, we visited stores and looked for things to bring home. There were no tourists and the stores were overstocked with merchandise, especially fine silks and perfumes. I thought of getting a silk dress and pajamas for Dag, while Spike was interested in an ivory chess set.

In the Kowloon Silk Shop, I saw a dress I liked and told the Chinese proprietor I wanted a size twelve. He smiled and rubbed his hands.

"Master velly lucky to have wife so young," he said.

I explained that it was size twelve, and tried to describe Dag to him.

"I savvy now, master," he said. "Please, one moment."

He went to the rear of the store and was gone for some time. He returned with four girls, each of different age, weight and height.

"Master, you lookie. Please, you tell which one all-same as wife. We have dress to fit. If not, we make fast."

The girls stood there patiently in line. Spike and I decided that the third girl was close to Dag's height and build. I pointed to her.

"That one," I said.

The proprietor went on rubbing his hands.

"Can do, master. Have size," he said, and he dismissed the girls while once more he disappeared and was shortly back with a dress. "Velly nice," he said. "Pure silk. Will fit wife."

We haggled over the price and eventually came to an agreement. Then I purchased a pair of pajamas which he assured me were the same size, and once more we bargained. He wrapped the dress and the pajamas and I paid him. As we were leaving, he walked to the door with us.

"Third girl velly nice," he said. "Velly young. Most anxious to accommodate. Please, you tell what hotel you stay and room, and I bring girl. You no like, no pay. Can do, master. Okay?"

"No, okay," I said.

"Most unfortunate," he said. "She nice girl. Same age your wife."

We left him there and walked toward our hotel. In front of the hotel, three Chinese youngsters, not over eight years of age, put out their hands and sang out, "No papa, no mama, no whiskey soda—cumshaw please, Mister Charlie." Spike and I reached into our pockets, but we didn't have any small change. "Not now," I said, "later."

Then we heard them yelling at us: "Son-of-bitch, Mister Charlie. Son-of-bitch, Mister Charlie."

The *Scharnhorst* was flying the Nazi flag and we didn't want to travel on a German ship. But in our room in Hong Kong we had counted our money and found we were running short; it would be at least one more week before we could pick up the *President Coolidge* for Japan, so we had booked passage second class on the *Scharnhorst*. We had a good cabin, the ship was clean and the food wasn't bad. Yet, we never felt comfortable during the five-day trip. There were portraits of Hitler in the dining room and in the lounge and at night they showed German propaganda films. We didn't care for the crew members either, the waiters in the dining room or the cabin steward. They were polite and attentive and at the same time we had the impression we were under their constant scrutiny and being tolerated only because we were paying passengers. They always seemed to be on their guard and there was a forced, mechanical precision to every move they made. Even their faces were, as Spike put it, chiselled out of cold steel. At night when we went to our cabin, we made a point of locking the door.

After the trip on the *Scharnhorst*, Japan seemed a paradise. If it were preparing for a full-scale war, it was not at first too apparent. Japan was peaceful, busy, industrious and the people exceedingly polite, good natured, and friendly. They were not capable, we tried to convince ourselves, of the bombings and the atrocities we had witnessed in China. Mr. Takahashi of the NYK Line and Carl Stanley, the manager of Hotel Del Monte had written about us to Mr. Inumaru, the managing director of the Imperial Hotel in Tokyo. When we registered at the Imperial, we were told we were to be guests of Mr. Inumaru and we were taken to one of the hotel's best rooms where we were greeted by two Japanese girls dressed in kimonos who bowed, giggled, and said that if there was anything they could do to make our stay pleasant to please call upon them. They bowed again, giggled some more and then they were gone.

Later in the day we called on Mr. Inumaru, a nervous little man with a sharp laugh and dancing eyes.

"I am going to see you enjoy your stay in Japan," he said and meant it. That night he took us to a dinner party at a geisha house and present were a group of government officials, representing the Japanese tourist department. In the beginning we had Scotch and then we sat at tables on the floor, drank sake, watched as the geisha girls prepared one food course after another on charcoal-burning hibachis. During dinner, which went on for hours, Mr. Inumaru and Mr. Den who was head of the tourist department, talked about the importance of tourist travel and of how much they wanted Americans to visit Japan.

I still like to think that Mr. Inumaru and Mr. Den and the others were not aware that the army and navy were planning a major war. Perhaps their talk and apparent kindness were part of a façade put on for our benefit. After midnight when we returned to our hotel room, we noticed that our luggage had been searched. They were not too careful about it, either; some papers I had left on top of the desk were in disorder, and the photographic prints Spike had were no longer in sequence.

Spike and I were seldom allowed to go out or to travel by ourselves. When Mr. Inumaru couldn't accompany us, he had a guide named Henry always waiting in the lobby. Henry was friendly and accommodating but he frequently stopped Spike from taking certain photographs. "Our government is very strict and does not like these types of pictures," he said. "Plenty of other photographs to take."

When we went on a trip along the coast, Henry was constantly at our side. "No pictures here," he said to Spike. "All of seashore restricted area. You must obey government regulations or we have trouble. Please, you excuse."

"What's the government afraid of?" Spike asked him.

"Government not afraid," Henry answered, "government careful."

"In the United States we let you take pictures of anything you want," Spike attempted to argue with him.

"U.S. and Japan very different." And that's about as much as Henry would say.

When we complained to Mr. Inumaru about it and told him how everywhere we went our luggage was searched, he laughed and passed it off lightly.

"Everybody suspicious these days," he said. "Everybody spies on each other. It is the new Japanese game. I do not like game, but game very popular. So sorry it happens."

One night when we all had had too much sake to drink, I said that the way things were in China, perhaps it would be best if the Japanese took over the country, as well as Hong Kong, Singapore and the Philippines.

"We don't want Singapore or the Philippines," Henry, drunk and off his guard, said. "For Japanese expansion program we need land west of the Rockies."

He quickly tried to cover the slip he had made by laughing

about it. But from then on, he was careful and we never caught him off guard again.

During the next ten days we traveled to all parts of Japan as Mr. Inumaru's guests. It was in the small towns where we occasionally stopped that we became more aware of the rationing of coal, gasoline, and food. Japan was stock-piling, preparing for the war that was already on the drawing boards, but Mr. Inumaru said it was the *incident* in China which brought about scarcities.

We enjoyed the small Japanese inns where we spent the nights while traveling in the interior and the friendliness and politeness of the people. They couldn't seem to do enough for us, and always they were apologizing when we asked for something that was not readily available. Each night before going to bed, we bathed in Japanese baths, and no one seemed to think anything of both men and women bathing together. After awhile, even we became accustomed to it.

"In Japan we are not afraid of sex," Mr. Inumaru explained. "Women and men different, but all the same thing. Here we recognize it—in other countries people afraid to face fact that people are naked under their clothes. Very difficult for Occidentals to understand. Japanese are very realistic. Sex very necessary and to be fully enjoyed at proper place and proper time. We respect it as most valuable."

Mr. Inumaru finished his sake, refilled his cup and ours.

"Perhaps you would like to try Japanese girl?" he now asked. "Very new experience for you. Can easily arrange—right now, if you wish. There are very pretty girls here—most accommodating."

We did not want to appear prudish, and perhaps as Mr. Inumaru maintained, it could prove an interesting experience. But the Japanese girls, with all their heavy make-up their strange hairdos and their giggling were not appealing or attractive—at least not to us.

"We are not in the mood," I said to Mr. Inumaru. "Perhaps

at some other occasion," and I couldn't help adding, "At the proper place and proper time."

"Sex is something that one should not talk much about," Mr. Inumaru went on, "but to be enjoyed. To be in proper mood is most important. Let us have some more sake. The sake here is very good, do you not think so?"

Our two weeks in Japan were almost over and we had booked passage on the *Chichibu Maru,* the same ship in which we had left San Francisco. We had been away close to two months, but it seemed longer. While we did not want to admit it, we were homesick and by now more than ready to go back.

When we reached San Francisco and were going through customs, I glanced over at one of Spike's suitcases. In a corner of the suitcase was an assortment of matchbook covers held together by a rubber band. He had not forgotten Leah.

CHAPTER ELEVEN

Visitor from Another Planet

It felt good to be home again, to be back with Dag, to be in the peaceful Carmel Valley, the hills already green from the winter rains, and the river below us running full. From the bathroom window as I shaved that first morning, I watched our cat, fatter than ever, standing motionless and waiting to trounce on a mole that was working away in a flower bed. In the pasture beyond, two horses were feeding on the high grass. Everything seemed to be the same and yet it wasn't; I had changed.

At Del Monte, Sam Morse said it was going to be a good season and that the economy was bright. But a war? Nonsense, there would be no war. In the afternoon I drove through Carmel and to San Antonio street, and slowed down by the house where Lincoln Steffens had lived. I went on along the ocean and the pounding surf, then I turned left at the Carmel Mission and continued on the winding Carmel Valley road. I thought of Spike. He, too, had moved into the valley and was living near us with his son. There had been no attempt at reconciliation; he and his wife had separated.

During the months that followed, I wrote a number of articles on what we had seen in China and sent them off with Spike's photographs of death and destruction. They came back; the editors weren't interested in China—their attention was now on Europe and on Hitler and Mussolini. The New York *Times* Sunday magazine section finally took one of our articles—about Japan.

At a dinner party one evening, the commanding general at the Monterey Presidio reiterated what Sam Morse had said: "There will be no war, and if the Japanese ever start something, we'll finish them off in a hurry."

We were complacent and uninformed, reassured by the news commentators and by Fireside Chats. For months this idyllic type of thinking went on, so much so that I began to believe it. Then it happened. Germany's panzer divisions moved into Poland and Hitler's hysterical shouting came booming through the radio. Soon afterwards Great Britain was at war with Germany and Italy.

"And we'll be in it next," I said to Dag and to Spike. "I'm going to enlist before I'm drafted."

"Better wait," Dag said.

"Wait for what?" I said. "I'm twenty-eight and of draft age. If I enlist now I'll go to officers' school and get a decent assignment."

I went on to San Francisco and to the navy recruiting office. They were friendly and firm. "Sorry—you wear glasses, and with your eyesight, the Navy just wouldn't be interested."

With the Army it was the same reception and perhaps more discouraging. "They'll never draft you," they said. "Your eyesight makes you 4-F. Know what 4-F is? Unacceptable."

I argued saying that the Japanese were getting ready for war. "I know," I said, "I just came back from the Orient."

"The Japs are nothing to worry about," I was told. "We can lick 'em with one arm tied behind our backs."

On the train returning to Del Monte, I thought it over. The war was going to be fought mostly in the air. There would be a need for trained pilots. If I learned to fly, I might get into the Air Force. The answer was clear; take flying lessons. I rang the bell by my seat in the clubcar and told Oliver, the porter, to bring me a Scotch. As I drank it, and then another, I could see myself in uniform, pilot wings on my lapel and taking off in a bomber. I was flying over Berlin . . . I pressed the button and I could see the bombs dropping . . .

"Did you ring, sir?" Oliver was standing by me. "The same thing?"

"Yes, Oliver, the same thing."

"Sure, I can teach you to fly," Larry Sweeney, the flying instructor at the Monterey airport said. "It will take you about five lessons to solo, and then it's up to you on how much time you put in. If you fly every day, you can log lots of hours and get plenty of experience."

"When can I begin?"

"Anytime. I have a Piper we can start you out with. Very easy to handle."

"Can we start now?"

"I see no reason why not," he said. "Let's talk about flying first, and then I'll take you up."

He spent half an hour or more describing the rudimentary instructions of taking off and landing and the importance of keeping the wings level. "Always fly level and never let one wing go lower, unless you're banking. And hold the stick easy in your hand. Don't tighten on it. Never freeze. Shall we start out?"

We walked across the field to the Piper.

"You wear glasses all the time?"

I nodded.

"Hope your eyesight is good. Lots of people disqualify, because they can't gauge distances."

We climbed into the plane which had dual controls. Larry sat behind me and we put on and tightened our safety belts. He started the motor.

"Can you hear me?"

"Yep."

"Taking off is a cinch. Just nice and easy. We'll taxi out to the runway."

We were out on the runway. "Okay, now. Put your hand on the stick. Just barely hold it. That's fine. We're going to gain some speed and then we'll be off. Here we go."

The motor roared, the plane started going down the runway, and in another moment we were in the air.

"Can you hear me?"

"I hear you."

"Now, slowly I'm going to pull back on the stick. Feel it? That's it. Never pull back too fast. Slowly and gently. See, we're gaining altitude." Then after awhile, "We're high enough. Your hand on the stick? Good. All right, take over. No! NO! You're freezing on me. Let go of the stick! LET GO! Okay, fine. You froze 'cause you're afraid. Let's start again. Hand on the stick. Hold it very gently, very easily. Good. That's it. Stay that way. NO! Hey, let go! LET GO! You're freezing again. Can't you get it through your head? Never hold the stick tightly. Let's start once more."

Larry Sweeney finally landed the plane. I unclasped the seat belt and jumped out of the plane. We started walking across the field.

"Scared, weren't you?"

"Plenty."

"That's why you froze. Once you get the hang of it, you'll be all right. When do you want to go up again?"

"Tomorrow."

"Okay. See you then."

Larry Sweeney had said that in five lessons I would be able to solo. I was soon on my tenth lesson and I still wasn't going up alone. My coordination was either poor or I just couldn't get the feel for flying. Each time Larry brought me down, he patiently went over all the things I had done wrong.

After every lesson my hopes of joining the Air Force and

becoming a combat pilot grew dimmer. Larry was also losing his patience. When we were in the air, he shouted and screamed at me. "No one can be that dumb," he yelled. "Can't you get anything through that thick skull of yours? Your right wing is low. IT'S LOW. BRING IT UP. Okay. Let's start again."

When we were back on the ground, he said with some encouragement. "You did better today. Tomorrow's your twelfth lesson and you're going to solo whether you like it or not."

I didn't think he meant it. I had no intention of taking up the Piper alone. I wasn't ready for it and I was certain he would not let me. Yet the next day when I showed up, he was standing in front of his office.

"Well, what are you waiting for? The plane's there. Go on. Get in it. Take it up."

"Alone?"

"Yes. ALONE. I've babied you enough. Go on."

"You'd better come with me."

"No—you're either going to fly that crate alone, or I am through giving you lessons. You know how to take it off and land it. You've done it plenty of times. Now, go on!"

"I'm scared to death—and not afraid to admit it."

"Everyone's scared when they solo the first time. Go on! The plane's waiting there for you."

"You sure you think I'm ready?"

"I'm sure."

I didn't move.

"Do I have to, Larry?"

"Yes, goddamn it. You have to."

I started walking toward the Piper, still convinced that Larry would follow. I climbed into the plane and as I looked across the field I saw that he was still standing in front of his office. I put on the safety belt and turned on the ignition and glanced at the instrument board trying to remember all the things Larry had told me. All at once I made up my mind I was going to fly the Piper and if I were to be killed in the attempt—well, I'd be killed.

I taxied out to the runway. I mentally crossed myself.

"Okay. Let's go now," I said to myself, pulled on the gas throttle and then as I was going down the runway, I began slowly pulling back on the stick. In another few moments I was in the air and gradually climbing. My eyes were on the instrument panel and then on the wings. "Don't freeze," I kept on saying to myself. "Level flight. Level flight. Can't you get anything through that thick skull. All right, you're doing fine. Getting up into the air and flying is easy. What about landing? I had better start thinking about landing."

For the next half hour I flew high above the clouds. I banked the Piper, circled the field several times, and was gradually gaining confidence. I was alone flying through space! It was worth it—all the lessons, all the shouting and the screaming. A great feeling of exhilaration came over me. I wanted to keep on flying—on and on.

Now for the landing. That was the most difficult part. I remembered Larry's instructions. Land against the wind. Study the runway. Gauge the approach. Then bring it in slowly. All right, I thought, here goes.

I started a gradual descent, watching the instrument panel. Everything was going well. The runway was clear. I was flying level. Now all I had to do was to bring it down. As I approached the runway, the ground seemed to be coming up toward me. I could feel my hand tightening around the stick. I was going to crash. Just in time I pulled back the stick and quickly gained altitude. I circled the field once more and prepared to land again. I knew I had to make it this time. I was approaching the runway. Slowly, now, I thought, slowly. I felt the wheels of the plane touch the ground and then I brought the plane to a stop. I taxied back to the field and climbed out. Larry was waiting for me.

"You see," he said, "it wasn't so difficult, though I was

kinda' worried that first time. Why the hell didn't you land it? Well, anyway, on the second try you did fine. It was a perfect landing."

I didn't tell him that in finally landing the plane as I approached the runway, I had shut my eyes.

One morning in July, less than six months before Pearl Harbor, as I went through the hotel lobby, John Powers, the registration clerk who had first told me about Gertrude Stein, called me over.

"Know who checked in? Salvador Dali, that's who," he said, and then leaning over the desk and in a whisper, he added, "He's a real screwball, waxed mustache and all. Makes paintings of melting watches and things like that. Going to stay here for awhile and we've put him in the old wing. If I know people—that wife of his—she's going to chisel for a rate."

I knew that Dali staying at Del Monte would make news, so I telephoned the room.

"Hallo, please who speaks?" came a loud, strongly accented voice.

"I'd like to talk to Salvador Dali," I said and explained I was the publicity man for Del Monte.

"Dali never talks to anyone on the telephone," said the voice, then after a thoughtful silence; "please you come to the room. We wish to see you."

Gala greeted me at the door. "This room is impossible," she said almost at once. "We will not stay here. You must find something better—very much better." Dali had been in the bathroom and as he came out, she introduced me and began talking in French with him. My French was not good, but I understood what she said to him.

Dali is Spanish and, because I was born in Latin America, I speak Spanish as fluently as English. I spoke to Dali in Spanish.

"We are happy to have you here," I said. "We want you to be comfortable."

"This room will never do," he answered in French. *"Cette chambre n'ira pas!"*

"Dali cannot work here," Gala joined in. "We need a bigger room with large windows that will provide more light."

Once more they began talking in French and I managed to understand part of the conversation. I told them that I would show them around the hotel and that I was certain they would find a room they would like.

As it turned out, it wasn't one room they wanted, but two. One would be converted into a studio for Dali to work in; the other would be used as a bedroom. I showed them various suites until they came to one which they said might do.

"This could be all right," Gala said, but not too enthusiastically. "What is the price?"

I told her. She let out a gasp.

"Trop cher, trop cher," she said. "It must be worth something for Del Monte to have Dali here."

"We get our share of celebrities," I said. "Clark Gable is here at present."

"Hotels are always happy to have us," Gala went on. "Dali makes publicity for a hotel. We do not ask for rates—they are given to us."

"I'll see you get a rate."

"We want better than a rate."

"Such as?"

"We will pay for one room and the room Dali uses should be free."

"These are expensive rooms—the best in the hotel."

"Dali always stays in the best. He is a great artist. He must have only the best."

"I'll see what I can do," I said.

"We must know now," Gala said, pressing for an answer.

"How long do you plan to stay?"

"If Dali is comfortable and he likes it, perhaps two or three months."

"I'll arrange for it," I said, and as we went down the hall I suggested they join my wife and me for cocktails and dinner. They accepted readily. It was a pleasant evening and Dali was amusing, though always talking in French. After we had left them and were on our way home, Dag said:

"They're different, all right—and I know you like them—but they're out to get everything they can. Dali paints, but it is Gala who does the thinking and the planning. She's cagey and schemes. Let's not get too involved with them."

But, of course, that's exactly what I did.

Dali was a visitor from a far-off planet, from Saturn, from Mars, certainly from another world. He was small, thin, and delicate to the point of appearing emaciated. There was a wild, animal look in his eyes, and his waxed mustache produced the proper dramatic effect. He was shy and sensitive, but when something interested him or caught his attention, he became enthused and excited and he spoke with great rapidity, even swallowing words as Frenchmen often do. Dag said that everything he said had an exclamation point tagged on it.

Gala was Polish, short and a little on the stout side. She gave the impression that life had not been easy on her and she had hardened to it—by now she had the skin of a rhinoceros and nothing seemed to bother her. She never asked for anything; she demanded. Her mind worked fast and her conversation was stimulating, particularly when she talked of her early days with Dali. There was a certain charm to her and she was dedicated to Dali and he, in turn, was entirely dependent upon her.

One evening, when they knew us better and they were relaxed, Gala described meeting Dali for the first time.

"We were determined to get married," she said, "but of

course there was my husband. He could not understand what
I saw in Dali."

Gala's husband finally agreed to a divorce, but even before
it was granted, Gala and Dali ran off together. Then Gala
said that, rather than register as man and wife in hotels and
in order not to imperil the divorce proceedings, they pre-
tended they were brother and sister. They soon learned this
would not work out.

"We were asked to leave the little hotel in France where
we were staying," Gala said. "The proprietor was very realistic and if guests were married or not didn't matter. But,
incest! He just wouldn't tolerate incest! We were thrown
out and from then on we obtained separate rooms, though
we could hardly afford it."

They did not know anyone on the Monterey Peninsula
and we began introducing them to some of our friends, including Robinson and Una Jeffers. Two or three times a week
we had dinner with the Dali's at Hotel Del Monte or they would
drive out to the valley and we'd barbecue steaks and Gala
would make the salad. When we were sitting at the dinner
table and Dali was talking, he occasionally would draw a
sketch to illustrate a point he was making; Gala would always destroy these drawings or drop them into her purse.

Whenever we went into the Del Monte dining room or
into a restaurant, Dali, in his velvet jacket and his waxed
mustache, would invariably attract attention. If he didn't, he
would think of something that would, such as ordering a
special dish that was not on the menu, or he would go into
a harangue in French with the waiter, gesturing with his
hands and making faces. Usually the waiter stood by, con-
fused and unable to understand a word Dali had said. Dali
was at his best when he had the limelight; Dag said that
Dali was an acrobat, leaping through space. He was, of
course, constantly putting on a performance, even when
the four of us were alone. He was Dali and he never forgot

it. Or, perhaps Gala didn't permit it. Sometimes I thought he was a pathetically unhappy small boy with great talent under the domination and protective care of his mother.

Dali worked hard, frequently as late as two or three o'clock in the morning, and by nine the next day he would be back at his painting. Unlike other artists, he did not use an easel, but instead a large drawing board placed across two wooden boxes I had obtained for him. When he was painting in a detail, he'd work with a magnifying lens, always with painstaking care and patience.

"*Voilà!*" he would exclaim when he was finished. "No one will ever know how much work went into that tiny leaf, but I know," and there would come a pleased expression on his face.

He didn't seem to mind my watching him; I think he enjoyed having an audience. He talked about giving us one of his paintings as a gift, but Gala quickly managed to get him off the subject. She was never going to let Dali give anything away, including those little sketches he drew on the backs of menus or envelopes.

Usually before lunch, he took a swim in the pool, being careful to keep his waxed mustache out of the water. He used a breast stroke or floated on his back. Anyone seeing him for the first time might well have thought we had a young, underfed walrus in the pool. After swimming he would stretch out in the sand and sunbathe. It was there one noon, as he lay in the sand, that he brought up an idea that had been incubating for some time in Gala's and Dali's fertile minds.

It was quiet and peaceful by the pool and the day was warm and mild. The cream-colored tower of the hotel stood out against the blue sky and the large expanse of lawns, only recently mowed, gave the hotel grounds a well maintained appearance. In the snack bar, hamburgers, hot dogs, and milk shakes were being prepared. Europe seemed far away

LINCOLN STEFFENS—
The great muckraking
journalist of the early
1900's was one of the first
of many notables to offer
Herbert Cerwin advice and
friendship. Cerwin and
his wife were frequent
visitors at Steffens'
Carmel, Calif. home.

ROBINSON JEFFERS—
The shy, sensitive but
powerful poet of the Big
Sur area constructed a
monumental home with
rocks and boulders. Cerwin
met him while still a
young newspaper reporter
and listened in awe many
evenings as Jeffers read
from his work in progress.

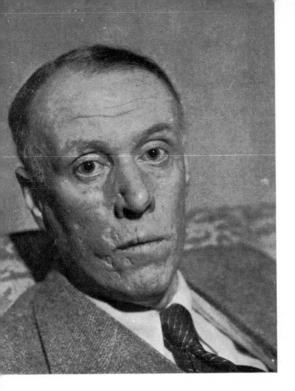

SINCLAIR LEWIS—A temperamental author of towering rages and biting sarcasms, Lewis did not like this photo, taken of him by Cerwin. But it delighted the noted photographer Edward Weston, who said it fully captured the author's personality.

MISS STEIN—Shown here in the patio of the Del Monte Hotel, the famed expatriot author was already something of a celebrity.

GERTRUDE STEIN—On a brief visit to the United States
with her friend, Alice B. Toklas, Miss Stein made a brief stop-over
at the Del Monte Hotel, where Cerwin met her, interviewed
her and fed her apple pie.

CHARLIE CHAPLIN AND PAULETTE GODDARD—The
noted comic actor and his attractive co-star came under Cerwin's
care when they stayed at the Del Monte Hotel. Chaplin
explained the creation of his most famous character, "The Tramp," to
Cerwin, then asked to be introducd to Robinson Jeffers.

DAGMAR CERWIN, HEITOR VILLA LOBOS, ERICO
VERISSIMO—The author's wife often presided over dinners attended
by the likes of the noted Brazilian composer and author. They are
pictured at the Cerwin's apartment in Rio, at the time of the
author's tour of duty with the U.S. State Department.

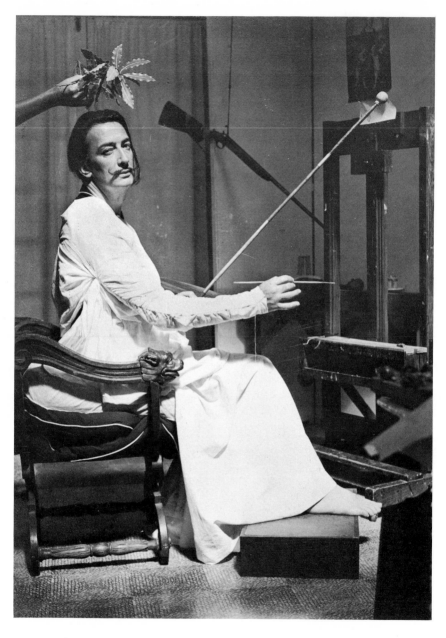

SALVADOR DALI—The world famous Spanish artist of
surrealistic fame brought his unique blend of super public relations, talent
and inventiveness to the Del Monte Hotel for a typically
unpredictable performance.

MR & MRS. DALI—In carefully selected costumes, the
artist and his wife make their grand appearance at the wildly
lavish benefit for the New York Museum of art,
sponsored by them at the Del Monte.

DALI, JEFFERS AND GINGER
ROGERS—News of Dali's lavish
benefit festival brought the shy poet
away from the Big Sur and the
glamorous motion picture actress
up from Hollywood.

BOB HOPE—The comedian is
shown here with an unidentified
guest, clowning at the outlandishly
served banquet dinner, which was
supervised down to the last
whimsical detail by Dali.

JOHN F. KENNEDY, RAYMOND C. LILLIE, CERWIN—The author and the Director of the Grand Teton Lodge in Wyoming were on hand to greet President Kennedy for his 1963 visit. Cerwin is wearing the leather tie he later gave the President.

NELSON ROCKEFELLER—Cerwin's "boss" during the diplomatic days in Latin America, the two men have remained close friends during the years.

and the war remote, despite the headlines and the news
broadcasts. France had capitulated long ago, though "The
Last Time I Saw Paris" was still being sung on the radio.
The draft was on in the United States and young draftees
were training at nearby Fort Ord with wooden rifles for the
army did not have enough rifles to go around. Yet no one
was too concerned, or aware of how close we were to war.
Many refugee artists, Dali said, had fled from Europe and
were in need of help.

"Gala and I were fortunate to leave France when we did,"
Dali said, "but the other artists were not so lucky. Now that
some have come to America they are in financial need. No
one thinks of the artists. They are forgotten. That must not
be. Dali will assist them."

"There are so many of them," I said. "What could you do?"

"Gala and I have been thinking—when one thinks one
thinks of ways—is it not so?"

He sat up and began picking up sand in his hand and
allowing it to pass through his long, thin fingers.

"How can Dali help? How can Dali assist the refugee
artists? Then it came to me. We will raise funds for them.
We will give a benefit party. It will be a big party—a party
such as has never been given before and only as Dali would
give it. And we will have many people come to it. And then
we will have money for the artists." He paused a moment.
"C'est un idée extraordinaire, n'est ce pas?"

"I'm sure it would be quite an affair." I said in Spanish.

He went on in French. "Yesterday Gala telephoned Mr.
Barr, the director of the Museum of Modern Art in New
York. He is most enthusiastic about the idea. He thinks it
is very good what we have planned. And the museum itself
will sponsor it! Already he has given the approval to it."

"Then you'll be going to New York shortly?"

"To New York? Why should we go there now?"

"To put on the party."

"But the party will not be in New York," his eyes gleamed with enthusiasm. "No—we will have it right here—here at Del Monte, and we will have people come from all parts of the country. Think of the publicity Del Monte will get! A benefit party put on by Dali! Everybody will talk about it—everybody will come to it! Who will want to miss a party that Dali gives? No one!"

As Dali went on describing his plans for the benefit party, he became excited, more enthused and his hands were gesturing in all directions. To Dali the party was already a reality and a success. He even had a name for it.

"We shall call it," he announced, *"A Night in a Surrealist Forest*. Is that not a good name? *A Night in a Surrealist Forest,*" and he chuckled. "We will startle everyone."

He got up from the sand where he had been sitting. "I will have another swim before lunch," he said, "and this evening we will talk more about it."

I stood by and watched him as he slowly got into the pool. He began swimming breast stroke across the pool, his head and mustache well above the water.

CHAPTER TWELVE

A Night in a Surrealist Forest

Many art critics are skeptical of the position Salvador Dali holds as a painter of major importance. While they lavish praise on Picasso, who incidentally was also born in Spain, their enthusiasm about Dali wavers. They admit there is greatness to Dali, yet the degree of greatness remains in a realm of limbo. But on one thing all the critics agree: Dali is skillful and his technique far superior to that of leading contemporary painters. Picasso paints as Picasso, but Dali does not always paint as Dali. He is many persons and the influence of his wife, Gala, on his art is dominant in almost all of his work; for a time, he included her name in signing some of his paintings. Her eyes, her hands, her face frequently appear in one form or another in his paintings.

How much Gala meant to Dali was evident during the three months we were with them. When decisions were to be made, Gala was always there. Gala spoke for Dali and Dali spoke for Gala. The idea for the benefit party to be given under the auspices of the Museum of Modern Art of New York, was probably not spontaneous—Gala and Dali must have thought it out long in advance.

Dali approached *A Night in a Surrealist Forest* with the same painstaking care that he gave to one of his paintings. It was to be a work of art, worthy of Dali's name and reputation and toward that end went his and Gala's efforts. They would discuss the smallest detail and very little escaped their attention. Everything they wanted was clear in their minds, though complying with their demands was not easily accomplished.

As we prepared and planned for *A Night in a Surrealist Forest,* Dag and I were in for an experience such as we could not have imagined. After a lengthy session with Gala and Dali, Dag would insist that Dali had reached a stage of madness that called for incarcerating him in an institution. "And I am sure, if this goes on much longer," she added, "I'll be ready to be committed, too."

On the day Dali had first spoken of the need of raising funds for refugee artists, we went to dinner with them. As we were having our coffee, Dali said rather casually, "I have prepared a list of a few things we are going to need."

We looked at the list. Each item was written in India ink and in Dali's heavy scrawl. On the list were: two thousand pine trees; four thousand gunny sacks; two tons of old newspapers; twenty-four animal heads; twenty-four store window mannequins; the largest bed available in Hollywood and two truckloads of squash, pumpkins, dried corn, melons, and other fruit.

If Dali thought he was going to startle me with this list, I had no intention of giving him satisfaction.

"We probably can get all of these things," I said. Dag sitting across the table just looked at me and didn't say anything.

"But the list is not complete," Dali said. "I have not included a wrecked automobile or the wild animals."

"A wrecked car?"

"Yes, it is very important."

"But, why, Dali?"

"Ah, soon you will see how it fits in. And, then there is the matter of the wild animals. We will have to have them."

"You mean real live animals?"

"*Naturellement*, and one of them must be a small, baby tiger."

"Where would we get them?"

"That should not be too difficult," Dali raised his shoulders. "Perhaps from a zoo, perhaps from a circus. Or you may have to find them in Hollywood. They have animals they use in their pictures, have they not? For a night in the forest we must have animals."

There was a long silence. "You are puzzled. You do not see how I will use all these things. *Voilà!* I will make a sketch to show how everything fits in." Dali picked up a menu, took out a pencil and on the back, began to quickly rough out a sketch. He worked fast and in about ten minutes he was finished.

"See, this is the way it will look," he said and showed us the sketch. "The trees—they will create the atmosphere of a forest. The gunny sacks, ah—we will fill them with crumpled newspapers and then we hang them closely together on wires across the ceiling of the ballroom. *Regardez*, do they not give the effect of a grotto? *Trés bien.* The bed—it will dominate one end of the room. It must be beautiful, very large, very elegant.

"Gala will be lying in the bed and from the bed, we will have a long table extending out into the room. Along the table and between every four chairs there will be a mannequin with an animal head. See the way I have drawn it? Good. By the trees, we will have some of the wild animals peering out. The effect we will strive for is of an enchanted forest. Now, as you can see, Gala is in bed with a tiger cub next to her. She is the princess of the forest and the guests sitting at the table are having dinner in bed! *C'est formidable, n'est ce pas?*"

Dali was talking with great enthusiasm.

"And the wrecked automobile—where does that fit in?"

"*Ce n'est pas difficile.* In America people are always in automobile accidents, is it not so? We will have a wrecked automobile that is overturned. In it, we will have a nude model who lies there dead. From the automobile there will emerge two dancers—their bodies bandaged—and they will perform a dance of death."

Dali stopped abruptly as if to make certain we had fully grasped everything he had said. Then he added, "When the guests walk in, it will be as if they had entered another world . . . a dream world . . . a world of fantasy."

"I'm quite sure of it," I said.

Later in the evening when we left Gala and Dali and started driving up the valley, Dag didn't say anything for a long time. Finally, "Do you realize what we are getting ourselves into?"

"I'm beginning to get some idea," I said.

"And the sketch he made . . . did you notice how Gala tore it into so many pieces?"

It was not too difficult to gather the props that Dali required. The Del Monte forest had to be constantly thinned of pine trees to make room for new growth. From the forest we could get the trees. The gunny sacks and newspapers presented no problem and neither did the truckloads of fresh fruit, squash, corn and pumpkins. The largest bed in Hollywood and the wild animals were something else again.

I was too intrigued and carried away by Dali's enthusiasm to foresee any obstacles. Undoubtedly he wanted to help the refugee artists, but he was also concerned with getting all the publicity he could for Dali, and in this he was thoroughly experienced.

Some people make news; Dali easily came under that classification. The party would make news, and Del Monte would get as much publicity as Dali.

"By all means, do everything he wants within reason," Mr.

Morse said. But, *within reason* was something Dali did not understand or accept.

Yet there was nothing impulsive about Dali. Every move was carefully thought out. He knew exactly what he was doing and why he did it. He was like a sales manager mapping out a sales campaign. Dali was selling Dali; he didn't need a publicity man—he was his own and an expert at it.

He wanted the largest bed in Hollywood because he knew it would make news. I went on to Los Angeles and contacted friends in the motion picture studios. My request for the largest bed in Hollywood was accepted in Hollywood without a murmur of surprise.

"The largest bed we have," said Jack Warner of Warner Brothers, "was the one used by Mae Murray in *The Merry Widow*. Ten people can sleep in it. Is that big enough?"

I contracted for the bed, and from another studio I obtained the animal heads. They had been used in a production of *A Midsummer Night's Dream*.

I flew back to Del Monte in triumph. The next day in an automobile wrecking lot in Monterey I bought a wrecked Chevrolet for fifty dollars. I. Magnin provided the nude store mannequins. The big problem that remained was to assemble everything. Then there were the live wild animals that Dali wanted. The best and most logical place to get these was from the Fleishhacker Zoo in San Francisco. Mr. Fleishhacker was president of the zoo, and I knew him.

I told Dali about the zoo and about Mr. Fleishhacker.

"But I need to know first what kind of animals you plan to use," I said.

"Tomorrow we will go to San Francisco," he said. "You and I, we will visit the zoo. We will look over the animals. We do not need many animals, but they must be very unusual animals. I will make the selection."

In the morning we drove to San Francisco and went to the St. Francis Hotel for lunch. As we passed through the lobby,

Dali, in his black velvet coat and his waxed moustache, began to attract attention. Then in the dining room, everyone seemed to turn and stare in our direction.

We finished lunch and started for the zoo. As we were driving down McAllister street which had many secondhand stores, Dali grasped my arm.

"Stop!" he called out. "Look over there! We must visit that shop. *C'est trés importante.*"

"Why? What have you seen?" I asked.

"Ah—I will show you. Come. Let us go into that store."

To me, it was just another secondhand shop, mostly junk in the window. But what had caught Dali's eye was an old anatomical chart, such as was once used in medical schools. It was hanging on a wire along the side of the window. The chart was in color; it had flaps and as each flap was raised, it revealed the lungs, the heart, the kidneys, the liver, the intestines, and about everything else.

"*Regardez!*" Dali would say as he turned one of the flaps. "Isn't it wonderful?"

He asked me to buy it and after bargaining, I managed to get it for fifteen dollars. But I still didn't see why this antiquated anatomical chart should interest him so much.

"What are you going to do with it?" I questioned him as we walked out with it and placed it in the back seat.

"It is superb. It is extraordinary," he said. "Never have I seen one as good as this. What a find! Ah—you have no imagination. You do not see what use I will make of it? Why, it will be my costume for the party! I will wear a black leotard and I will have the chart sewn on the front. As I greet people, I will open one flap and I will show them my heart—or my lungs—or my kidneys. It is just perfect! Is it not fate that we should take this street and pass by that shop? Everything we do, everything that happens to Dali, is predestined. Now, let us go to the zoo."

I had a difficult time keeping up with Dali at the zoo. He rushed from one cage to another, calling to the animals in French and Spanish. He made faces at the animals and then would go through a pantomime routine, imitating their expressions and their antics. He was putting on an amazing performance, and was thoroughly enjoying it.

When we came to the spider monkeys, he stood there motionless, fascinated, as if in a trance. The monkeys, too seemed to be aware that they had a perfect audience, for they began to chatter away happily and then gave an exhibition of their acrobatic skills, jumping from one swing to the other. Finally, Dali applauded and shouted: "*Bravo! Bravo!*"

Then, turning to me, he said: "What a great error God made when He didn't allow us to remain as we once were. We would all be better off as monkeys. *Quel dommage!*"

I looked at my watch. We had been at the zoo almost two hours and soon it would be closed. Dali had not made his selection of animals he wanted for the party. I reminded him that it was getting late and we still had a long drive. But Dali was having too good a time to be rushed.

"I have not yet seen the tigers and the giraffes," he said.

We went across the zoo to visit the tigers. As we stood in front of the iron bars that separated us, he called to the tigers. When one approached us, Dali's voice softened.

"How beautiful you are." he said. "Come near me and let me pet you."

The tiger kept its distance. It opened its jaws and then yawned, as if bored by the whole thing. Finally it turned and walked away. Dali wasn't pleased.

"It does not like me," he said. "Tigers are very feminine." He took me by the arm. "Come and let us go and talk with the giraffes. There you will see the difference. With the giraffes I have great understanding."

Dali was right. The giraffes were far off, grazing in the grass, but when they heard us approach they stopped and stretched their long necks. Their heads went up as they listened attentively to our summons. Two of them began to move slowly in our direction, and one came close to us. It looked down from its great height, then lowered its head and sniffed on the ground near Dali. Dali was in ecstasy.

"*Chulona grande,* you are the most magnificent of all," he spoke to it endearingly in Spanish. "You do recognize me— do you not? Yes, we are old friends, you and I. Come near me. Let me touch your beautiful head."

The giraffe brought its head close to Dali. He put his hands through the bars and began petting the giraffe and talking to it.

"It's time we leave," I said.

Dali gave the giraffe a final pat and we started walking down the path. Suddenly he stopped, turned and looked back at the giraffe. The giraffe's neck and head were up high again and it was staring at us.

Dali seemed unhappy and he was silent most of the way home. When we eventually reached Del Monte, his mood changed, and he was in better spirits.

"I must not forget my costume," he said. "I must show it to Gala at once. She will be very pleased with it. How wonderful that I found it!"

Dali had made mental notes of all the animals we had seen at the zoo, for on the following day he had prepared a list and brought it to me. There were twenty animals on the list, including a tiger cub and a giraffe.

"The giraffe," he said, "will be the hit of the party."

The San Francisco Zoo had been donated and named after Mr. Fleishhacker. That morning I telephoned Mr. Fleishhacker, told him about the party, about Dali and why we needed the animals.

"It is a very unusual request," he said. "Ordinarily the animals never leave the zoo, as you must know."

"This is an unusual occasion," I said, "and besides, it's for a benefit."

"Which are the animals you want?"

I read the list off to him.

"All right, my boy," he said, "I'll see what I can do. I will call you later in the day, but I can't promise anything."

At four o'clock Mr. Fleishhacker was on the phone. He had talked to the zoo director and he would permit the animals to leave the zoo, as long as they were accompanied by four guards and if we provided the transportation.

"But the giraffe is out," Mr. Fleishhacker said. "On that point the zoo director was definite. A giraffe is too valuable and too delicate to be transported even a short distance."

"They come from Africa and that's a long distance," I argued.

"They don't go from the zoo to Del Monte, however."

"No giraffe then?"

"Sorry, no giraffe."

"Dali will be disappointed."

"That can't be helped."

"The giraffe was the one animal Dali wanted."

"He just can't have it."

"The director won't change his mind?"

He was adamant. "No giraffe."

I thanked Mr. Fleishhacker and I began to worry how I would break the bad news to Dali. He wasn't going to like it. He would be furious. I decided not to tell him until the very last, when it would be too late to do anything about it.

By this time, stories about the Dali party and the props he was going to use were appearing in the newspapers and people started telephoning and writing in for reservations. As Dali knew it would, the search for the largest bed in Hollywood hit the front pages. Dali was making news and reporters came to Del Monte to interview him and to describe the preparations for the party.

A week before the party, the props were assembled and a crew of ten men began to transform the huge ballroom in the lower floor of the hotel into an enchanted forest. The two thousand pine trees were brought in and strung against the walls. The gunny sacks filled with the crumpled newspapers were hung from the ceiling. The bed was flown in and placed at one end of the room; on the other side went the wrecked automobile. Dali was present most of the time, directing the workmen, making suggestions and always demanding more props.

"We're going to need at least twelve hundred shoes," he suddenly announced.

"But why, Dali?" I protested. "You are getting in so many props there won't be room for the guests."

"The shoes—it is evening slippers with high heels that I want—they will not take up space. We will use them only at the table—to serve the first course in."

"Inside the slippers?"

"*Exactement.*"

Stores in San Francisco were telephoned and combed for evening slippers—any color, shape, or size. Within two days we had them and they arrived at Del Monte and then the chef had to be persuaded to use them. The chef didn't like it, but Dali charmed him.

The chef who only a few moments before had been red-faced and angry and ready to throw me out of the kitchen, said to Dali: "*Oui, Monsieur, avec plaisir.*"

That same day Dali had to choose from the six models the one that would lie nude in the overturned automobile. At first I thought he was going to ask them to strip in front of the workmen, but Dali merely lined them up. He stood back, stared at them very professionally, and then he pointed to the third girl in line, a well developed brunette, and said, "Please, you walk."

She walked back and forth in her tightly fitted dress.

"*Trés bien,*" he said, "you will do," and he immediately lost interest in her. To him, she was only a prop. I told her what she had to do.

"Lie there without clothes?" she asked.

"Yes, in the nude."

"Completely nude?"

"That's the way he wants it."

She hesitated for a moment. "I guess it will be all right," she said, and she looked very innocent and demure. "Never done it before, but no reason why I shouldn't—is there?"

"None," I said. "You will be here on time?"

"I've always been on time," she said and she left along with the other girls. I went over to talk to Dali.

"That girl," I said, "if she's only going to lie nude in the car, why did you make her walk?"

He looked at me bored. "When a woman walks," he said, "she reveals everything. Every woman knows that. Now, let us go on with our work."

By noon on the day of the party, the forest was as enchanted as it was ever going to be. Every prop was in place, including the naked store window mannequins with the animal heads. The truckloads of fruit, squash, corn, melons, and pumpkins had arrived the previous afternoon and in the evening they had been put on the tables. Two electricians, working under Dali's direction, had tried different lighting effects until Dali was finally satisfied. Dali had had his way and the result he had achieved was startling and remarkable. He had created an enchanted forest, weird and mysterious. Only the wild animals were missing now, and they would be in by late afternoon.

The hotel was sold out and the reservations continued to come in. William Parker, the maitre d'hotel, was looking for us and he found us in a corner of the enchanted forest. Where, he wanted to know, were he and his captains going to put the people who had bought tickets and made reservations?

"There is no room, not enough tables—we can only seat several hundred at the most," he was saying. "There are more than a thousand people coming. Where, Monsieur Dali—where are we going to put them?"

Parker was right, of course. Dali had so many props, he had left practically no space for tables.

"If that overturned car was removed," Parker went on, "we could put in more tables . . ."

Parker didn't finish. Dali just stared at him.

"Nothing is to be moved," he said. "Nothing is to be touched," and he walked away from the enchanted forest.

When Parker, who had lost his usual, calm maitre d' manner, appealed to me, I told him it was Dali's party and I couldn't do anything about it.

"We're going to put tables outside, all along the halls," Parker said, "but even so, we'll have to turn down hundreds of people. What am I and the captains going to say to them?"

"Blame it on Dali," I said. "He's the one who is putting on the party."

I managed to get out of the enchanted forest and up to my office. Two of the assistant managers were waiting and they were holding lists in their hands. Did I realize that the Vanderbilts, the Hitchcocks, the Sanfords and the Winston Guests were flying in from New York—and from Hollywood there were Bob Hope, Bing Crosby, Ginger Rogers, Clark Gable, and dozen of others. They all wanted—and were demanding—ringside tables, but there were not enough tables to go around. Something had to be done, they said.

Mr. Morse was buzzing me on the telephone. "What's this I hear about the lack of tables?"

And then the chef came in and he was holding a black evening slipper in his hand. How, he asked, was he going to serve the first course inside a woman's shoe? Besides this one was too small to put anything inside.

"Line them with waxed paper," I said, "and put in just enough food to fit."

The chef walked out, shaking his head, murmuring that Dali was mad and that I had gone mad, too.

We made a room chart; the most important guests were to be seated inside and the rest would have to wander in and out of the enchanted forest and find such tables as were being strung out in the halls.

On the afternoon of the party, newspaper reporters, society editors, feature writers, newsreel cameramen, and photographers from *Life* and from *Look* began checking in and wanting to photograph the enchanted forest. But Dali had ordered the doors locked and would not let anyone in. The party was scheduled to start at eight o'clock in the evening and finally he agreed that at seven o'clock the newspapermen, the newsreel cameramen, and the photographers would be permitted to take photographs before the room was filled with guests.

The log for the party went something like this:

4:00 P.M. Arrival of wild animals from Fleishhacker Zoo, including six-months-old tiger cub.

4:30 P.M. Conference with doctor as to whether or not the nude who was to lie in wrecked automobile should be given mild sedation. It was agreed she should have sedation so that she would lie motionless and comfortably.

5:00 P.M. Call from Dali. Could my wife get him a seamstress or could she help to sew on his costume? Dag decided to go to his assistance.

5:30 P.M. Photographers break into Dali's room and take pictures of him putting on his costume. (Comment by Dag: "I was photographed sewing on Dali's kidneys.")

6:00 P.M. Brunette nude arrives.

6:30 P.M. Wild animals are located and placed where

Dali had previously indicated. He still does not know about the giraffe.

6:45 P.M.   Doctor arrives to bandage dancers who will perform dance of death from wrecked automobile.

6:50 P.M.   Brunette undresses and gets inside of wrecked automobile. Complains she feels cold.

7:00 P.M.   Unshaved and without time to shower, I start out for Dali's room to pick him up and take him to the enchanted forest for press preview.

At seven-fifteen, fifteen minutes behind schedule, I led Dali through the rear of the hotel, in order to avoid the crowds gathering in the lobby and halls of the hotel. In the back of the hotel was the dimly lit freight entrance, and by it was a six-foot high platform with a wooden ramp that gradually sloped into the courtyard.

On reaching the edge of the platform I suddenly realized that the ramp, usually there, had been removed. It was too late. As I started to fall, I yelled to Dali to stay back. I landed on my right arm on the cement courtyard.

"I'm hurt," I said as I managed to get on my feet. "I think my arm is broken."

Dali, still standing on the platform, looked down at me and began to laugh. It was a long, hysterical laugh.

"The party will be a great success," Dali shouted in great mirth. "Always when there is an accident, it means success!"

I was in too much pain to care what happened to Dali or to the party. Holding onto my arm, I took a service elevator to the third floor and went to the room where Dr. Mast Wolfson was bandaging the dancers.

"I think I'm hurt," I muttered.

Mast examined my arm. "Come on, we're going to the hospital," he said.

At the hospital the X-rays showed that I had three fractures.

"Do you want to stay in the hospital or go on to the

party?" he asked. "If you do want to go, I can put on a temporary splint and we can set the arm tomorrow."

"I'd like to go to the party," I said, glancing at the hospital clock. It was now after eight o'clock.

He put on a splint, bandaged my arm, gave me some medicine to kill the pain and a half-hour later we were at Del Monte. Everyone thought that my bandaged arm and splint were part of my costume for the evening.

Around ten o'clock I saw Dali. He gave me one of his strange, wild stares. He didn't inquire about the accident or how I felt.

"You didn't get me the giraffe," was his only comment, and he walked away.

The next day, while they were placing my arm in a cast, the auditing department ran tapes on the cost of the party and the receipts taken in. The expenses went far beyond any profits. Dali held me responsible and as we argued, both in Spanish and in French, our short-lived friendship was shattered. A few days later he and Gala left Del Monte.

Shortly afterwards letters from Mr. Barr at the Museum of Modern Art in New York began to arrive. Dali, he said, had told him that the party had been tremendously successful. Where, Mr. Barr demanded, was the money for the refugee artists?

We sent him a list of the props, including the evening slippers, and a break-down of expenses. After that, we never again heard from Mr. Barr.

CHAPTER THIRTEEN

A Sunday Excursion on the Lake

The doctor removed the cast, massaged my arm and assured me I would have no trouble with it.

"Keep on exercising it to get the stiffness out," he advised. "But what you need is a rest. Go away somewhere and forget about Dali and Del Monte."

So when Witter Bynner, the poet, invited us to spend the Christmas holidays at his home in Chapala, a little Mexican town on the edge of the lake and an hour away from Guadalajara, we accepted.

"Not much to do there and the Indians are always sending up skyrockets at five in the morning. But there's a quiet charm to the place," Bynner said. "If you get there before I do, look up Isadoro, he takes care of the house. Make yourself at home. I'll write you a note to give him."

We took the train to Mexico City toward the end of November. In the dining car, we met a doctor and his wife from Nashville, and Brigance, the dress designer from New York. It was their first visit to Mexico, too, and the doctor kept on warning us about the food and the water and I could see that Brigance was worried.

"I think I'll just eat bananas and drink beer," he said.

It was a short ride from the railroad station to the hotel, through the narrow streets and past buildings painted brilliant reds, pinks and greens along with splashes of yellow. In the distance were the snow-covered peaks of Popocatepetl and Iztaccíhuatl, silently guarding the city. We went down the Reforma and then on to a tile-floored hotel with high beams and ceilings where we had reservations.

For some, Mexico is a state of mind—an escape from reality. There is beauty and tragedy to Mexico and there is also something beyond it that is far reaching and casts a spell of enthrallment over many people. One either falls under the hypnotic trance or, instead, there is violent repulsion to the country. "I hate Mexico," tourists have said. "There is too much poverty and filth."

For me, that first visit to Mexico brought back childhood memories. My brother and I were born and raised in Guatemala and until I was ten, Spanish was the only language I spoke. In Mexico and with the Mexican people I felt at home; the Indians I saw and heard talking on the streets were like the Indians I had known as a boy. They were a part of me; I was rediscovering my youth.

I did not expect Dag would like Mexico but she reacted much as I did. Her Nordic background was so different from that of the Mexicans; yet there was an instant acceptance on her part. There is a legend in Mexico of a bearded, blond god, Quetzalcóatl, who landed on its shores centuries before, about the time the Aztec empire was established, and who had promised to return. No explanation exists as to who he was, except that he might have been a wandering Viking, and perhaps he was.

One afternoon, as we walked through the flower market on Dolores Street, the sidewalk stands filled with poinsettias, carnations, violets, gardenias, and greens, I said to Dag that I hoped someday we could come to Mexico and spend several months, rather than a few weeks. "Perhaps we can," she said.

We were still exhausted from the Dali party and each

morning we slept late and had breakfast in our room. On the front pages of the newspaper, brought with our breakfast, the news was not encouraging. But we had been so assured that there would be no war with Japan, that we were not too perturbed. We dined at Prendes, and ate *gusanos de maguey* and washed them down with good Mexican beer. We lunched at Paolo's while a Mexican marimba on the sidewalk played "La Feria de las Flores" and "Adios Mariquita Linda." Each day we went to a different restaurant and ordered such typical Mexican dishes as *mole poblano* and *pulpos en su tinta.* Late at night we visited the Tenampa bar and listened to the mariachis, and long after midnight we went to the car barns to sip hot chicken soup as Mexicans did who were out on the town.

The next day the Nashville doctor told us he had rented a car with a driver and a guide, and he and his wife were going to Cuernavaca and Taxco. He invited us to come along and we agreed to share the expenses, but I said there was no need for a guide. He said the guide was included in the price, and that was how we first met Alfredo Gonzales, a handsome Mexican with olive complexion and thick, black hair. He had studied at the University of Pennsylvania and he spoke English fluently with barely a trace of an accent. We liked him and he liked us and by the time we returned to Mexico City we were friends.

"You don't act like *gringos*," he said.

"How are *gringos* supposed to act?" I asked.

"They rush around—wanting to see churches, museums and ruins, and night clubs—and are afraid to miss anything. You and your wife are different."

"How?"

"You are relaxed, in no hurry. You're more like Mexicans," he said, and it was a compliment that we did not forget.

When we took the night train to Guadalajara, Alfredo came to see us off at the station.

"If you come to Mexico again," he said, "I hope you will call me."

I told him we would and he gave us a card with his address and telephone.

We arrived in Chapala on the third of December, long before Witter Bynner was expecting us. He had said he wouldn't be there until the tenth or fifteenth, but we had decided to go anyway. Instead of going to his home, we went to Chapala's only hotel, *El Nido*. In Spanish, *nido* means nest, but it was also the name of Señor Nido, the proprietor, a tall heavy-set Spaniard with black horn-rimmed glasses. He was standing at the doorway, a toothpick in his mouth, as we climbed out of the taxi that had brought us from Guadalajara. We went through the lobby—only it wasn't really a lobby—it was the hotel's dining area and there was a bar which also served as the registration desk. Señor Nido, now rubbing his hands, was right behind us.

"Welcome to Chapala," he said in his broken English. "We are happy to have you here."

"We are friends of Witter Bynner," I said, "and we would like a room for a week or so."

"Of course," he said, "very happy to take care of friends of Señor Bynner." Then turning to his assistant, Guillermo, who was behind the bar, he said in Spanish. "*Son Americanos* —give them one of our better rooms.

"With a view of the plaza," I said in Spanish.

He looked startled and kept on rubbing his hands.

"So you speak Spanish—very good Spanish."

"A little," I said.

"It is very strange to hear an Americano speaking Spanish," he said. "We are happy to have an Americano who speaks Spanish here." Then he told Guillermo to hurry up and take our luggage to the room.

It proved to be their best room. It had a view of the *zocalo* with its park benches, and in the center the usual bandstand. Across the square was the church and the bells were ringing the noon hour.

"Do the bells ring all day long?" I asked Guillermo as he brought in our luggage.

"No señor," he said. "Only at noon, at five, at six, and then again at five in the morning, at six, at seven, and at eight. Except when there is a *fiesta*. Then they ring more. But, they will not bother you. One becomes accustomed to them. I myself do not hear them—only when I want to hear them." He put the luggage down. "Is there anything else you wish?"

"Besides the hotel, where's an interesting place to have a drink before lunch?"

"Señor Bynner likes *La Viuda's* and perhaps you will too. It is two blocks from here on the edge of the lake. Ask for a *tequila con sangre*—it is her specialty."

"The bar is owned by a widow?"

"*Si señor*. In true reality, *La Viuda* is not a widow. She has been married three times and is now married again."

"Then why do they still call her the widow?"

"You see, when her first husband died, she naturally became *La Viuda,* and everyone referred to her as *La Viuda.* After she was married the second time it did not make much difference. They kept on calling her *La Viuda.* Now that she is married to her fourth husband, perhaps it is just as well she is still called the widow as it was in the beginning—is it not so, señor?"

After Guillermo left and we had unpacked, we walked down to *La Viuda's*. It was an open air *cantina,* and there were mariachis playing and singing. From *La Viuda's* we could look across the lake at a group of islands. Fishermen in their white cotton pantaloons, rolled up to their knees and wearing white shirts and straw hats, were returning in their boats after being out all morning. We ordered *tequila con sangre*. The *sangre* was tomato juice with chili; a forerunner of the Bloody Mary. After two tequilas we went back to the hotel and had lunch. It wasn't "lunch;" it was the *comida*, or dinner, and there were at least six courses. When we were finished, we went up to our room and fell asleep. By now we were getting used to taking a siesta.

We liked Chapala, primarily because it didn't pretend to be anything but a small Mexican fishing village. Bynner was about the only American who owned a home and the nearby town of Ajijic was still undiscovered. The water in the lake was muddy, but it was warm and pleasant to swim in and the black sandy beach wasn't too bad for sun bathing. Except for the hotel, few houses had running water and always there were men transporting barrels of water from the lake on their shoulders or on burros. Guillermo was right; after a few days we became accustomed to the church bells and the loud rockets the Indians fired into the sky. There were no newspapers in Chapala and we soon forgot there existed a threat of war.

Witter Bynner's home was across the plaza from the hotel, and one afternoon we stopped by to inquire from Isadoro, his caretaker, if Bynner had been heard from. Isadoro said Bynner was arriving about the tenth. He also wanted us to move from *El Nido* into Bynner's home, but we thanked him and told him we liked the hotel and planned to remain there.

In addition to being Bynner's caretaker, Isadoro operated a business of his own. He moulded clay figures and artifacts, much as his Indian ancestors had done centuries ago. He treated them with acids and buried them in the ground for several months. Eventually, he shipped them off to Mexico City where they were sold as rare pre-Columbian archeological pieces. "Very few can tell the difference," he admitted and laughed about it.

Isadoro was taller and heavier than most Mexican Indians. He had a fine face, slightly slanted eyes and a determined nose and jaw. There was nothing submissive about him and yet he was friendly and pleasant. He wore the same cotton trousers, shirt and leather sandals as the fishermen. He felt badly about Bynner not being there to entertain us.

"Perhaps you will permit me to show you around Chapala," he said, and when we agreed he took us to a number of native bars where we drank straight tequila with salt and lemon.

"Why is it, Isadoro," I asked him when we were in one of the *cantinas,* that every morning they fire rockets?"

"Perhaps because they make a loud noise," he replied, and the answer was so logical I never pursued the subject further.

As we became better acquainted, he told us stories about Chapala, about his people and of *brujos* who had the ability to bewitch.

"Señor Bynner says such things are not possible," Isadoro said, "but I personally do not take chances. One is never sure about these matters. The devil, as the priests say, is all around us."

Then he told us about an American woman who had come to Chapala. According to Isadoro, she had had many affairs, but never with an Indian. "So she talked to me about it, and asked me if I were willing. I said, 'I am a man—*porqué no?* But first you must speak to my wife. I do not do anything without her permission. Occasionally, and if she is in a good mood, she gives the permission if a proper fee is paid.' So she talked to my wife and they came to an agreement. I was rented out for two weeks." He laughed. Then he showed us his wrist watch. "She became a good friend and before she left she made me this present. She also made a present to my wife."

It was on a Friday that we were together with Isadoro and as he walked back to the hotel with us, he suggested that on Sunday we should rent a boat and go for an excursion on the lake and visit some of the nearby islands. He said he would make all the arrangements and he would bring the food and invite a group of mariachi players to come along. They would play and sing, he said, as we sailed around the lake.

"How much will it cost?" I asked him.

"*Pues nada, señor.* You will be my guest."

I nevertheless gave him fifty pesos. "Will that be enough, Isadoro?"

"With all this money, we will have a big fiesta," he said, and he was smiling and laughing as we parted at the doorway of *El Nido.*

I half suspected that on Sunday morning Isadoro would fail to show up, but he was waiting for us when we came down to the lobby for breakfast. He waited while we finished, and then we went on to the beach. He had arranged for everything, including the boat, baskets of food, plenty of tequila and six musicians. We climbed into the boat and the mariachis with their instruments followed us.

It was a warm, pleasant day on December seventh, and the water in the lake was smooth. All morning long the musicians played and sang as we sailed around the lake; at noon we stopped at one of the beaches and had our lunch. But, the tequila went faster than the food, and soon the musicians were drunk and their music took on a quality of sadness and melancholy. Every so often one of the mariachis let out a soulful, tear-jerking screech. After a while they stopped playing and, leaning on each other for support, they managed to get into the boat. By the time we returned to Chapala it was three o'clock and the musicians had passed out and were asleep on the bottom of the boat. Isadoro told us to go on to the hotel and he would take care of the musicians.

"I am full of embarrassment," he said, apologizing for them.

At that time of the afternoon in Chapala, there was no one on the streets, and even the juke box at *La Viuda's* was silent. When we entered the hotel there was no one in the lobby or at the bar. I went behind the bar, picked up the room key and, as we started climbing the stairway, we heard Señor Nido calling us.

"*Madre de Dios*—where have you been?" he cried out, and there was an excited look on his usually calm face.

"On the lake with Isadoro. Has something happened?"

"Has something happened? *Dios mío!* Have you not heard the news? The Japanese, they have bombed you! They have bombed Pearl Harbor! And you ask 'has something happened?' "

We were silent, unable to grasp fully what he was telling us.

"If you do not believe me, come and listen to the radio," Señor Nido added.

We stood there motionless, his words gradually getting through. But our first reaction was, as it must have been to millions in the United States and in other parts of the world, of disbelief and shock. How could the Japanese bomb Pearl Harbor? Pearl Harbor was an armed fortress. It was absurd! And even if it had happened, incredible as it might be, we would quickly retaliate.

"Do not worry, Señor Nido," I said. "If they did attack Pearl Harbor, our fleet will destroy Japan in no time."

Dag and I looked at each other. We were still hanging onto that false security which had been drummed into us for so long. It was not possible, it was beyond comprehension. We followed Señor Nido across the empty lobby and through a French glass door and into his room. Señora Nido was there and so was Guillermo and two hotel guests. They did not say a word as we came in; they were sitting as if at a wake and the coffin was the radio.

I looked around the room. There was a large, old brass bed with a dip in the middle and a faded, crocheted bedspread. Against one wall was a wooden *armario* that held clothes, and next to it on a stand, an enamel wash basin and a pitcher of water. By this hung two soiled towels. Nearby was a small cabinet; the door was open only slightly, but enough to reveal a white chamber pot. It was a dismal room and I remember it very well, for we remained there until midnight, occasionally switching Señor Nido's radio set to stations in Laredo and San Antonio. The news was all the same, whether in Spanish or in English.

In the morning the church bells rang and the Indians sent off their rockets. At breakfast no one any longer seemed excited or upset. Life went on in Chapala as it had been going on for many years. We had *huevos rancheros* and *pan dulce,* and the waiter, Antonio, said that it would be another fine day as he brushed away the flies with a napkin.

We decided to leave Chapala and take the night train from Guadalajara to the border and asked Guillermo to arrange for a car. We also sent word to Isadoro about our departure and he arrived while we were packing. He asked if he could ride with us to Guadalajara, and we told him to come along.

"Is the war serious? Will Señor Bynner be in the Army?" he asked.

"I hardly think so," I said.

"I wish I were a *gringo* and in the war," he said. "Nothing very exciting happens in Chapala."

Isadoro helped us with the luggage and Señor Nido and Guillermo shook hands with us and said how sorry they were that we were leaving. In the car as we drove on toward Guadalajara, we heard on the radio that the President had asked Congress to declare war.

Isadoro spent the day with us in Guadalajara, and as we waited at the station, he brought out from under his shirt, one of his clay figures.

"It is not very much," he said, "but perhaps you will keep it and remember Isadoro."

The train at the border was packed with soldiers going to San Francisco. They looked so young, in their trim uniforms, joking and laughing and telling each other what they would do to the Japanese. After the first shock of Pearl Harbor, they too felt as we did, that it would be a short war.

"Why, it will be over before we get to the Pacific," one of them said.

When we finally arrived in Monterey, there were no longer any signs of complacency. Barbed wire was stretched across the beaches and everywhere there were armed soldiers and machine guns. The Army was expecting the Japanese to land momentarily along the California coast. The frightened expressions on the faces of people were like those I had seen in Shanghai and in Canton.

Once again I tried to get into the Army and the Navy. I made telephone calls and sent telegrams to Washington. I got nowhere and felt useless, unwanted. I saw friends who had been in the reserves, in uniform and with the rank of majors and colonels. I was furious and envious.

Even Spike Graham was not very consoling. "What are you worrying about? Didn't all those generals and admirals tell you it would be over in no time? If Washington needs you, they'll come after you."

When I had about given up hope, a telegram came from the Office of the Coordinator of Inter-American Affairs, ordering me to report for duty in Washington, D.C., within forty-eight hours. The Coordinator's Office was a government agency set up to help transport strategic war materials from Latin America and to carry out an extensive propaganda program. I suspected that my knowledge of Spanish had something to do with my going to Washington, though there was no indication of what my duties might be. I was also convinced that being given forty-eight hours in which to report meant that I was urgently needed.

But when I reported to the reception desk in the Department of Commerce building, the girl glanced at the telegram and said in a strong Brooklyn accent. "Oh—so you're another one of 'em. Go to the fourth floor. Ya gotta be processed first."

It took all day, going from office to office, filling out applications and signing papers.

"And now," said another girl, this one from the deep South, "you've got to get your medical. Come back tomorrow."

The next day the girl from the deep South said: "You got your medical so soon? Better return tomorrow. They haven't decided where to place you."

I spent the rest of the day going to various museums, visiting the Lincoln Memorial and then, like any tourist, I stood on Pennsylvania Avenue and gazed through the iron fence at the White House. In the evening I bought a mystery novel, had dinner, and went to bed. At eight-thirty in the morning I reported to the Coordinator's Office.

The girl from the deep South was kind and apologetic. "I still have no instructions about where to send you. Do you mind coming back in the morning?"

I returned to the hotel, went up to the room and tried to read the mystery story, but the words were meaningless. I telephoned the few friends I had in Washington, but I couldn't get through. I left my name and set out again on another sightseeing tour. Late in the afternoon I checked at the hotel desk. There were no messages and no one had returned any of my calls. In the morning I was back at the Coordinator's Office.

"Oh, it's you again," said the same girl. "I am sorry, but really, there is not a thing for you so far. I reckon you just have to wait."

"But, there's a war going on . . ."

"We sure all know that, and that is where the trouble is. We have too many people reporting in. You come back tomorrow. I sure hope I have better news for you then."

Now began two of the longest weeks I have ever spent. I was in the nation's capital where great decisions were being made. The streets and the hotel lobbies were crowded with military personnel, all carrying briefcases. Every one seemed to be busy, going somewhere—except me. I had nowhere to go, nothing to do. During these two weeks I followed a routine: I reported each morning at eight-thirty at the Coordinator's Office. At eight-thirty-five I was told to return the next day. At nine o'clock I would start for a walk and wait for the Mellon Art Gallery or the Smithsonian Museum to open. At noon I would be back in the hotel to check for messages. There were never messages. Then I would have lunch and afterwards would visit one or two historical sites. By four o'clock I would walk back to the hotel, check in again for messages. The next stopping place would be a bar. Then dinner, and up to my room to read or I'd take in a movie. At ten o'clock I'd listen to the news. The news was all bad. Finally I would go to bed and read some more.

It was not difficult to dislike Washington and everything about it. Each day I became more discouraged and depressed. Then late one afternoon when I was in the bar of the Mayflower Hotel, I saw a familiar face.

"Pat," I rushed over to greet him, "remember me?"

"Oh, sure," he said, "what are you doing here?"

"Working for the Coordinator's Office. And you?"

"Working for the Coordinator's Office," he said. "Have a drink."

His name was Sylvester "Pat" Weaver and he was in charge, he told me, of programming the short wave stations from New York which were beamed at Latin America. But every other week, he said, he had to come to Washington. "I'm having a hell of a time finding people who speak Spanish," he said.

That was all I needed to hear.

"Pat, I was born in Latin America," I almost shouted the words out, "and I speak Spanish—spoke it before English. I hate being in Washington, not doing anything. Can't you get me out of here?" I was now pleading. "Get me transferred to New York?"

"I'll see what I can do," he said. "I'll call you tomorrow. I have to go now. Nice seeing you."

He left me at the bar. I had another drink, wondering if I would hear from him.

In the morning as usual, I reported in at the Coordinator's Office and went for a walk. Then I returned to the hotel and as usual, I stopped at the desk.

"Any messages?"

"No messages. Say, wait a minute—there is a message for you."

I returned Pat Weaver's call.

"I've managed to get you transferred to New York," he said. "I'm taking the four o'clock train. Why don't you get on the same train?"

As we sat in the club car, I thanked him.

"Don't thank me—you speak Spanish—I can use you," he said.

CHAPTER FOURTEEN

Just Call Me Nelson

As a nation we have not taken the countries that make up Latin America too seriously and our interest in their development and their political antics we have found at times more entertaining than important to our own future and security. Not until the bearded Castro came into power in Cuba did we begin to show great concern over Latin America. We are also prone to forget that we had our Marines in Nicaragua, and that for ten years (1913–1923) we had no diplomatic relations with Mexico, our closest neighbor.

A year or so before Pearl Harbor, Nelson Rockefeller, then in his early thirties, and possibly already looking at his own political destiny, foresaw that the friendship of Latin America could prove significant in the event of war with the Axis. He persuaded the President to establish the Office of the Co-ordinator of Inter-American Affairs and Rockefeller, who was learning Spanish, was appointed to head this agency. The Department of State, under whose jurisdiction comes all activities abroad, was not at first alarmed over the formation of this agency. It was considered more of a plaything for Rockefeller. Furthermore, the Department of State was too preoccupied with Europe to give much thought to Latin America, to which it usually assigned less experienced diplomats.

After Pearl Harbor, the Department took a second reading

on Latin America. The United States, with no stockpiles of essential war materials, found its supply lines cut off. Many of the materials we urgently needed were available in Latin America. Military strategists also saw that Brazil might well be a jumping off place for invasion forces going into Africa. With its diplomats withdrawn from occupied countries in Europe and the Orient, the Department began sending them to Latin America, and at the same time increasing the size of its embassies.

It also discovered that its prerogatives in Latin America were being threatened by the still infant, but possibly powerful Office of the Coordinator of Inter-American Affairs, to whom Congress had appropriated, through Rockefeller's initiative, ample funds. The Department proceeded to snipe away at the Coordinator's Office and by bureaucratic entanglement, took steps to reduce its influence. Nelson Rockefeller had to fight the Department of State at almost every turn. That he was mostly successful and held his own in this squabble was something of an achievement in itself.

This, then, was the situation at the time, but unknown to me, when I reported for duty to the Coordinator's Office. Before Pearl Harbor, the Coordinator's Office had less than a hundred employees; after Pearl Harbor, its employees numbered over a thousand and eventually it doubled. I was one of the first thousand hastily hired.

Over the years, German nationalists had entrenched themselves in Latin America and had established a propaganda offensive. One of the responsibilities of the Coordinator's Office was to combat this activity and to break the stronghold held by the German Nazis. As an initial step in this direction, the United States began to beam news and propaganda programs via short wave to Latin America.

Pat Weaver, who had had me transferred from Washington to New York, was in charge of these short wave broadcasts. His staff consisted of writers, producers, and executives from

the major networks, who had volunteered their services and
who had been hurriedly drafted by the government. They
were experienced men, but few if any, had ever been to Latin
America or were too familiar with the problems of these
countries and neither did they speak or understand Spanish
or Portuguese. The Coordinator's Office was as unprepared to
direct an effective propaganda program as were the soldiers
at Fort Ord marching with wooden rifles.

Weaver was forced to recruit Puerto Rican or Mexican
waiters, bellboys, and even janitors, for announcers, actors,
narrators, and translators. About their only qualification was
that they spoke Spanish. Even more difficult to find were those
who knew Portuguese, the language of Brazil. With this untrained group, Weaver and his staff had to fill from four to
six hours of short wave daily.

In Washington I had been frustrated and angry, not realiz-
ing the difficulties faced by the Coordinator's Office. I had
been turned away, not because I was not needed or wanted,
but because the Coordinator's Office had mushroomed too fast
to assign jobs to the people it hired. There was not even
adequate office space or desks, and government bureaucracy
was not keeping up to the sudden change in pace; it was
still trying to operate as it had before Pearl Harbor.

In Washington, the Department of State was attempting to
curb the activities of the Coordinator's Office. The situation in
New York was somewhat different. Radio broadcasting and
propaganda was new to the Department, and it left Weaver
and his staff very much to themselves. Yet Rockefeller and
Weaver knew that short wave broadcasts were at best only
an expedient. Men had to be sent out from the Coordinator's
Office to establish and organize programs in each Latin
American country. Later I was told I was to be among the
first to be sent out into the field, though I was also cautioned
that it might be months before such an assignment material-
ized. I didn't care. In New York I felt at home. I had always

liked New York. It is big and impersonal as are all big cities.

The evening I arrived on the train from Washington with Pat Weaver, I registered at the Waldorf Astoria for I had always stayed there when I had worked for Del Monte. During the early months of the war, there was no scarcity of rooms and the clerk was even happy to see me. I was given a room on the tenth floor. I bathed in luxury and then went to dinner at Christ Cella's where I had once dined with Ludwig Bemelmans. Unlike Washington, the restaurant was uncrowded, the food and the service was excellent for there was still no rationing.

In the morning I reported for duty and Weaver put me to work. This in itself was a relief and a satisfaction. I read radio scripts, watched productions, listened to the news being broadcast in Spanish, and attended rehearsals. I sat in conferences and studied the directives being sent from the Department of State. For once my knowledge of Spanish was proving useful and helpful.

For a week I remained at the Waldorf, and then, being on a government salary, I knew I had to move and find a reasonably priced room. Frank Ready was the manager of the Waldorf and on those occasions when I had stayed at the Waldorf, he had complimented the room or given me a rate, because of my association with the Hotel Del Monte. Even now I had been extended a special rate on the room I occupied, but it was far more than I could afford.

I had packed my suitcase, but before checking out, I went to thank Mr. Ready, and also to explain why I was leaving.

"I venture to guess that before this is over," he said, "we'll all be working for the government. How long will you be in New York?"

"Perhaps two or three months."

"Where are you going to move?" he inquired.

"There are a number of small hotels where I can get a low-priced room. With my wife still in California I have to keep expenses down. I might even look for a furnished apartment that won't cost over a hundred dollars a month."

"That might not be easy to find," he said kindly.

"I know, but I'll get something."

"That room you're in—it's one of our better rooms," Mr. Ready went on. "There's always a demand for them. But we have some suites on the fourteenth floor that are vacant. I could let you have one of them."

"But, Mr. Ready, as I explained, I can't even afford the room I am giving up."

"Suppose I gave you one of these suites for a hundred dollars a month?"

"You're joking."

"But I'm not. They are vacant, so why not put them to use for our friends. I think you should take it."

He pressed a buzzer on his desk and one of his assistant managers came in.

"This is Ed Hastings," Mr. Ready said, and introduced me to him. He told him about my planning to check out and the reason for it. "I'm giving him one of those suites on the fourteenth floor at a special rate," he added. He got up from his desk and walked to the door of his office with me.

"By the way, if you entertain don't order drinks from room service. Buy it by the bottle from the liquor store on Lexington. It's cheaper and there's plenty of ice in your refrigerator."

Ed Hastings, who later was to become manager of the Waldorf, took me up to the suite. It was huge and it overlooked Park Avenue.

"If there's anything you want, be sure to call me," Hastings said. "I'll have them bring the luggage from your room."

He walked out and left me alone. I still found it difficult to believe that I had this suite for a hundred dollars a month. Everything was turning out well. My luck was holding out.

That afternoon after work I went to one of the Gristede

stores near the Waldorf. I bought cheese, crackers, and a quart of milk to put in the refrigerator.

Next day I went to Macy's and bought a small electric hot plate, a few dishes, and some tableware. From then on, I began cooking breakfast and frequently dinner. Gristedes would deliver promptly any groceries I needed.

On several occasions I had some of the fellows who worked in the Coordinator's Office for drinks. The first time I did, one of them looked over the suite.

"You sure live in style," he said. "How does Rockefeller get all you rich guys to work for him?"

I was being trained as a propagandist, the only trouble was that no one knew exactly what a propagandist was supposed to do. Every two or three weeks I'd ride the crowded train to Washington, where there would be long conference sessions behind closed doors. They were called "policy meetings," though it all seemed vague to me. There was also no inkling of when I and others working with me would be assigned to Latin America. In fact one of the men being trained with me wrote out a skit about the delay in being sent abroad. Hitler had been defeated. Japan was about to surrender. Suddenly a messenger from the Department of State rushed in. "I have your passports," he announced. "You can go out on your assignments."

The months passed, the conferences in Washington went on. Dag remained in California attempting to dispose of our home in the country and of our furniture. Then one day I was summoned to Washington. Nelson Rockefeller, I was told, wanted to talk with me at ten o'clock in the morning.

Within the Department of State, Rockefeller was at first looked upon as a young upstart, an interloper who was trying to break into an inner circle exclusively restricted to career diplomats. If he could be stopped early in the game, he would be no problem and while his ideas would be politely listened to, they need never be acted upon.

When the Department found it could not curb Rockefeller, it began to compromise, permitting some career diplomats assigned to Latin American countries to improvise their own road blocks.

One such diplomat was George S. Messersmith, the American Ambassador to Mexico. Messersmith, as a former assistant secretary of state and a long time career diplomat, had no regard for Rockefeller or his Office of Inter-American Affairs. Furthermore, Messersmith was determined not to allow Rockefeller to extend the operations of the Coordinator's Office into Mexico.

On the morning I went to see Rockefeller, he was sitting at his desk and near him was a man lounging in a leather chair, his long legs stretched out. When I came in, Rockefeller rose, greeted me and then introduced the man in the leather chair.

"This is Wally Harrison," he said. "He's my chief assistant. How about some coffee?"

He didn't wait for me to answer. There were some heavy mugs on the desk and a large percolator. He poured the coffee into a mug and handed it to me. I sat down in a chair near his desk.

Rockefeller was in shirt sleeves, and there was a friendly smile on his face. But I noticed there were deep lines around his eyes and a look of concern; he seemed tired. I reached for my pipe and began filling it.

"Would you mind not smoking?" he asked, and added, "I've been having sinus trouble. Smoke seems to aggravate it," and he said this almost apologetically. "You probably wonder why I called you in." Then in Spanish, which was heavily accented, "I understand from Pat Weaver that you speak Spanish fluently."

"*Un poco,*" I said.

"I gather more than *un poco,*" he said, and then switching

to English again, "Pat thinks you might be right for a job I want done. But, let me say it's a tough one."

"He's putting it mildly," Wally Harrison interrupted. "I think it's impossible."

"Perhaps it is and perhaps it might not be," he said. "With the right break you might swing it. Besides it's worth trying." He stopped for a moment. "I suppose you know of our problems with the State Department."

I nodded.

"Our relations are improving. We've been through the worst part and they are beginning to accept us. But we're not getting far in Mexico. Let me tell you about it."

He was brief and to the point, describing Messersmith's efforts to keep the Coordinator's Office out of Mexico. "I sent Wally Harrison to talk with Messersmith. The trip was futile." Rockefeller turned to Harrison: "Wally, tell him what happened."

Harrison, a distinguished architect, a close friend of Rockefeller and later chosen to design the United Nations building, had obviously had a bad time with Messersmith. His sensitive face, his quiet eyes quickly revealed the vexation and humiliation he had undergone.

"The Ambassador refused to see me," Harrison said. "Sent word that I had twenty-four hours in which to get out of Mexico. Imagine getting a message like that!" He hit his open palm with his fist. "He's no person to toy with, and he's dead set on not having anyone from the Coordinator's Office. He's stubborn—convinced the Embassy can do it alone and without help. Yet he must know that Mexico is vitally important to our war effort. But he won't cooperate and never will, unless he gets orders direct from the White House."

"The President has enough on his mind," Rockefeller broke in. "I want to solve it without asking his help. But I will, if necessary. I have no intention of letting Messersmith stop us. We have a job to do, and we'll do it!"

"You want me to go to Mexico, then, Mr. Rockefeller?"

"You are going to Mexico, and yet you aren't," there was a sparkle in his eyes and he was smiling again. "We're going to request the Department to issue you a passport to visit the five Central American countries. You are stopping in Mexico only enroute, and once more on your return trip. You see, by doing it this way, Messersmith can't keep you out."

"I could go on a tourist card."

"No, you're traveling on official business," he paused for a moment. "And while we are doing this thing above board, I have found that there is more than one way to skin a cat."

I looked at him, still uncertain what he wanted me to do. Rockefeller now seemed younger, almost boyish, fully enjoying the scheming. I couldn't help thinking of his grandfather, as I sat there—old John D.—and the photographs of him that showed him shrewd and cunning. Some of it had obviously passed on to his grandson.

"Here's what I want you to do," Rockefeller began to explain.

I was to have two days in Mexico and I was to see and talk with Guy Ray, the first secretary of the Embassy. I was to attempt to get his assistance.

"Guy Ray, we have reason to believe," Rockefeller went on, "is not entirely opposed to us. He recognizes that the Embassy could use outside help and the funds we are ready to provide. We also know that he is close to Messersmith and that the Ambassador listens to him. If you can persuade Ray about the urgency of the matter and he opens the door, then we're partly in."

Wally Harrison got up from the leather chair on which he had been lounging. He walked several times across the room.

"I don't care for this approach, Nelson. We should get tough with Messersmith."

"But perhaps it won't be necessary. It could work, Wally." Then to me: "We've picked you because of Pat Weaver's recommendation. Besides you were born in Latin America and speak Spanish. Messersmith can't say we are sending untrained people who don't know the country and can't speak the language."

"When do you want me to go, Mr. Rockefeller?"

"Within the week, but first I'll arrange to have you briefed some more. Even if you fail in Mexico, I want a report on the Central American countries. As soon as we can, we'll set up offices in each country you visit."

He left his desk and I, too, got up. "I can't give you any further advice. When you get to Mexico, you'll have to play it by ear. Think you can handle it?"

"I'll do the best I can, Mr. Rockefeller."

He was standing next to me. "Look, we're going to be working a lot together. I would prefer if you'd just call me Nelson."

"Yes, sir," I said.

He walked to the door with me. "Good luck, fellow," he said and we shook hands.

I checked in at the Geneve Hotel, a few blocks from the Embassy and where not too long ago Dag and I had stayed. As I went up to my room, I thought of Brigance and of the doctor from Nashville and of the guide, Alfredo. Everything seemed different now. There were no tourists; the hotel was empty.

I had a cold and was tired from the long flight. I was also concerned as to how I would be received by the Embassy. I wanted to get it over with, so I didn't bother to unpack, but put some cold water on my face, combed my hair and started out for the Embassy.

At the reception desk I asked for Guy Ray's office and went up to the second floor. The door was open and I walked in.

He was reading the afternoon newspaper, his feet on his

desk, a cigarette hanging from his mouth. He glanced up at me.

"Well?"

"I was told I should report in to you."

"From Rockefeller's office—don't tell me," there was a look of disgust on his face.

"I'm just passing through—going on to Guatemala and as far as Panama."

"Well, you reported in. Have a good trip." He was about to start reading his newspaper again.

"It's almost five o'clock—couldn't we have a drink somewhere?"

He appeared mildly interested, or perhaps curious about what I was up to.

"I suppose so," he said, but his voice was indifferent.

He locked his desk and we walked out of the Embassy and went to a bar a block away. We had one drink and then a second. He seemed to thaw out a little. I thought it was as good an opportunity as I was ever going to have to talk with him.

"Rockefeller asked me to see you and ask your advice and help," I said. "Sooner or later, he's going to force his way into Mexico. He's determined to set up an office here."

"Over the Ambassador's dead body," Ray said. "He has no use for Rockefeller."

"But, we're at war."

"You don't know the Ambassador."

"I don't want to know him," I said. "But you do. He'll listen to you."

"Not about Rockefeller."

"He might."

I told the waiter to get us another drink.

"No use beating around the bush," I said. "I'm going to be quite open with you. I am leaving day after tomorrow for Central America and I'll be gone for three weeks. My reason for being here is to try to get your help in setting up an office in Mexico."

"I sort of figured that. Rockefeller doesn't give up easily, does he? Well, you're wasting your time. The answer is plain no."

"You know what will happen? Rockefeller will go to the White House."

"Let him go. To hell with him."

"Rockefeller is asking now for your help," I went on. "He doesn't forget a friend. He's close to the President. At some future time he could be helpful to you."

"I'm doing all right."

"Yes, but friends in the right places can be important."

"I suppose so," he said, giving a little. He was more relaxed now.

"You and I could work together. If they sent someone else here eventually it might be different."

Perhaps it was intuition, but I felt I was reaching him, getting through. I sipped my drink. I must be careful now. I had to win him over. If I did, I would be living in Mexico and Dag would be able to join me. Guy Ray was from Alabama and a Southerner. He liked flattery, I was sure that he was an opportunist, as are most career diplomats.

"If you could swing this for Rockefeller—"

"I'm not against him. An office here and with the funds he has—it could be helpful—I have to admit that."

"Then talk to the Ambassador. He listens to you, and, I understand, has great respect for your judgment."

"Let me mull it over. The Ambassador has been known to change his mind, but not too often."

"Perhaps you can do it. You're the only one who can. Rockefeller told me just before I left that he had a talk with Sumner Welles."

"He talked with Welles?" Welles was then Under Secretary of State, and next to Cordell Hull, the most influential man in the State Department. "What did Mr. Welles have to say?"

"He told Rockefeller that the only person who could persuade Messersmith was you."

"Hmm," he paused and drained his drink. "I'll see what I can do. But don't put your hopes too high." He lit a cigarette. "I tell you what—you go on with your trip. Stop by when you get back. I'll see what I can do."

I went on to each of the Central American countries, including Panama. On the way back, I visited my brother in Guatemala again and spent a week with him, playing for time. I sent on my reports to Washington and then I took a plane to Mexico. In the morning I went to the Embassy. Guy Ray saw me right away.

"You're a week overdue," he said.

"I had a lot of work to do," I replied.

"How was the trip?"

"Fine."

"I talked with the Ambassador," he said. "He'll let you stay —for a few months, anyway. Then we'll see how it works out. We'll have to work together and under the guidance of the Embassy."

"I understand. I won't do anything without your advice."

"Come to my house for dinner tonight. At seven. We can talk further about it." He reached into his desk. "I see you smoke a pipe. Good tobacco is hard to get here. Try some of this," and he handed me a can of tobacco.

I walked out of the Embassy and started back to the hotel. I telephoned Dag in California, and although aware that the censor was listening in, I said, "We've skinned a cat. Get to Mexico as soon as you can."

CHAPTER FIFTEEN

"Come In Mexico, Come In . . ."

In Mexico at the time of Pearl Harbor, many of the news broadcasts were sponsored and controlled by German interests. The newspapers were similarly influenced and in the motion picture theatres, Hitler and his panzer divisions, when shown on the newsreels, were applauded, while our armed forces and Roosevelt were hissed. In public demonstrations, there was an open antagonism to the United States.

The American Embassy was aware of this situation, but did not want to face up to it. Guy Ray, as he later told me, became convinced that some counter measures had to be taken, and this was probably the reason why the Embassy had relented and allowed me to stay in Mexico. The Rockefeller office, and not the Department of State, had the funds to carry out a concentrated propaganda program.

One of the first and most important of our efforts was to call a meeting of the leading radio station owners and newspaper publishers. Radio stations needed power tubes to continue to operate and stay on the air; newspapers required newsprint. The stations were assured that they would receive power tubes from the United States and newspapers, paper on which to print. In exchange, Guy Ray told them we wanted radio time for news broadcasts, and from the newspapers, we asked for a fair treatment of the news.

The radio station owners and the newspaper publishers were wise enough to realize that with the submarine warfare underway, ships from Europe would have difficulty in keeping them supplied. They readily accepted our offer, not because they were anxious to help the United States, but because they were convinced we could and would keep our word. They also began to think that we might even win the war.

Guy Ray was not difficult to work with. I flattered him, always asked his advice and approval and in time he trusted me to the point of being cooperative and friendly. I was aware, of course, that I was in Mexico by tolerance of the Embassy—any false step and I could be ordered out.

On that first trip to Mexico before Pearl Harbor I had been impressed with Alfredo Gonzales, who had gone with us to Cuernavaca and Taxco. Within a few weeks he was working in our newly opened office and in time, he became one of my assistants. I relied on his judgment and understanding of the Mexican people, which always proved to be excellent.

We bought radio time and soon we had news programs with Mexican news commentators on the air, who were fairly interpreting the news. There was no radio network in Mexico and, in order to get our news programs on stations throughout the country, we organized and financed the first radio network in Mexico. *Radio Programas de Mexico,* a network which still exists today, was made possible through the Coordinator's Office.

A press department under Paxton Haddow began providing material to the newspapers. Then a motion picture department was organized with an extensive film library and motion picture equipment that was loaned out to schools, churches, and organizations. We obtained permission from the Mexican government to open a lending library in an old brick building on Avenida Reforma. Rockefeller sent the former head librarian of the New York Library to get it underway. All books were provided by the Coordinator's Office.

There were many libraries in Mexico, but they were poorly lighted and books could not be taken out. The Benjamin Franklin Library, as it was to be called, was to be the first lending library. We anticipated that, in the beginning, many books would disappear but after it opened, the librarian reported that losses were less than in most libraries in the United States. What was stolen were not books, but the toilet seats in the men's room. Why they should be taken was not much of a mystery. Books were hard to dispose of and had little value; toilet seats, however, had a quick turnover.

In November, for Thanksgiving Day, we invited several friends for dinner. We had much for which to be thankful. The outcome of the war was still uncertain, but we were getting stronger. In Mexico, the Coordinator's program had made some progress, and while the Ambassador remained unfriendly, he had allowed us to stay. Dag had purchased a turkey to be served with a chestnut stuffing and I was going to make the gravy and do the carving.

Then two days before Thanksgiving, a telegram from Washington instructed me to attend a conference in Peru scheduled to start the day after Thanksgiving. This meant that I would have to leave on Thanksgiving Day for Panama, and take a connecting plane for Lima on the following day. Dag was left with the task of putting on the dinner herself.

It was a full day's flight to Panama. I arrived late in the afternoon, checked in at the Tivoli Hotel, and went up to shower and change. At five-thirty I went into the bar for a drink before dinner. I was self-conscious wearing civilian clothes and would have preferred to be in uniform, but at least I thought I was proving useful.

Sitting in the bar of the Tivoli Hotel, I rationalized about how much better off I was than our soldiers fighting in foxholes. It did not seem fair, but neither did the attitude of the State Department and our Ambassador in Mexico. It was also unpleasant to know that, at a time when we were losing the war, Mexican politicians, industrialists, and American businessmen were taking advantage of the war in order to make a profit. When Mexico should be giving us all the assistance it could, it was constructing, of all things, a luxury race track and clubhouse using materials we needed.

I finished my drink and started for the dining room. The lobby was crowded with high ranking military and naval officers in their dress uniforms and their wives in dinner gowns. At the entrance of the dining room a line was forming. I went around the line, located the headwaiter and asked for a table.

"You have a reservation?" he asked.

"Of course I haven't," I said. "I just arrived and am leaving at five in the morning."

"Sorry can't help you," he said. "All these officers in the lobby and in line have had reservations for weeks."

"You mean I can't have dinner in the hotel?"

"That's it."

"What about room service? Couldn't I have a sandwich sent up to my room?"

"We have no room service," he said, and then sarcastically, "don't you know there's a war going on?"

I walked away staring at the line of officers in their dress uniforms with gold braid and at their wives. They had a right to be there and perhaps these men had already risked their lives or would be risking them a week or a month from now. Yet it all seemed in bad taste and inappropriate. I couldn't help thinking of the soldiers on the war fronts—of the millions of refugees in Europe and of the volunteers who were fighting underground.

I left the hotel and went out on the street. The tropical night was hot and humid. I walked for a long time and finally returned to the hotel, trying not to glance in the direction of the dining room where a dance orchestra was playing "Don't Sit under the Apple Tree." I stopped at the newsstand, bought a can of peanuts and a chocolate bar and went up to my room. I opened the can, sat on the side of the bed, and ate most of the peanuts. Then I undressed slowly and took one bite of the candy bar. That did it. I made the bathroom just in time to vomit up everything eaten that day. I crawled into bed. The room was stifling hot, though the windows were wide open. From the dining room below I could hear the dance music. After awhile, I must have fallen asleep, the telephone rang. It was four-thirty and time to get up.

Nelson Rockefeller wanted to come to Mexico to confer with government officials and discuss the further expansion of the Coordinator's program. But without the Ambassador's approval, such a visit was not possible. There was one way that the Ambassador could not stop Rockefeller and that was for the Mexican government to invite him officially as its guest, and that's exactly the way it was done.

Before Ambassador Messersmith could do anything about it, an invitation from the Foreign Minister, Ezekiel Padilla, went to Rockefeller. Within a week Rockefeller arrived as an "official guest" of the Mexican government. Messersmith was too well trained as a diplomat to lose face and he went to the airport, welcomed Rockefeller and arranged for him to stay at the Embassy residence.

By now I had been in Mexico almost a year, but this had been the first time I had seen the Ambassador. Rockefeller's intelligent and realistic approach to the problems in Mexico as they concerned the United States and the war effort, I was certain, would win over the Ambassador. The two appeared to get along and by the time the visit came to a close, Rockefeller assured me that from now on, I would have no further obstructions from the Embassy. "I am very pleased," he said at the airport. "Everything's going well."

However I did not see Messersmith again and whatever business we had with the Embassy went through Guy Ray, who continued to act as the intermediary.

Mexico's role in the war effort grew in importance and freight trains loaded with strategic materials were now going out regularly supplying the United States with exports that we required and that had once come from the Far East. Mexico had become our ally and our efforts went toward keeping these supply lines open and making the Mexican people aware that we were fighting the war together.

After Rockefeller's visit, additional funds were provided to intensify our propaganda program and eventually we had about two hundred persons, all Mexicans, working in our operation. I never gave orders. I left this to Alfredo Gonzales, for I soon found that Mexicans resent an American telling them what to do. It was also through Gonzales that Father John, a Catholic priest, came to work for us. Father John volunteered his services and we put him in charge of contacting priests, Catholic institutions, and visiting factories.

Propaganda was a word that the Department of State refused to use; yet we were in the propaganda business. Our work was not only to counteract the activity of German agents who knew how to play up the nationalistic feelings of the Mexicans, but we had still another and far more influential group to combat. This was the Sinarquista movement, closely tied to Franco, to Spain and which worked adroitly with the Spanish wing of the Catholic Church. The Sinarquistas, were fascists and did all they could to create animosity toward the United States.

While propaganda was our main concern, Rockefeller also recognized the importance of appealing to the cultural side of the Latin Americans. This was one of the reasons that Leopold Stokowski agreed to conduct the Mexican Symphony Orchestra for a series of concerts, including a program that was to be carried by the three radio networks in the United States. This was to be an hour-long program with fifteen minutes devoted to Mexico. Orson Welles was in charge and was to act as narrator.

We were instructed to give Stokowski all the assistance possible. I met the Maestro at the airport and took him to his hotel where he telephoned the Ambassador and made an appointment to see him.

"I want you to come as there are many phases of my visit here that I'd like to discuss with him," Stokowski said to me.

"Perhaps it would be best if you went alone," I said. "I will meet you afterwards."

"No, I think you should sit in," Stokowski said.

It was then that I should have pointed out that I was not welcome at the Embassy, but I assumed he must have been briefed in Washington.

"I'll do as you say," I said, and waited while Stokowski changed into another suit of clothes. Then we drove to the Embassy.

Stokowski was a man of great energy and, despite the long flight, he did not seem tired. He kept on asking questions about Mexico and the people and he told me of how many years ago he had visited the Mayan ruins in Yucatan. When we arrived at the Embassy I parked the car and went in. We entered the reception room and the Ambassador's secretary told Stokowski that Messersmith would see him in a few minutes.

After a brief wait, the door opened and the secretary asked us to go in. The Maestro was tall and lanky and his bushy hair made him seem even taller. The Ambassador, in contrast to Stokowski, was small in stature and was sitting behind a huge desk, the American flag at his side. He rose as we came in and smiled warmly at Stokowski, but for me there was only an icy stare. The Maestro sat down; I found a chair as far back as I could from the Ambassador.

During the conference with Messersmith which lasted for half an hour I remained silent and tried not to look obtrusive. When Stokowski rose from his chair I also got up. The Ambassador left his desk and started to walk across the room. He had a friendly smile as he shook hands with Stokowski at the door.

"Good afternoon, Mr. Ambassador," I said and made the mistake of extending my hand to shake his.

Messersmith froze, and for those few seconds, a chill from the north came into the room. He turned away and left me standing with my hand outstretched.

Stokowski, sensitive, instantly aware of the situation, took me by the arm and led me through the reception room, down the hall, and to the courtyard where the car was parked. I was angry and humiliated. I was in a rage, murderous thoughts going through me.

But it was the great Stokowski, known for his temperamental outbursts, who calmly, and with firmness, brought me back to reality.

"You hate him. You could kill him," he said.

"That would be too good for him."

"He was rude—immeasurably so."

"He's an insulting little man. The things I could tell you about him."

"I have felt the way you feel many times." He climbed into the car. "Let's take a drive and we can talk."

I was still so angry, I almost stripped the gears. We started toward town.

"I've never been treated like this before," I went on.

"What just happened—it is often that way in the world of music—jealousies and intrigue and the snubbing that goes on. I've been through it. Every musician has."

"I was merely trying to be polite."

"He was letting you know he was the United States Ambassador," Stokowski said.

That night he took us to a little French restaurant. He went into the kitchen, introduced himself to the chef and discussed what dishes he wanted prepared and what wine served. The chef, flattered and impressed, outdid himself. It was one of the best dinners I ever had in Mexico.

The Maestro knew the importance of the radio program he was going to conduct from Mexico. He would be directing an orchestra made up of musicians he had never worked with and who might resent him as a foreigner. Millions would hear the program.

"It has to be good. It has to be sharp, brilliant, and forceful," he said a number of times, as if trying to reassure himself. "I must get everything I can from the musicians. It's expected of me."

As soon as he could, Stokowski began a series of rehearsals with the members of the Mexican Symphony Orchestra. Many were accomplished musicians, but they were poorly paid and because they were seldom allowed enough time for rehearsals, they did not have the discipline Stokowski demanded. But he was patient and thorough. While there were quarrels and bitterness during some of these rehearsals, the majority respected him. Within a short time, he had the orchestra playing as he wanted them to play.

He came from these final rehearsals exhausted, but confident that the program would be successful and worth all the efforts he had put into it. I also made certain that we did not let him down. On the day of the broadcast, five persons from my office, including Alfredo Gonzales, went early to the studios of Station XEW. We checked over all of the facilities, saw that the microphones were correctly placed and that the engineer in the main control room knew what he was to do and to do it at the right time. The program would be picked up by New York from a direct telephone line.

I was to be in the studio control room where a short wave radio set had been installed and tuned to New York. At exactly eight forty-five, I would get my cue from the radio and then cue Stokowski. The program was to originate in New York, switch to Washington, then Dallas, San Francisco, and finally Mexico and back again to New York.

At seven-thirty I talked to Orson Welles in New York. The line was sharp and clear, he reported. We went over last minute details and synchronized our watches. The studio soon began filling up with important guests who had been invited to hear the performance. The musicians took their places on the stage.

The facilities at XEW were limited. Stokowski, therefore, would have to depend on my signals and we went over them again. Five minutes before we were to go on the air, I was to hold up my hand with the fingers spread apart. One minute before broadcast time, I was to hold up a single finger and then I was to raise my hand and bring it down quickly at the exact broadcast time.

At eight-twenty, from behind the heavy glass of the control room, I saw Ambassador and Mrs. Messersmith arrive. With them were Guy Ray and his wife; they took seats in the second row which had been reserved for them. Far in the back, in the last row, I caught a glimpse of Dag.

The short wave radio in the control room had been on since seven o'clock and the program we were to be on had started at eight o'clock and was coming in clear. It was being broadcast by all three networks and it was also being beamed to Latin America and our fighting forces overseas.

At eight thirty-five, Stokowski came from backstage and bowed to the audience, which responded with applause. He looked up at the control room and at me, waiting for the five minute signal.

At eight forty I gave him the five minute cue. The orchestra, which had been warming up, stopped as Stokowski motioned for silence. At the one minute cue Stokowski raised his baton. On the radio I heard a San Francisco announcer saying, "and now we take you back to New York and Orson Welles."

Welles spoke for about thirty seconds. Then at exactly eight forty-five: ". . . and now Mexico, come in. Come in Mexico."

I cued Stokowski in and the orchestra began playing. But on the short wave radio, I heard Orson Welles repeating, "Mexico, please come in. Mexico, come in, come in."

I signaled to Stokowski to stop. We were not prepared for this eventuality, but he understood my signal that he was not on the air. He stopped the orchestra abruptly and, as I cued him in again, once more the orchestra began playing.

The music filled the control room, but above the music on the radio, I heard Welles saying: "Due to technical difficulties, we are unable to get Mexico. One moment, please. You will now hear again the NBC Symphony Orchestra in New York."

I couldn't believe what I heard. I yelled at Gonzales who had been standing by me to rush out and check the main control room. I picked up the phone and tried to get through to New York, but couldn't. Out in the studio, Stokowski went on conducting and the musicians of the orchestra faithfully followed his directions, all unaware that their music was not being heard by millions, but only by the small studio audience.

I sat there in the control room for fifteen minutes, listening to an orchestra playing to dead air, and shouting into a telephone, still trying but unable to get to New York. During all those minutes, I kept on thinking about Stokowski and the many hours of rehearsals and how hard he had worked with the musicians. What was I going to say to him? How was he going to take it?

Then Gonzales returned to the control room.

"Everything's in order," he said. "I've talked with all the engineers. No one knows what's happened."

"All right," I said. "But, I am sure going to find out."

Stokowski had carefully clocked the time he was to be on the air. At exactly eight fifty-seven, he brought his baton down. He had conducted brilliantly and the orchestra had responded to his direction. As the piece finished he looked up at the control room waiting for me to give him the signal that all went well. Instead, I walked out of the control room.

I did not have to say anything to him. He must have guessed it from the look on my face. He was holding his fists very tightly and the veins on his forehead stood out. He was making every effort to hold his temper.

"Maestro," I said, "something went wrong. You were playing to dead air."

"No one heard the program?"

"No one except those in the studio."

"Please don't say anything more about it," he said, and quickly left the studio alone.

In the morning we had a conference in the office of Emilio Ascarraga, owner and general manager of XEW. His chief executives, producers, and engineers were present. I was certain, and so was Stokowski, that the lines had been tampered with, that sabotage was at the bottom of it.

But nowhere was there any evidence of it. Ascarraga explained it very simply and then apologized in the name of the station and of Mexico.

"We have gone over it step by step," he said, "until we found out what did happen. The engineer who has been with me for fifteen years, somehow, in the excitement of putting on this program, plugged the main trunk line into the wrong outlet. He cannot explain it. *Así pasa.* So it goes."

There was no anger, no recriminations. The engineer was looking at us and we at him. But, I did not feel sorry for him.

The evening before I had felt sorry for Stokowski. But not any more. Stokowski would get over it.

What I would never forget was the calmness of Ascarraga. *Así pasa.* So it goes. He really didn't care. With the aid from the United States, he and so many prominent Mexicans grew wealthy and influential. I could not forget either that on his station he had once broadcast programs sponsored by the German Nazi movement.

CHAPTER SIXTEEN

An Exchange of Cards

During our first year in Mexico our home was a small furnished apartment on Avenida Luis Moya, near the flower market. Half the time the plumbing failed to work and there were sewer smells and the odor of fried, rancid grease seemed to permeate the building. We had just the clothes we'd been able to get in three suitcases and a steamer trunk; our books, our silver, our dishes, and our cooking utensils, along with other things we would have liked, remained in storage in California. We lived from day to day, never certain whether or not the Ambassador would continue to let us stay in Mexico.

My office was in a newly constructed building, adjacent to Avenida Reforma. There was a penthouse apartment seven floors up, which was unoccupied. One afternoon the concierge showed it to me. The apartment had a huge outdoor terrace, a living room, two bedrooms, and a narrow, circular stairway leading to a tiny kitchen. From the terrace there was a sweeping view of Mexico City and of the two volcanoes, Popocateptl and Ixtaccíhautl. The moment I saw the apartment I knew it was for us. It had remained vacant because the owner thought it had been badly designed and was inadequate for his family.

After Dag looked at it, we talked with the owner, who was

willing to rent it without a lease. We took the apartment and began furnishing it. Some pieces of furniture we had made, while the rest we bought at the various open-air markets. On Sunday mornings we'd go to Lagunilla, or the so-called "thieves market," where we'd pick up old, but attractive, second-hand articles.

Renting this apartment and furnishing it was something of a gamble; at any time the Ambassador might have had a change of heart and sent us packing. Nevertheless, we thought it was worth taking a chance. We hired a maid named Socorro, and Concha a cook, and gradually we had a feeling of permanency and of having a home again.

Adjoining the kitchen were the servants quarters and there, high above the city, a large, flat roof. Concha, the cook, thought this roof top was being wasted and she convinced Dag that we should have chickens and a turkey on it. It seemed incongruous that in the heart of Mexico City we were permitted to have chickens, a turkey, and a rooster that awakened us each morning.

Everything went well until, on a late afternoon during the worst traffic rush, the rooster flew away from the roof and into the street below. Concha rushed down the circular staircase, down the seven stories without waiting for the elevator and began chasing the rooster.

Dag phoned me. "The rooster's flown off!" she said excitedly.

"The rooster? What rooster?" I asked.

"Concha's rooster. It's taken off from the roof. It's somewhere below."

I went to the window of my office and looked out. Sure enough, there on the street was the rooster walking along with great dignity, and Concha after it. The rooster would stop, allowing Concha to come near, and then just as she was ready to get a hold of it, it would start out again. Now, the rooster approached Avenida Reforma, Mexico City's main thoroughfare. It stood for a moment on the edge of the sidewalk, poised like a fighting cock. Then it proceeded to cross the Avenue, over which thousands of cars were passing. If it had been a pedestrian, not a single Mexican driver would have stopped. But, suddenly, the traffic halted as the rooster, taking its time, hobbled across Avenida Reforma with Concha after it. The chase soon came to an end and Concha, a triumphant expression on her face, started back with the rooster grasped tightly in her arms.

"You could have been hurt, Concha," I said to her that evening. "Why didn't you let it go?"

"Oh, I couldn't, Señor." she said. "Not that fine rooster! Anything might have happened to it, and if it had, I would never have forgiven myself."

A week later, on Sunday morning, we heard the rooster crowing loudly up in the kitchen, and then there was a dead silence. Dag went upstairs and was soon back.

"She's killed it!" she announced. "Chopped its head off. We're going to have *gallo en mole* for lunch. That poor rooster," she sighed.

Slowly we began to adjust to living in Mexico. Each morning Dag accompanied Concha to the market to buy meat, vegetables, and fruit. Every day at noon a woman arrived with freshly made tortillas. Concha was an excellent cook and made a variety of native dishes which took hours (and sometimes, days) to prepare. We ate the main meal of the day around one-thirty in the afternoon, and a light supper after eight in the evening.

In the same building where we lived, Sam Rosoff, a well-known New York contractor who had moved to Mexico, had his offices. He had them elaborately furnished with a divan of down, and thick, heavy carpets. Neither he nor we knew until much later, that his office after midnight was the "love nest" of our maid, Socorro, and the concierge. We learned about it when Dag noticed that Socorro was no longer as thin as when she had first come to work for us. She was filling out, and her face was plump.

At first we thought it was because of all the good food she had been eating. Then Socorro admitted she was pregnant.

"But, do not worry, Señora," Socorro reassured Dag. "I will visit my cousin in Toluca and everything will be all right. There is a doctor there who has special medicine."

Within five days, Socorro, a little pale and weak, was back, no longer pregnant. During the four years Socorro worked for us, she made at least two visits a year to her cousin in Toluca, even though Sam Rosoff had a new lock installed and his offices were no longer available to Socorro and her boy friend.

Now that we had our penthouse apartment furnished, we began to entertain and to meet new friends, most of them Mexican. Some were archeologists, doctors and others, painters, writers, composers and musicians. Among them was Jesus Guerrero Galvan, at the time one of the best of the younger painters. Through him we met Diego Rivera, José Clemente Orozco, David Siqueiros, Rufino Tamayo, Carlos Merida, and Augustin Lara, who, small and delicate in appearance, had a deep scar on his face. Lara was famous for having composed "Granada" and other songs about Spain. He had almost no voice; but that which he had was very husky and when he went to the piano and sang some of his compositions, he did it with so much feeling, that it was easy to forget his ugliness. Mexican women were enraptured by him, but he was cold and indifferent to them. His one big love was Maria Felix, the actress. When she left him and went to Spain, he composed "Madrid," a song of forsaken love that was soon being played on every juke box in Mexico. He was the idol of all the servants and cooks and even Concha, old and toothless, would say of Lara when he came to our home: "I die every time I see him. *Qué hombre!*"

And Socorro, would blush and her hands would tremble when she served him. "Ay, Señora," she would say to Dag, almost gasping for breath, "what pleasures he must give to women."

As we widened and increased the activities of the Coordinator's program, I began calling on newspapers and radio stations in the principal cities and towns of Mexico. Usually, Alfredo Gonzales went along on these trips, and always we were well received. By now, over a hundred stations were carrying our news broadcasts every night, and they were being heard by millions of Mexicans. Newspapers, too, even those in the interior, were using and publishing the material we were sending them, and editorially they were supporting the United States and its allies. But it was the radio that had its biggest impact and which effectively was getting our story over to the Mexican people.

In time our combat forces on the war fronts and Roosevelt were no longer hissed at in the theatres—instead, they now brought loud applause. Mexican politicians who could usually count on being cheered when they attacked or criticized the United States, turned to other issues. Public demonstrations, including those of university students, either ceased or were of small consequence. The fact that we were winning the war certainly had much to do in bringing about a more sympathetic and friendly attitude. But there was no question that the programs Nelson Rockefeller had initiated were also hitting hard and reaching the Mexican people. Even the Embassy reluctantly had to admit it, and the most startling of all was the changing opinion of the Ambassador.

Guy Ray and I saw each other once or twice a week, and were on the telephone almost every day. So it was not unusual when, one morning, after we had been in Mexico two years, he called me. Yet there was something about his voice that was different and alerted me; he sounded especially friendly.

"Your wife doing anything this afternoon?" his Alabama voice drawled.

"Not anything that we couldn't change," I said.

"Uncle George (he always referred to Ambassador Messersmith as Uncle George) thinks it's about time you should be leaving cards at the Embassy Residence. Think you could do it today?"

Leaving cards at the Embassy Residence meant that the Ambassador was about to accept us socially as well as officially. But I was still skeptical.

"What's brought all this about?" I asked.

"Oh, Uncle George is not as bad as you and Rockefeller think," he went on. "I told you once he's been known to change his mind, but not often. Now he's changed his mind. Wants to be more friendly. We're all going to be one happy family. Here's what should be done . . ."

That afternoon at five o'clock, Dag drove to the Embassy Residence, which up to then had been out of bounds. In accordance with protocol we were to leave three cards, one from her and two of my cards. On the bottom of two, we were to write our address in pencil. The right-hand corner of each card was folded over since they were being personally delivered.

On the following afternoon, Dag told me when I came in from work that evening, our call had been returned. The Embassy chauffeur had stopped by and had dropped off cards from the Ambassador and Mrs. Messersmith. Because it had not been a personal call, the cards had not been turned down on the right-hand corners. But no matter we had been officially recognized!

The exchange of cards was to make a great difference. It meant that our stay in Mexico was no longer on a day-to-day basis. We were now eligible to be invited to Embassy luncheons and receptions and more important, we were permitted free entry into Mexico of the few things we had in storage in California and we could bring in an automobile on a government priority. In the past we had depended on taxis and on the use of the cars of friends.

A few weeks later we flew to Larado to pick up the car that Washington had delivered for us. We didn't realize how much we had missed the United States and how much it meant to be back in our own country, if only for a few hours. We gorged on hamburgers and milk shakes; then at the J. C. Penny store, we bought many things that we needed and which, in Mexico, were either difficult to find or too expensive.

At intervals, the Ambassador asked me to attend meetings of members of his staff and of American businessmen residing in Mexico. Also, I was present whenever he called a press conference. The Ambassador was always austere and cold, but, as I got to know him, I learned to respect him.

Mexicans never fully understood him, for he lacked the warmth to make friends easily. Yet in his strange way he loved Mexico. Many years later, long after he retired from the diplomatic service, he returned to reside in Mexico. There he died and was buried.

"Uncle George," was probably a good Ambassador. He was unbending, firm in his decisions and the Foreign Office knew he could not be pushed. Mexicans like strong men; perhaps it reminds them of their Spanish conquerors. But I will always remember Messersmith as the man who left me with my hand extended in midair.

Of the Mexican painters we met, we found Diego Rivera boastful, at times unpleasant, and ready to create a situation to serve his interests. As an artist there was a greatness in Rivera, but as a person he was a windbag, opinionated, at times vulgar, and he could be extremely rude. He was huge and fat; yet his hands were small and delicate, almost effeminate in appearance. He acted and felt important, and he lived as lavishly as the rich Mexican capitalists that he portrayed so devastatingly in his murals and paintings.

José Clemente Orozco was the opposite of Rivera. He lived quietly in a small, unpretentious home and he seldom took part in a controversy. He wore heavy rimmed glasses with thick lenses that magnified the size of his eyes. Despite his success in the United States and that much of his income came from sales in American art galleries, he had only contempt for us as a country. Like Rivera, he was an avowed Communist. David Siqueiros maintained that Orozco's hatred for the United States was due to the years he spent working in a Brooklyn factory, painting kewpie doll faces.

Siqueiros was no friend of the United States, but of the three major Mexican painters, he was the most colorful. Rivera and Orozco were passive Communists; Siqueiros was an active participant. He had master minded the first attempt to assassinate Trotsky, when the former revolutionary leader lived in Mexico. Siqueiros would have been successful, if Trotsky on the night of the attempted assassination, had not moved into another bedroom. Siqueiros enjoyed describing in detail his part in the plot, and later, his experiences in jail. But, one evening at a party which we attended, Siqueiros was quickly subdued by his wife, Angelica. Angelica was no angel; when she discovered that her husband was paying too much attention to the young wife of a Mexican poet, she struck him on the head with a highball glass.

Many Mexican painters, particularly the younger ones who were striving to gain a reputation for themselves, were friendly and understanding of the United States. These included Rufino Tamayo, Guerrero Galvan, Carlos Merida and others. They came often to our apartment or we would visit them at their studios. They were pleased at our interest in their work, although the Embassy generally ignored them.

Not all the artists we met were Mexicans. Some, such as Pablo O'Higgins and Michael Baxte, were Americans who had come to Mexico many years before and had made it their homes. Michael Baxte liked and painted in and around Uruapan, where the earth is rugged and volcanic.

"The country is primitive and unpredictable—almost explosive in texture and in character," he said at dinner one evening. "It is one of the most beautiful and untouched parts of Mexico."

We bought one of Michael Baxte's paintings that conveyed this feeling of the land. It was this painting that interested us in going to Uruapan and resulted in our being there about the time that a strange drama was unfolding in the nearby town of San Juan de las Colchas, or St. John of the Bedspreads.

A Mexican farmer, Dionisio Pulido, owned a small acreage just outside the town where he planted corn. On this particular morning when he was working his field, he saw a small mound, much like that created by gophers. He pushed down the mound with his foot and continued with his plowing. But when he passed by a few minutes later, the mound had increased in size. Again, he tried to stamp it down, but couldn't. As he stood there startled and unable to move, the mound began to grow in size; then smoke and flames shot out of the earth. Convinced that the very devil was emerging from hell, Dionisio Pulido ran into San Juan de las Colchas, summoned the priest and the villagers. They followed him to his corn field in time to see the birth of Paricutín, a volcano that within a short time was to reach the height of 6500 feet. The priest made the Sign of the Cross, and the villagers kneeled and prayed.

We saw it that first night, the fiery mouth of this baby volcano, sending up massive flames into the sky. We stood there, fascinated by what we saw, awed by the mysterious doings of nature. Man, we thought, could never rival anything like this. We did not know, of course, that at that very time when Paricutín was having labor pains, scientists in the

United States were giving birth to another explosive force, much more destructive and threatening than anything nature had ever produced, the atomic bomb.

The village farmer, Dionisio Pulido, was right; the devil had emerged from hell on that quiet spring day.

We were winning the war in Europe and in the Pacific. Our great military might was gaining the respect of the world and the admiration of the Mexican people. It felt good again to be an American. Our relations with Mexico had never been better.

The anti-American sentiment which had existed before had gradually disappeared, or at least so we thought. But it was still there, lying for the time dormant, ready to break out at the slightest provocation. At first, I believed it was a prank when Alfredo Gonzales brought in a peso note with the wording written on the back: *If you are a Catholic, do not buy Palmolive soap.*

Within a few weeks, however, thousands of peso bills began appearing with those words; then walls were painted with this warning: *With gringo money, anti-Catholics are attacking our faith.* Sale of Palmolive soap, manufactured by an American company in Mexico, came to an abrupt stop. The propaganda campaign was having its effect and could spread and become serious.

We knew that something had to be done about it. But first we had to discover what was behind it and why it was carried out.

We soon found the reason. An officer and a large stockholder in the Palmolive soap company had died in the East, leaving the bulk of his estate to a Protestant organization doing missionary work abroad. A group of Mexicans, a handful of zealous Catholics, and a few priests, tied in with the fascist Sinarquista movement joined in this anti-U.S. campaign.

I asked Father John, who was working in our office, for advice. He said that only one person, the Archbishop of Mexico, could curtail this campaign. The following day, Father John came with word that Archbishop Martinez would see me that evening at nine o'clock. As Father John preferred not to accompany me, I asked Alfredo Gonzales to come along.

While Mexico is a Catholic country, Catholicism is practiced somewhat differently there than in the United States. Virtually every president of Mexico has been a Mason, and Benito Juárez, its greatest patriot, was responsible for putting in stringent laws regulating the Church. Nevertheless, the influence of the Catholic Church in Mexico is tremendous.

On our way to talk with Archbishop Martinez, Gonzales told me of his own views about the Church. Then he said: "When I go in with you, I will not kneel and kiss the Archbishop's ring. I am a Catholic, but in name only."

At a few minutes before nine o'clock we arrived at the Archbishop's Palace. We were ushered into a small waiting room, and shortly afterwards we walked into a sedate, but spacious, audience room where the Archbishop received visitors. He was standing in the center as we entered, a small wiry man, with the typical Mestizo features that revealed his Indian ancestry.

As we approached close to him, Gonzales did what he told me he wasn't going to do. The many years of his Catholic upbringing were inherent in his character, and now it was simply reflex action. He dropped to one knee before the Archbishop and kissed his ring. Then as Gonzales got up, there was an astonished look on his face. He could not believe what he had done.

Archbishop Martinez asked us to sit down on the high, straight-back chairs that formed a semi-circle. He sat next to me and he expressed interest in the work we were doing in Mexico. I explained that I had come to see him, not in an official capacity, as I did not have Embassy approval, but had made the call at Father John's suggestion.

He asked me a number of questions and said that he hoped that at some future time he might meet Rockefeller. Then we talked about the strong labor movement in Mexico and the Communist labor demonstrations which frequently took place with thousands participating.

"They do not worry me," he said. "If we wished, the Church could put on quite a few demonstrations." Then he smiled. "We are not as weak or as badly organized as some people would like to believe."

Then he got up, as an indication that the audience was at an end. He walked toward the door with us. I was disappointed. We had failed to discuss the reason for this visit. But as we shook hands, there was an understanding look on his face.

"Do not be further concerned about the matter you wanted to talk to me," he said. "I have already taken care of it. I regret it happened. It was most unfortunate."

We left the Archbishop's Palace and, as we drove back, Gonzales was silent. When I dropped him off at his apartment, he barely said goodnight.

The Archbishop had impressed me. It had been an eventful evening, and I found it difficult to erase it from my mind. There had been an air of mystery to the sedate room—the high, straight-back chairs—the little man with Indian blood who had so much influence—and, when I finally went to sleep, I dreamt of Montezuma and his palace and his priests and the sacrificial altars where, with a knife of jade, they cut out hearts and offered them to their ancient gods—always, in one way or another, religion has been important to the Mexican people.

In the morning, when I went into breakfast and opened the paper, there was a manifesto from the Archbishop printed on the front page. It was short but strong. American money was not being used against the Church. The soap company was absolved of blame. Catholics were ordered to stop writing on Mexican peso notes. The manifesto was broadcast every hour on radio stations, and it appeared in most newspapers.

We are not weak, the Archbishop had said. I have never since questioned the strength or the influence of the Catholic Church in Mexico, or the great faith of the Mexican people.

Our cook, Concha, had this great faith, and so did our maid, Socorro. We had planned an outdoor party on the terrace and we had many important Mexicans invited. The party had to be on the terrace, for the living room in our apartment was far too small to accommodate many guests.

But on the afternoon of the party it began to rain and we wondered what we were going to do with all the people we had asked.

"Do not be preoccupied," said Socorro, and she ran upstairs to the kitchen. She was down in a minute holding a big butcher knife in her hand. "You will see," she said. "I will stop the rain."

We watched her go out on the terrace. In the distance barely visible were Popocateptl and Ixtaccíhuatl. Socorro stood there looking up at the sky and then, with the knife in her hand, she made the Sign of the Cross.

"I have cut the rain," she announced as she returned from the terrace. "You will see, Señor; it will no longer rain."

After awhile it did stop raining, and in the late afternoon the clouds disappeared and even the sun came out. Socorro mopped the terrace dry.

"It will be a beautiful evening for the party," she said, completely convinced that she had stopped the rain.

CHAPTER SEVENTEEN

How to Meet a Mistress

He didn't belong there and he looked out of place in his well tailored suit, his custom-made initialed shirt, and his blue silk tie. We were sitting in *Mi Corazón*, a Mexican *cantina* in a Mexican village. He had a tequila in his hand, not sure whether or not he had had enough. He wanted to see Mexico, and I had taken him to Tenancingo and Taxco, and to Puebla, and now we were in Guadalupita, above Toluca.

Eugene Reynal was a New York book publisher and he had seen, in the short time he had been in Mexico, many parts of the country and he had listened to me talk on endlessly about Mexico and the people. He had apparently enjoyed himself and he had even learned to drink his tequila straight, with salt and lemon.

Now as he reached for his gold cigarette case, he glanced around the bar and then at me. He was sensitive and intelligent and this, his first visit to Mexico, had made a definite impression.

"You think a lot of Mexico, don't you?" he asked.

"I suppose so," I replied. "After you've been here for awhile, Mexico gets into your blood."

"Why don't you write a book about it? With all the material you have and the way you feel about the country, you might do something interesting." He gulped down the tequila, bit into the lemon and made a face. "I'll tell you what," he went on. "You write it and I'll publish it."

"You're serious about it?"

"Enough to sign a contract," he said. "Now let's get out of here and go back to Mexico City. I want to take a shower and eat in a good restaurant—no more Mexican food."

Later that day, we went to the *Ambassadeurs*, where the place plates are of heavy silver, the cuisine is French and the waiters wear white gloves. For the first time, Reynal seemed relaxed and comfortable.

"This is more like it," he said. "All those strange places you took me to are all right for color. But the food was horrible and they were so dirty. Here I feel at home, as if I were in New York."

Most visitors to Mexico feel that way. They say they want to get off the regular tourist run and go into the back country, and see the "real Mexico." But they don't. And so, they stay in hotels which have been constructed especially for them and resemble the hotels back home. They eat in restaurants that feature American or French dishes and are frequented almost exclusively by tourists. Even the bars seem like the bars in Chicago, New York, or San Francisco. Everyone talks English, including the waiters, and the prices are American, too.

"They come to Mexico, because it seems different for them and it is a change," Alfredo Gonzales, who used to be a tourist guide, insisted. "They prefer not to mingle with the people or see too much. It would frighten them. And one must not frighten tourists. They like everything to be as they think it should be, and not as it really is. To them, Mexico is something of a fantasy that does not exist except in their imagination."

Reynal had been willing to be uncomfortable and he had seen more than most tourists. But it was an experience not to be repeated. At the *Ambassadeurs,* Reynal no longer felt ill at ease and so, during the rest of his stay, we either had lunch or dinner there.

When Reynal returned to New York he wrote about how much he enjoyed Mexico and how he would always remember "the strange places and villages." He also kept his word. A contract was enclosed. "With your knowledge of Mexico, you should be able to turn out a good book," he said in his letter.

I was not as confident as was Reynal. In the beginning I was enthusiastic as is any man who is going to have a book published, but as I thought about it, I soon realized how little I knew about the country and the people. There was so much that I did not understand, or ever would. I'd have to dig in deeply, learn much more than I had during the years I had been in Mexico. *Mexico Gets in Your Blood,* I wanted to call it. I had the title, but that was about it.

There were friends, however, who would help: Alfredo Gonzales, Guerrero Galvan, Augustin Lara, Frans Blom, the archeologist: Oscar Martinez, a young doctor who came from an old Mexican family; and then there were the Mexicans who worked in the office. From them and many others, I'd have to seek answers to all the questions that came to mind.

We began making trips to the back country. With Frans Blom we went on a five-day horseback trip, sleeping on the floors of school houses and in native huts. We went to remote villages and talked with the Indians about their land, their problems, and their religious beliefs.

The Indian huts were comparatively clean, but whenever we stayed in a hotel or in a pension, there were bedbugs and fleas. We dusted the beds with DDT powder, but somehow one bedbug always managed to survive and it invariably bit Dag.

"Why are there so many bedbugs?" she asked the owner of one of the pensions.

"Who knows?" the woman shrugged her shoulders. "They have always been with us. But after a while, one gets accustomed to them, and the bedbugs do not bite. They lay in wait for strangers. They like new blood."

In Mexico City, Dr. Martinez took me along as he made the rounds of his social security patients, allowing me to get into homes that it might not be possible to visit otherwise. In each home there was usually a crucifix and a picture of the Virgin of Guadalupe. The people lived poorly and in crowded rooms, but they seldom complained. One old man, lying in an iron bed, reached out and took hold of my hand.

"Am I going to die?" he asked me.

I looked at Dr. Martinez who was preparing an injection, and I saw in his eyes that there was no hope for the old man.

"We all have to die at one time or another," I answered evasively.

The old man smiled and continued to hold on to my hand.

"I do not mind dying," he said. "I just wish to prepare for it, so I will be ready. It is foolish to resist it. I am not afraid."

Mexicans, especially those who are poor, do not seem to fear death as much as we do. Perhaps they welcome it as a release from the misery in which they live. When one of their children dies, they put wings on the tiny shoulders and the relatives and friends sing and play music. When they are so young and without sin, they have a better chance to get into Heaven.

With Guerrero Galvan, the painter, in Taxco one Sunday morning, we saw a funeral procession for a child who had just died. They were carrying the small coffin and behind it were a group of musicians playing. It was colorful and dramatic and very Mexican. I asked Galvan to sketch this scene and later he made it into a water color. When I saw it in his studio, I knew how I would use it. It would be the jacket for my book and I immediately wrote Reynal about it.

"You're the only writer that I know of," he answered, "who has a jacket made before even writing the book."

I was still too busy gathering material to start writing. I went on talking with politicians, bankers, labor leaders and with old men who had taken part in the Revolution of 1912 and with others who had ridden across the countryside with Zapata. In Chihuahua I spoke with the widow of Pancho Villa.

"He had many women," she said. "But I was the only one he cared for. He never drank or smoked. Pancho was a good man."

The time we had left in Mexico was running short. We wanted to see everything we could, but the more I saw, the more I talked with people, the task of preparing and interpreting the material I was gathering became a formidable challenge. Yet I felt that if in a minor way I could create a better understanding of Mexico, it would be worth it.

I went into the agrarian problem, into the political picture and into the human side of the Mexican people. Then I ran head-on into their sex life.

"Almost everyone who can afford them has mistresses," I said to Alfredo Gonzales. "Why?"

"*Así pasa*," he replied. "That's the way it is."

"But how do the women feel about it?" I pressed him.

"They accept it," he said. "They close their eyes to it."

I began questioning wives, although at first I didn't think they would be willing to say much. But they did and they were frank. They did not accept mistresses; they simply tolerated a situation which has always existed.

"Man is rarely faithful to one woman," the wife of a high-ranking cabinet member pointed out. "So, why should I expect my husband to be any different? He has his mistresses and he knows I know it. It happens everywhere, except that here in Mexico it is accepted and no overt criticism is attached to it. Naturally, I wish it wasn't that way, but there's little we can do."

"You could divorce him."

"We are Catholics and the Church would not permit it," she went on. "Besides what would I gain if I divorced my husband? Self-respect? I'd rather keep my family together and the security that comes with it. Don't feel sorry for us. We are women and we get back at our husbands in devious ways."

"A lover, perhaps?"

"Some wives have lovers but many don't. They do not seem to have the need for it. We try to make a man think he is running us, his family, and the home. We make him feel important. This is vital to any man. But we are the ones who make the decisions, whose advice they seek, and who as they say in your country, 'call the shots.' We are subtle and shrewd and we usually get our way. You must also remember that to a Mexican, his family comes first. Divorce my husband because he has a mistress? Only a wife who is a fool would do that."

The Catholic Church, which prohibits divorce, prefers to remain silent on the subject of mistresses and adultery. Mexican civil laws do not recognize adultery as grounds for divorce except under the most unusual circumstances. Also, by law, a Mexican woman cannot vote, engage in any profession or business without the consent of her husband and she may not leave the country unaccompanied by her husband unless she has his written permission.

But Mexican wives are not tied down as much as it would appear. They may not be as independent as American women, nevertheless they manage to do almost anything they wish. The husbands with the mistresses are more understanding, more tolerant of their wives, than American men.

"They are warm in their affection, they are thoughtful and they do all those little things that mean so much to a woman," another wife said to me. "They do not take us for granted. They are attentive and considerate in so many ways. Perhaps because they have mistresses they hold us in higher regard and with greater respect."

That was one side of the story. What about the mistresses? How did they feel about the passive role that they had to play? If the wives had social status, the Church and security, what did the mistresses have to cling to?

I again turned to a Mexican, whom I shall call Antonio, for help.

"How does one meet a mistress?" I asked him while we were having lunch.

His eyes brightened. "So you want to meet a mistress," he said with enthusiasm in his voice. "That can be arranged."

I don't think Antonio ever felt as close to me as he did at that moment. I was on a subject dear to his heart. I wanted to meet a mistress. I was becoming very Mexican.

"But I don't want to sleep with her," I said. "I only want to talk with her. And not only one. Perhaps three or four or six."

"Oh," he said, and there was disappointment in his voice and in his eyes. I wasn't really very Mexican after all. I was letting him down. I then explained why I wanted to talk with them.

"All right," he agreed. "I'll set it up for you to meet Lucia late this afternoon, if you like."

"Tell me about her," I said. "Who is she?"

"I met Lucia about a year ago," he went on. "She works in a government office. We liked each other and I rented a small apartment for her."

"I didn't know you had a mistress," I said. "I didn't think you could afford one."

"I just take care of the rent and help her a little," he said. "She's a nice person. You'll like Lucia."

Late that afternoon, after work, Antonio and I went downtown to Lady Baltimore, a small tea and pastry shop on Avenida Madero where they serve coffee and tea. I thought Lady Baltimore was a strange place to meet a mistress, but after a while, Lucia came in and joined us. Lucia was small and she must have weighed less than a hundred pounds. She had the bronzed skin of many Mexicans and black, sharp eyes. She was attractive, well dressed and on the shy side. She didn't talk very much at first.

Antonio ordered coffee and cake. He explained to her that I was his friend and that she could talk freely to me. I asked her first what she did and she told me she was a secretary and knew typing and shorthand.

"There are seven in our family," she said. "It is very crowded where we live. I've always wanted an apartment of my own and when Antonio and I started going together and he said he would help me with the rent, I accepted."

"How old are you, Lucia?" I asked.

"Twenty-two."

"Your parents don't mind?"

"They would prefer to see me married."

"You eventually want to be married?"

"Yes, if God wishes it."

"Are you and Antonio in love?"

She looked at him and he at her. He took her hand in his and he gently squeezed it. "Naturally," he said. "We wouldn't be together otherwise."

"But, Lucia," I went on. "You know he's married."

"Of course."

The way she looked at me, she must have thought I was stupid.

"That doesn't make any difference?"

"*Así pasa,*" she said: "That's the way it is."

We went on talking for an hour. Then I left them and they said they were going out to dinner and later to the theatre.

Lucia was one of ten mistresses with whom I spoke during

the next few weeks. They all had about the same story to tell and they all emphasized that they were not promiscuous, but faithful to the men they cared for.

"I live with Juanito, because he loves me and I love him," another of the women with whom I talked said. "I see him only once or twice a week. I wish we could be together more often but that's not possible. We cannot have everything in life the way we want it, so we do the best we can."

"Suppose you have children—what then?"

"I have a child by Juanito. He's six years old now. The Mexican law does not recognize illegitimacy. He bears his father's name and when he grows up he will have the same rights as his other children."

"But you would prefer to be married to him?"

"Who knows? perhaps I would, and perhaps I wouldn't. We care for each other and that's the most important of all. Because we have so little time together, we are never bored with each other. I always look forward to his visits and he looks forward to being with me. He does not take me for granted."

Most Mexican mistresses dress conservatively and their *casas chicas* are usually apartments where they reside, often with a mother or some other relative they help to support. Those who are ostentatious in their appearance are often the *queridas,* or girl friends of bullfighters, movie stars or wealthy politicians. They frequent the expensive restaurants and night spots, and not all of them are faithful to one man. They will accept favors and affections primarily from men who can afford them.

"Mexicans are not the great lovers they would like everyone to think they are," one of the girls we chatted with admitted. "They have girl friends because they are trying to prove they are *muy macho.*"

Muy macho means much man, and every Mexican wants to be that, even to the point of being supersensitive about it.

He will shrug his shoulders about political corruption and criticism of his country, but anyone who throws the slightest doubt on his masculinity, will have a fight on his hands.

Mexicans like to be known as ardent, romantic lovers and many have mistresses as further evidence of being *muy macho*. Having a mistress has also become something of a status symbol. They are proud of it and will admit it openly. But despite all this crowing and chest pounding, Mexicans are rather puritanical, especially when it comes to the woman they are going to marry and who will be the mother of their children. They insist and demand virginity. Young daughters, therefore, are carefully watched over and guarded until they reach a marriageable age. But not all girls remain pure and, as a result, there are a half dozen surgeons in Mexico who specialize, not in abortions, but in, of all things, restoring virginity.

As I dug deeper into the behavior pattern of the Mexicans, I found it difficult to assimilate and understand the many phases and contradictions of the material I was gathering. I needed help from someone who was well qualified and could be objective. Fortunately, I was soon to find just such a person.

By now we were frequently attending diplomatic receptions, luncheons and dinners. The protocol at many of these official functions was puzzling. At a formal diplomatic dinner there was a seating chart which had to be followed, and always on the table there were hard rolls, but never butter. At a luncheon, fingerbowls were brought out on a dessert plate with a spoon and fork. Under the finger bowl there was usually a doily. The correct procedure was to take the bowl and the doily off and lay them aside. Then the waiters came with the dessert. There is a story about a visiting dignitary from Washington who failed to remove the doily, and as he ate his dessert, he also ate the doily. Everyone afterwards wondered whether or not he suffered any ill effects.

At first we enjoyed going to these functions, but after a time it became an effort, for we often met the same people.

There was one reception being given which I did not want to attend because I was tired. But as the Embassy had requested us to be there, I had several drinks at home before making an appearance, and I was feeling the effects when we arrived. After two more drinks I noticed a woman dressed in a severely-cut, tailored suit, and there was something about the way she looked that irritated me. I went up to her.

"Are you a missionary?" I asked, "here to convert the Indians?"

For a second she was stunned and there was anger in her eyes. Then she smiled and promptly put me in my place.

"I'm afraid not," she said. "I am a psychiatrist—a lieutenant commander in the United States Navy—attached to the Merchant Marine."

I apologized and briefly told her of my recent experience with the Archbishop and how I felt about missionaries. She said she was on her first leave in three years and had borrowed the suit because she learned at the last moment she could not wear her naval uniform into Mexico. We invited her for dinner for the following night and she accepted.

Her name was Florence Powdermaker and she had both a Ph.D and an M.D. degree from Johns Hopkins and a long-established reputation both as a psychiatrist and a psychoanalyst. It was Florence who had the training, the penetrating mind and the necessary perception that was to prove so helpful in putting together the material I had on Mexico.

The war in Europe and in the Pacific was almost at an end and our work in Mexico was about over and soon we would be leaving. But we did not want to go. Mexico had become our home and we wanted to stay.

"Uncle George" was still the United States Ambassador, but he was friendly and urged me to join the diplomatic service and become a foreign service officer. We also had other offers and we were in a quandary as to what we should do, when a cable came from Guatemala. My brother had suffered a stroke and was semi-paralyzed. I flew to Guatemala and visited with him and we agreed we would come and stay with him. I would help him with his business interests and it would still leave me the necessary time in which to write the book on Mexico. At the time it appeared the logical thing to do.

In December we packed everything we were going to take, and filled a huge lift van with our furniture. Father John had arranged for a freight car to transport our automobile to the Guatemalan border where we would pick it up and then drive to Guatemala City.

We were leaving on an early morning plane for Tapachula. We did not expect anyone to be at the airport at that hour—but most of our Mexican friends were there. They had hired a group of musicians and they were playing some of our favorite pieces. Our friends and the musicians followed us to the ramp of the plane and they sang "La Golondrina," a sad and moving song. We took our seats on the plane and waved as the plane taxied down the runway.

CHAPTER EIGHTEEN

A Most Unusual Luncheon
with a Most Unusual Friend

There is an amusing story of how Tapachula, which is on the Mexican–Guatemalan border, was given its name. During the early colonization period, the native women did not wear any clothing above their hips and the missionary priests would say to them: *Tapa té chula,* or "cover thyself, little one." It was here in Tapachula that we were to pick up our car and meet Father John.

Father John wanted to be certain that the car would be there upon our arrival and he had volunteered to travel on the train transporting our car. When we landed in Tapachula by plane and came down the ramp, Father John greeted us and helped us with our hand luggage. But he appeared concerned.

"I have a confession to make," he said as we walked toward the airport building. "The engineer invited me into the caboose, and while I was asleep, the freight car with your automobile was switched. But we have traced it. It is sure to get here by tomorrow."

Father John was an optimist. The freight train bringing our car was delayed for three days and while we waited we visited a number of Indian villages where the natives were participating in traditional ceremonies which took place as the new year approached.

Tapachula is hot and tropical and malaria is prevalent. Each night we had our hotel room sprayed and we slept under mosquito nets. Finally our car arrived and Father John saw us off at the border.

The drive to Guatemala City was long, dusty and over a narrow, winding road poorly maintained. But the countryside was rich with tropical flora, including tall tree ferns. Beyond San Marcos, the road climbed through the mountains and onto a plateau that was temperate and cool.

Once the great Mayan empire stretched across from Honduras, to the Petén jungle of Guatemala and then through southern Mexico and much later it flourished on the Yucatán peninsula. Their temples and their advanced culture thrived in the lowlands which must have, at one time, been free of malaria and other tropical diseases. Today the descendants of the Mayas have their villages and towns in the highlands where the cold mountain air provides the best protection from malaria-bearing mosquitos.

We stopped the first night in Quetzaltenango at a hotel where it felt good to undress in the warmth of the fireplace in our room. We fell asleep listening to the sounds of the burning embers. In the morning, even before we were awake, a native boy quietly laid a fire and started it with a piece of pitch. In a few minutes the logs were burning and the room grew warm again.

We breakfasted and once more started on the road. As we drove through the mountains, in the distance was the great Cuchumatanes range and the continental divide at an altitude of over thirteen thousand feet. By evening we reached Chichicastenango and the Mayan Inn, managed by Julio and Mary Matheu. I had gone to school with Julio. He and his wife were waiting for us at their cottage near the hotel.

Julio was erratic and hot tempered, but a good friend. He fixed martinis and then we had dinner, including chicken *pepian* with freshly-made tortillas. The native boy who served at the table was dressed in a colorful Mayan costume.

"Don't you ever get lonely up here, far away from everything?" Dag asked Mary.

"No, we're happy, and we enjoy it," she said. "Besides there's so much we have to do we are always busy."

"What about the Indians? Don't they make trouble when they have their fiestas and get drunk?"

"The Indians?" Julio broke in with a laugh. "They are our friends. I keep a loaded revolver around, but I've never had to use it. We have had trouble only from an insolent tourist guide." He stopped for a moment. There was sudden anger in his eyes. "Don't mind me," he said. "He makes me sore." His anger subsided and he was smiling again.

We had one more drink, and went to bed.

We arrived in Guatemala City the next day long after dark and managed to find our way to my brother's home. We rang the bell by the high iron gate. Dogs began barking and then lights were turned on and Macedonio, the gardener, opened the gates and we drove in.

Maria, the cook, and Josefina, the maid, were at the door and welcomed us. But where was Don Alfredo, my brother? Had he suffered a relapse and was he bedridden again?

"No, señor," said Maria. "He did not think you would arrive until tomorrow."

"But then, where is he?"

"It is New Year's Eve, señor," Maria went on. "He is away for the evening. But you must be tired and hungry. Come and we will take you to your room. I shall have supper ready for you very soon."

"But he should be here," I said to Dag. "He must have known we were coming. I don't understand it."

We stayed up, turned on the short wave radio and listened to stations in New Orleans, Texas, and Mexico. At midnight we heard the church bells ringing, ushering in the New Year, and shortly afterwards my brother, Alfredo, arrived. He was apologetic, convinced we had misinformed him about the day we were getting in. I was angry and irritated with him; it was, I thought, not a good beginning.

My brother loved animals and birds, and his menagerie included Arturo, a vicious macaw; Tiburcio, a pet alligator; Anastasia, a female deer; Policarpio, a male deer; Hermanegildo, a goat; and Constantino, a long-nosed pisote that resembled an ant eater. There were, of course, dogs, properly named, and on his *finca,* or farm, near the city he had three horses which he called, Stalin, Timoshenko, and Eisenhower.

Only he could handle Arturo, a beautiful and graceful bird that seemed quite tame on his perch. But when Dag approached him the first day, he almost bit off her finger. However, it was Constantino, the pisote, that gave her the most trouble. Constantino was unusually dexterous with his front paws and drank bottles of Coke and beer easily although he enjoyed going after women's calves most of all; Dag had a daily battle with Constantino until she began tapping him on the snout with a rolled-up newspaper.

Our stay at Alfredo's home was to have been temporary or until our furniture arrived; then we would move into a home of our own. The furniture had been shipped ahead from Mexico in a large lift van which weighed several tons. But almost two months passed before we located the lift van in the border town of Suchiate, near Tapachula. I flew to Tapachula and then had to spend the night in Suchiate where there were no screens on the windows or mosquito nets on the bed. I was able to get the lift van on a flat car and send it on its way. We wanted to have our house ready with our furniture, for Dr. Powdermaker had written that she was planning to visit Guatemala and we had invited her to stay with us.

During those first few months we were in Guatemala we tried occasionally to eat out, but the few restaurants that existed were not good. Then we discovered Los Arcos, not too far from the airport and near my brother's home. We started going there at least once a week, and often went with friends.

Los Arcos was a huge, old house that had been converted into a restaurant with private dining rooms. Guillermo, the owner of Los Arcos, brought by air from New Orleans, prawns, lobsters, fresh oysters, and other food delicacies generally unobtainable inland.

Guatemala City, small and provincial was a change after Mexico City. However, I kept busy helping my brother with his business and working on the book on Mexico. Dag occupied herself collecting orchids of which there are hundreds of varieties in Guatemala. On weekends we went to my brother's *finca*, where we went horseback riding and swam in his pool. Gradually Alfredo regained the full use of his leg and before long he did not need a cane.

We made new friends and among them was Paul Nesbitt, who was designing the new Guatemala Museum, and Edwin Shook, who was at that time with the Carnegie Foundation doing archeological research. With their wives they joined us almost every week at Los Arcos. But one evening, when we went there for dinner, Guillermo, the owner called me aside.

"Will you have a drink with me?" he asked and led me to a little bar near the kitchen, while our friends and Dag went into one of the private dining rooms.

I knew Guillermo had something on his mind, but like most Latins, he did not come to the point right away.

"Your brother, Don Alfredo, never comes with you, does he?" Guillermo said.

"My brother doesn't like to eat out," I said.

"Did he tell you about Los Arcos?"

"No, I had to discover it myself. And I am glad we did. You have the best food in the city, Guillermo. You can't get prawns and lobsters anywhere else."

"I fly them here by air—it is very expensive."

"I am sure of that. But your prices aren't high."

"Will you have another drink?" he asked.

He poured me a Scotch. He was getting ready now to get to the point. I was growing impatient and wanted to join Dag and our friends.

"Do you know why I bring in these prawns, lobsters, and oysters?" he asked.

"Because people like them."

"There's another reason. You are certain your brother has not told you?" He hesitated for a moment. "You see it is this way," he went on searching for words. "The restaurant—it offers seclusion and privacy. It is something the politicians like—the privacy—and they come here with their girl friends —their *queridas. Los políticos,* they are big spenders. They order all these things I import. They like to show how important and big they are before their *queridas,* and always they order champagne. You have no idea how much champagne they and their girl friends drink. And as you know—it is in the champagne on which I make money. You understand then—what is happening?"

"No, not exactly," I said. "You want us to order champagne —is that it?"

"*No, hombre,*" he protested. "*No es eso!* You see, when you come here, you bring your wife and your friends. They also bring their wives. *Dios mío!* Do you not see what is causing the trouble? It is the wives! They do not belong here and the politicians, they do not like it and they are no longer coming with their *queridas.* They complain and they say to me, 'Guillermo, what is happening to Los Arcos? All these men and their wives—it is not good to have them here. We will not patronize Los Arcos anymore.' So I am losing my customers. You are making the place respectable. Please, do me a favor—do not come with your wives."

Guillermo was smiling, relieved that he had put his point across. "You are not angry? Ah, good. We must not be angry over these matters. Now you and I, we will have a drink together and I will send champagne to your table. It makes me happy to send it with my compliments."

Our furniture had been unpacked and we had the house about ready when Florence arrived. We met her at the airport in the morning, took her for a short ride and then returned in time for lunch. We were sitting in the dining room and the soup was being served, when I felt a chill and my teeth began to chatter and I started to tremble. I left the dining room with Dag and Florence right behind me. I went to bed and they covered me with blankets. They brought me brandy and I gulped a glassful. I was still freezing and shaking. Then I felt warm and began perspiring. Florence took my temperature. I had a 104 degree fever.

"I think I know what's wrong," Florence said. "But we better have some blood tests made."

I had malaria, probably picked it up during the trip to Suchiate. Florence now used her skill as a physician and psychoanalyst to get me well. If I had to be ill, if I had to have malaria, it could not have been under better circumstances. She had me take strong doses of atabrine, and every hour, she stood by the bed until I finished pitchersfull of water and fruit juices. Gradually under Florence's care, the fever went down and I began to feel better. Within the week I was up, though still weak and unsteady.

Nevertheless we made plans for a trip into the back country of Guatemala, including a visit to the Mayan Inn at Chichicastenango where we would stay with Julio and Mary. I knew Florence would like it there, and then we would go on to the village of San Francisco El Alto and later, Lake Atitlán.

The day before our departure there was a story on the front page of the afternoon paper that was to change our plans. Our friend, Julio Matheu, had shot and killed a tourist guide in the lobby of the Mayan Inn. The story went on to say that the shooting was the result of a long feud between the two. Julio was under arrest, charged with murder and had been taken to the prison at Quiché, pending trial. The story also said there was unrest among the Indians, many of whom had come to Julio's defense.

We were shocked by the news. We postponed our trip and took Florence instead to Coban and other parts of Guatemala. But a month later, and just before she was getting ready to leave for New York, we decided we did not want her to go before visiting Chichicastenango and the Mayan Inn.

"I'm sure everything is quiet by now up there," I said, and on the following day we started out, stopping the first night at Lake Atitlán.

From Atitlán to Chichicastenango is only a short drive. In the afternoon as I drove over the narrow and dusty mountain road, I turned to Florence.

"Suppose Mary is still there—what should we say to her about Julio?"

"Why, you just act natural, inquire about her husband, and let it go at that," Florence replied.

I thought it was fine to be traveling with a psychoanalyst who knew the answers. But none of us was prepared for what was to take place, least of all, Florence.

On Sundays, in Chichicastenango, the natives who come down from their villages gather in front of the church steps to burn incense and to worship as their ancestors have for centuries. The ceremonies are half pagan, half Christian. Later in the morning they move on to the open-air market where they enjoy haggling and arguing over each purchase.

One would not expect to find a comfortable, modern and well operated hotel here in this somewhat isolated area. But the Mayan Inn was constructed to accommodate tourists and its success from the beginning was due to the efforts of Julio and Mary. In time they became a part of the town and when they were not busy catering to the tourists, they tried to help the natives. While their knowledge of medicine was limited, they nevertheless opened a clinic and made an effort to take care of the sick, especially children and expectant mothers. Julio and Mary paid for most of the medicines which were given away free.

They were well liked and, according to the story we eventually pieced together from various sources, the trouble originated with the same tourist guide who in the past had irritated and heckled Julio. The guide began calling Mary, *la curandera,* or midwife. Other times he referred to her as the housekeeper of the hotel and often, Julio and Mary maintained, the guide was drunk and used offensive language. Julio complained to the tourist company about the guide and asked that he should not bring tours to Chichicastenango.

The tourist agency ignored his pleas, and one afternoon the guide came again to the Mayan Inn. He became involved in an argument and Julio took out the revolver he kept in his desk and told the guide that if he came to the Mayan Inn once more, he would shoot him. The guide did not take him seriously for on the following week he was back.

Julio refused to let him in the hotel. They began to argue and fight, and the guide hit Julio. Julio, in a rage, rushed into his office, took out the revolver, and shot him. Julio called the local police, convinced he would be set free after a brief investigation.

In the meantime the widow of the guide swore out a murder complaint. Julio was arrested and, because there was no jail in Chichicastenango, he was taken to the state prison in Quiché, an hour's drive away.

While he was imprisoned, Mary took on the running of the Mayan Inn, and she was there when Florence, Dag and I arrived. We asked about Julio and expressed our concern over him.

"He's all right," Mary said reassuringly. "When I found out you were coming, I phoned him. He would like to have you visit him."

I turned to Florence. "Would you mind?"

"Of course not," she said, and then in a more professional tone, "it might prove interesting."

The next day when we were getting ready to leave, Mary came to the car, followed by one of the native servants from the hotel carrying a large basket. He put the basket in the back of the car.

"I had the cook prepare some chicken," Mary said. "I thought we might all have lunch with Julio."

"But is that permitted?" Florence asked.

"Oh, yes," Mary replied. "They are taking good care of him. The governor of the state is an old friend. He and Julio were in the Military Academy together. He has given instructions that Julio should be comfortable."

The road through the mountains is winding and narrow and it was after twelve o'clock when we arrived in Quiché. We drove around the plaza and to the prison which was nearby. As we parked the car we saw Julio. He was leaning against the gray wall of the building, wearing a sport shirt, khaki trousers, and sandals.

"Where have you been? You are late," he said as he approached the car. "I've been waiting for you."

He kissed Mary, embraced Dag and me and we introduced him to Florence.

"Doctor Powdermaker is a psychiatrist and a psychoanalyst," Mary said.

"Doctor, I'm glad to meet you," Julio said. "You're exactly what I need."

I started to take the lunch basket out of the car but Julio stopped me. "No, I don't want you to carry that. Just a moment."

He put two fingers to his mouth and whistled loudly. A flunky came out of the prison and Julio told him to carry the basket inside.

We followed Julio through the main gate of the prison. There were soldiers with rifles guarding the gate but no one paid the slightest heed to Julio or us. He led us through a narrow passageway and then to a barred cell, which was open. "Come on in," he said, "and we'll have lunch in here."

The cell was spacious with a high ceiling and there were two beds, six chairs, and a table. I looked around and noticed there was a radio and an electric razor there, too.

Once we were inside the cell, Julio closed the grated door. "Please sit down," he said, "and we'll have some drinks in a moment."

He walked over to the far corner of the cell and tapped on the floor. A trap door opened and a native boy in a white jacket came up the steps from the cell's basement. He made several trips bringing glasses, soda water, and ice.

"What will you have?" Julio asked. "We can give you a martini, Scotch or an old fashioned."

Florence continued to be professional in her attitude but finally she relaxed and said, "I've had many experiences, but this is the first time I've ever had cocktails in jail. I think I'm going to enjoy it."

Julio took orders for the drinks and helped the boy prepare them. Then turning to Mary, "I hope you brought enough lunch. Pepe is going to join us."

While we were having our first drink the native boy set the table with a white tablecloth, dishes, silverware, and glasses.

During our second drink, a man in a well tailored military uniform appeared at the cell door.

"Sorry to be late, Julio," he said.

"You're just in time," Julio opened the cell door.

The man greeted Mary and then she introduced him to us.

"This is our friend, Pepe," Mary said. "He also happens to be the Governor," she added.

The Governor was about Julio's age with a ruddy complexion, rather thick hair, and light brown eyes. He was a handsome man and he made, I thought, an immediate impression on Florence with whom he talked in English.

After a while we sat down to eat. Mary had brought chicken

Gallantine, a potato salad, green beans vinaigrette, and, for dessert, chocolate cream cake. There was probably an electric plate in the basement, because after we finished eating the native boy served hot coffee.

The Governor liked Florence and during lunch they chatted together, but little was said about Julio and why he was in prison.

Around three o'clock, the Governor expressed his regrets that he had to leave and return to his office. "I wish we could see each other again," he said. Then after a thoughtful glance at us, he added, "Are you staying at the Mayan Inn through tomorrow night?"

"We are not going until Sunday," I said.

The Governor turned to Mary. "Why don't we plan to have dinner at your house? We could leave here after dark and if I get Julio back before morning, there would be no problem."

Then to Julio, "What do you think, *Chino?*"

"*Porqué no, viejo?*" Julio replied.

"Let's plan on it," the Governor said.

"Do you really think you could manage it?" Mary asked. "Oh, if you only could. It would do Julio so much good." There was a worried look in her eyes and it was obvious that Mary, though she would never admit it, had been badly hurt and had suffered much from what had happened. "Would it not be a risk—if it was found out—both for you and Julio?"

"No, it will be done with discretion. No need to worry," the Governor said. "We'll see you tomorrow night, shortly after eight," and he shook hands and left.

We stayed on a few minutes longer. By now the native boy had collected the tableware and had repacked the basket. Julio led the way back to the car, kissed Mary, and waved to us as we drove away. From the rear mirror, I saw him slowly walk back towards prison.

On Saturday evening, after we had dressed, we picked up Florence in her room. I knocked at her door.

"Come in," she said. "I'm ready."

Florence was wearing a brown silk taffeta dinner dress and a pearl necklace. I helped her on with her wrap.

"You really think Julio and the Governor will be there tonight?" she asked as she started out from the Mayan Inn for the cottage where Mary was living.

"I'm sure of it." I said.

"I just can't believe it," Florence said. "The whole thing is most amusing—the Governor picking up a prisoner and bringing him here for dinner. One does not expect it to happen, and yet it is happening."

Mary greeted us at the door of the cottage. She was smiling and there was a pleasant expression on her youthful face.

"They should be here any time," she said. Mary had planned a buffet supper, and on a table there was caviar and champagne chilling. She asked us what we wanted to drink and as I went to help her, there was a knock at the door. It was the Governor and Julio. They were dressed in Indian clothes and each had a straw hat and a false mustache. They were made up so well that anyone who might have seen them would have never recognized them. We had drinks and then dinner. Later, Florence began asking questions and Julio described the events that led to the shooting, and details of the shooting itself.

"But you will go on trial?" Florence wanted to know.

"Not if we can avoid it," the Governor interposed. "Julio and I are working on a plan that might prove successful."

"I shouldn't be prying," Florence said, "but you have aroused my professional curiosity—what are you proposing to do?"

"It is what might be called a practical approach," the Governor said. "First you must understand—the guide was a drunk and a trouble maker. Julio had warned him many times and he could even plead self-defense and he might be exonerated. But we have the widow of the guide—she's pressing the charges—creating the difficulty. It is she whom we have to deal with and pacify."

"How then, do you propose to handle her?" Florence asked.

"She likes men—this we know," the Governor went on. "So we have arranged with a friend to be most attentive to her—to have her, if possible, fall in love with him. If she does, he will convince her to drop the complaint against Julio and then it will not be necessary to have a trial. Of course," the Governor hesitated for a moment and added, "it will be necessary to compensate our friend accordingly and Julio might have to make a cash settlement to the widow."

"The approach you are taking is very Latin," Florence said, "I suspect it will work out exactly as you have planned. But do you know, if I tell my friends in New York this story, they will not believe it."

It was after two o'clock in the morning when the Governor and Julio left and we returned to the hotel. As we took Florence to her room she was shaking her head. "I've heard the most incredible stories from my patients—but never anything to match this one." She laughed. "Weren't they something in those clothes they were wearing, and those false mustaches—it was just the right touch, wasn't it?"

On Sunday we left Chichicastenango and for the next four days we traveled through the back country of the Guatemala highlands. Then we return to Guatemala City in time for Florence to catch her plane for New York.

It must have taken longer than Julio and the Governor had anticipated for their friend to court the widow of the guide sufficiently. It was eight months after Florence's visit that there appeared a brief item on the back page of the Guatemala newspaper. It stated that the murder complaint against Julio had been withdrawn and he had been given a two year probationary sentence.

CHAPTER NINETEEN

Man Falling down a Marble Stairway

We had looked forward to living in Guatemala, and we should
have been happy in this land where I was born and spent my
childhood. There was a soft mildness to the climate; the
scenery was dramatic and we liked our home with its high
rock wall and garden. It did not take us long either to become
devoted to Juliana, our cook who had an extraordinarily delicate hand in the kitchen, and Felipe, our houseboy who
served at the table and took care of nearly everything. Life
was easy and with my brother's varied business interests, with
which I was becoming identified, there would be in time—if
this was what we were searching for—financial security and
independence.

There was much about Guatemala we enjoyed. On weekends we'd usually go to my brother's *finca*, where we'd lie in
the sun, swim or ride horseback; occasionally we'd travel into
the remote back country as far as the Rio Dulce, looking for
ruins or orchids, or we'd drive to Iztapa, on the Pacific side,
to fish or to swim in the warm surf. There was time to write,
and eventually the book on Mexico was finished and sent off
to the publishers. I now had time to concentrate on another
project I had in mind.

While we were in Mexico I had read many books about the
country, among them *The True History of the Conquest of*

257

Mexico by Bernal Díaz del Castillo. This eyewitness account of the Conquest intrigued me; I wanted to know more about Bernal Díaz. He was a soldier in the army of Cortéz, but how did he happen to write a book which was still being read four hundred years after his death? What was his background and what kind of a man was he? What happened to him after the Conquest? But there was little on him in print. I was told that the original manuscript of the *True History* was in Guatemala where he had gone in 1541. The archives there, I also learned, might be the only source of material on him.

Knowing Spanish and reading it fluently, I did not consider it a problem to go through old documents. So one morning I went to the archives and talked with Joaquín Pardo, the director, and asked for whatever he had on Bernal Díaz. He was soon back with a high stack of dusty folios which he put on a table in front of me.

I started going through them, but I could only make out a word here and there. The handwriting was in sixteenth century Spanish and done by notaries using abbreviations or their own style of shorthand. It appeared an impossible task and I was ready to abandon the whole thing, when I became aware of a man standing by me. I looked up; he was a priest.

"You are interested in Bernal Díaz?" he asked.

"I was," I said, "but I can't make a thing out of these documents."

"I am also trying to find out about Bernal Díaz," he said, "and perhaps I can help you."

He introduced himself as Carmelo Santa Maria, a Spanish Jesuit who had been only a short time in Guatemala. Each morning after that we met at the archives, and with the use of a reading lens and a list of symbols—and great patience— Padre Santa Maria taught me how to decipher sixteenth century documents. In three months I could do it on my own. Historical research, I found, could be exciting, and not unlike uncovering clues in a detective story.

One day I came across the dowry Bernal Díaz received when he married; another time it might be a document with the number of chickens, corn, and other agricultural products he was given from Indians who worked his land. Sometimes weeks would go by without finding a thing; then suddenly would come pay dirt—valuable source material.

By now, Joaquín Pardo, the director of the archives, and I had become friends enough for him to show me the original manuscript of the *True History* which was kept locked in a safe. It was considered the most valuable document in Latin America. I was fascinated going through it; the handwriting was clear and easy to read. However, as I turned the pages I noticed that the handwriting changed. I asked Joaquín Pardo about it.

"Of course, it changed," he said. "He worked on it for many years and he was getting older."

I turned some more pages and once again the handwriting differed. I didn't say anything more to Pardo, but I was certain now that something was wrong, for Bernal Díaz' handwriting indicated that he was getting younger again.

That afternoon I talked to Padre Santa Maria about it, and while he was puzzled, he said there was no question about the authenticity of the manuscript; it had been examined by the best historians in the United States and Latin America. But Santa Maria did admit that it was strange about the changes in handwriting.

In my youth, I had met and written an article for *Reader's Digest* about Dr. Edward O. Heinrich, a criminologist and expert on disputed documents. I now wrote him about the problem and asked him for advice on how best to determine the authenticity of the handwriting of the manuscript. Within a week there was a letter from Dr. Heinrich with detailed instructions. First I was to photograph the signature of Bernal Díaz as it appeared on the official *cabildo* or city council records, of which he had been a member. Then I was to get photographs of at least a dozen pages of the manuscript, specifically where there was a variance in the handwriting.

It was not easy to persuade Joaquín Pardo to allow photographs to be taken of the manuscript, but with the help of Padre Santa Maria, we were able to do it. Two months passed, and then the report came from Dr. Heinrich.

The manuscript in the Guatemalan archives, he concluded, was not in the handwriting of Bernal Díaz, but a copy prepared by various notaries or secretaries, and that was why the handwriting changed. The original manuscript, Dr. Heinrich pointed out, was probably sent to Spain, and this was only a copy which Bernal Díaz kept. There were corrections on the manuscript, and these, Dr. Heinrich said further, were in Bernal Díaz' handwriting. His findings were helpful, for it now explained to historians the many discrepancies between the first edition of the *True History* published in Spain in 1632, and the manuscript in the Guatemalan archives.

Everything was just as we might have wanted it to be in Guatemala, and yet it wasn't. I enjoyed working in the archives on Bernal Díaz, but there arose difficulties with my brother that should have been minor irritations; and yet they grew out of all proportion. We were probably at fault in failing to understand him better, and in not adjusting as well as we might have to our new way of life. Florence, from the first, was aware that we should not live permanently in Guatemala, but she was too wise to say anything about it. However, as the publication date for the book on Mexico approached, Florence invited us to visit her in New York and we decided to go east early in October.

This was our second year in Guatemala and as we planned to be away for three months, we rented our home to an American Army colonel and his wife, and at Puerto Barrios, boarded a banana freighter for New York. Florence met us at the pier and took us to her apartment on Park Avenue, where she lived and had her offices. It was exciting and stimulating to be in New York. We found it a welcome change to be meeting and talking with some of her friends; we enjoyed going to the theatre, shopping in the stores, and even the crowds and the traffic.

It was during our first week in New York, while we were having dinner one evening, that Florence brought up Dr. Theodor Reik's name.

"While you are here, why don't you have some sessions with Dr. Reik?" she said to me. "I have a hunch he would be helpful to you. He was with Freud for thirty years and I consider him one of our better analysts."

"But Florence, I don't need analysis," I said.

"I didn't say you did," Florence went on. "I am just suggesting that some talks with him might make you see things more clearly. We all carry emotional burdens on our backs. Analysis often lightens the weight of these burdens."

Then she changed the subject and we did not talk any more about it that night. But in the morning while Florence was with her patients, I discussed it at breakfast with Dag.

"It can't hurt you," she said. "And you like new experiences —this might prove quite interesting for you."

"All right," I said. "I'll call him and see him just once and that's it."

I went to the telephone and dialed Dr. Reik's number.

"Hallo," I heard a loud voice answer; and then in a strong, foreign accent, "vell, vat is it? Who is talking?"

I gave him my name, told him I was a friend of Florence's and asked when I might come and see him.

"So," the voice went on. "You vish to see me, yes? Just a moment, pleeze. I look in my book." There was a half-minute silence and once more he was on the phone. "At three o'clock this afternoon, I see you. Yes?"

At noon we had lunch with Florence and she seemed pleased that I was going to talk with Dr. Reik.

"He's just right for you," she said. "He's very intuitive and you'll be surprised how helpful he'll be."

Dr. Reik at the time lived in an old apartment building on West Fifty-sixth Street. I walked over from Florence's and arrived there about ten to three, rang for the elevator, and asked for Dr. Reik's apartment.

"Eighth floor to the right," the elevator operator said, and I thought he looked suspiciously at me.

I felt self-conscious and frightened as I approached the door with his name on it. Florence had told me not to ring, but to walk in and go into his waiting room. I followed her instructions. The apartment was clean, but old and shabby; it had a European feeling to it. I didn't like it and I was certain now that I wasn't going to like Dr. Reik. I was sorry I had come.

At exactly three o'clock I heard footsteps. Then he was standing in front of me, a heavy-set man, quite bald and with a long beaked nose that seemed to dominate his face. He spoke in a loud voice and with a thick accent.

"Vill you pleeze come in now," he said. I followed him into his office and he went to his desk. The desk was covered with papers, and books were piled high on it. Above it was a photograph of Freud, and near the desk and against the wall was a leather couch.

"Pleeze, you sit down," he said, and he motioned me to take the chair next to his desk. "So, you vish to see me? Vot about? Feel free to talk. I vill listen."

It was a bad beginning. I was certain Florence had talked to him about me. He must have known the purpose of my visit. He was not making it easy for me. I thought of the *shamans,* or medicine men of the Indian tribes in Mexico and Guatemala. This Dr. Reik, I decided, was a man who also dealt in black magic.

"So, pleeze, you tell me about yourself," he went on. "Vot is that you are doing in New York? You come from far avay, no?"

Suddenly I began to talk. I forgot about the shabbiness of his office, of the general disorder of his desk, of the ugliness of his face. I found myself telling him things I had never said to anyone before. Then he stopped me.

"It is most interesting," he said, puffing at a cigarette. "Now, ven do vee start? Ven do I see you? I vill make room for you tomorrow. Is four o'clock goot? I vill give you a full hour then. Now, vee just make the acquaintance. Yes?"

He was up from his desk and I was following him down the hall; then the door closed and I was in the elevator again, and once more on the street. I glanced at my watch. It was only three-fifteen. I had been with him less than a quarter of an hour.

"I'll never see him again," I said to myself as I walked toward Park Avenue. "He's nothing but an old charlatan—a quack."

But the following day I was back in Dr. Reik's waiting room and at four o'clock he ushered me into his office. This time he asked me to lie on the couch and he sat down behind me.

"So," he said—always in that loud voice of his—"Pleeze, you introduce me to your family. Tell me about father and mother. And, your brother, yes?"

The time went quickly, and only once or twice did he interrupt to ask a question. Then before I knew it, I was out walking on the street again. One did not linger with Reik. The partings were abrupt and deliberate.

"How is it?" he asked on my third visit as he sat down. "Any dreams last night?"

"No, no dreams," I said, and then a dream did come back to me and I began telling him about it. "He was a man quite fat and he was standing on top of a marble stairway. I came up behind him and pushed him. He went tumbling down the marble stairway."

All at once, it came to me. No wonder Florence had wanted me to have analysis. I was a potential killer!

"I murdered him, didn't I?"

"Yes, but everyone is a murderer. People want to kill father, mother, brother, friends, and enemies. But it is in the mind only. It is repressed."

Then, after a moment's silence; "The man you pushed—vas he not bald and did he not have a big nose?"

"That's right—how did you know?"

"Vell, that is so simple. That vas me. Your unconscious, it does not like my probing. So it tries to send me falling down a marble stairway. That happens vid many patients. It is goot; it is very goot sign. Now, vy do you not tell me vat you really think of me? Pleeze, you be honest vid me."

"Florence says you are a fine analyst."

"I ask you—vat is it you think of me? Vy do you not say it? I am a dirty old Jew vit a big nose and that big nose—it is prying into everything. Yes? Is it not so? Vell, vy do you not tell me? It does not bother me. It is goot—very goot—to have patients express their aggressions, hatreds, and their hostilities. Now I tell you a liddle story . . ."

Dr. Reik always had little stories to tell about himself, about his children, about some of his patients. Unlike most analysts, he did not just sit by the couch and listen; often he would interrupt to stress a point, to ask a question, or to tell one of his stories. At first I resented when he broke in.

"You do not like ven I tell you a story? You think I am taking up valuable time that costs money. I tell you how you can save money. You do not make visits to me. Very simple, yes? But I must probe until I find vat you are repressing. Your father—you do not remember him well. Ve must search for him. Now tell me about your brother—you feel sorry for him?"

Sometimes I would be so angry at Dr. Reik that I would lie on the couch tense without saying a word. But always he was patient and understanding, helping me with one of his stories, hoping they would recall some childhood memory or a remnant of the past that might prove helpful.

During that first week we were in New York there was another person I telephoned and whom I was to see almost every day—Eugene Reynal. When I called him, he invited me for lunch and said he would have proofs on the book by the end of the week.

"Everything is going on schedule," he told me at lunch. "We'll have the book out in time to catch the Christmas sales. The book is good—my editors like it—but it will need the right promotion for it to have a good sale. By the way," he dug into his files, "have you ever been inside of a publishing house?"

"No, I haven't."

"Tell you what," he went on, "you have a lot of ideas and from what you have told me, you are not going to be too busy while you are in New York. How would you like to give us a hand in promoting the book? I can give you an office and you can work right along with us. It will also give you a chance to see how a publishing house works. How does it strike you?"

"I'd like it," I said. "Quite a break, I'd say, for an author with a first book."

"I realize that," he continued, "and we usually don't give authors that opportunity. But you are no ordinary author," he appeared amused. Then he added, "After lunch we'll go over and I'll show you around."

Reynal introduced me to his associates and then he arranged for me to use a small office near his own. I went there each morning and worked with his editors and his sales and promotion department. I had brought with me a large collection of photographs of Mexico, and from them we selected the ones to go into the book. The painting that Guerrero Galván had made of the funeral scene in Taxco was to be used as the

four-color dust jacket. I was disappointed, however, to learn
that Reynal, his editors and the sales manager had turned
down the original title: *Mexico Gets in Your Blood,* and instead were calling the book: *These Are the Mexicans.*

Within a short time I knew most of the people in Reynal's
firm. I first thought they would resent my being there, but
they seemed to enjoy talking to me about Mexico and Guatemala. Often I went to lunch with some of them and after a
while I was made to feel part of the staff. I had always had
the impression that editors were cold and indifferent. But I
found them friendly, warm, and generous.

Every day in the middle of the afternoon I left the office
and took the bus or the subway to Dr. Reik's. Sometimes they
asked me at Reynal's where I was going, but I was evasive,
saying I had appointments to keep. My visits to Reik's took
on an undertone of mystery. I felt as if I were doing something that was improper and should be concealed.

I found too, that usually it was better in introducing Florence to our friends, not to say she was a psychoanalyst. When
we did, it seemed to frighten people. One friend in the adver-
tising business failed to keep a dinner date with us on learning Florence's profession, and that she was joining us.

In the evenings and on weekends when we were with
Florence, we seldom discussed analysis, and she would stop
me if I ever talked about my sessions with Reik.

"That's between you and him," she would say. "You'll have
to work it out with him. Leave me out of it." But Florence was
perceptive and she was convinced that Reik was being helpful.

"It is hard in the beginning, I know," she said. "Everything
in you fights against it. Then you begin to have a better picture of yourself. Analysis does not solve everything. It merely
helps you to understand yourself—what you do, why you do
it—and you start to understand other people and you become
in time more tolerant of them."

I found this true as I continued to see Reik. I no longer resented him and rather, I looked forward to seeing him. Gradually my hatred toward him disappeared and now he became a father image. My father died when I was quite young. I remembered very little about him. But in my sessions with Reik, my father came to life once more and I realized how important he had been to me and how I had repressed his existence and then his death.

"So you have found father," Reik said one afternoon. "He vas not such a bad person, vas he? But you are very moralistic —not in the sense of being moral—you understand, but you set too high standards on yourself. Most people do. Everyone vants to be a Jesus Christ and ven they do not think they are, then they hurt and they punish themselves. Be yourself and accept yourself as you are—that is important, yes?"

All my life, probably because we had so little of it, I had feared the lack of money. In Guatemala, I would have the financial security I had always sought. But now I learned from Reik that there was no security, except in oneself and in what one believes in.

During some trying sessions, Reik would shout out at me: "Vell, so you think you vill end in the poor house. Then I vill go to the poor house vid you. In the poor house they vill take care of you. But is it not a bore to be taken care of? Do you know something? Vell, I vill tell you. Rich people—you know vy they are afraid? Always they fear they vill lose their money. The more money they have, the more they are frightened."

During these sessions that went on, day after day, Dr. Reik never gave advice. Then one day, everything seemed to become clear. I knew we had to leave Guatemala; I must no longer be dependent and lean on my brother. Guatemala had only been a temporary refuge. I had constructed in my unconscious false illusions about it and about my relations with my brother. Suddenly it came out! My brother's illness had probably been imaginary. His wife had left him—he was alone and lonely—he had used his illness as a means to get us to Guatemala and to be with him. Florence had suspected this all along, so had Dag, I was to learn later. But now lying on the couch in Dr. Reik's office I blurted this out.

That evening when we were having a drink before dinner, I told Florence and Dag that we were going to leave Guatemala and the reason for the decision I had reached.

"I have never told you this before," Dag said, "but from the day we arrived I've hated it. I thought you'd be happy there, and so I kept it to myself. I'm glad now we can talk about it."

I have always been close to my wife; I was convinced she had shared my feelings about Guatemala. One thing Reik taught me is how little one really knows about people—even those whom you love and to whom you are very close . . .

Having a first book published can be compared in some respects with having a child. There are doubts and great expectations. What will it look like? How will it be received? What will people think of it?

All the toil, all the months one has worked over it, are forgotten. It comes off the press in huge sheets. They are gathered together, mechanically cut, and then once again, mechanically bound together, and put between hard covers. Finally the dust jackets are slipped on, and the books are stacked up in the bindery to be shipped out.

Yet what a wonderful feeling it is to hold this first book in one's hands, to thumb through the pages, to admire and gloat over it and to walk down the street with the book under one's arm. Then come the days of waiting impatiently for the reviews. What will they say of it? So much depends on the reviews and the attention it receives.

Before the publication date, Reynal gave a party. Book critics, book salesmen, and many others were present, including a few of our friends. There were over a hundred people invited, and they drank and talked while a three-piece mariachi orchestra played Mexican music.

Eugene Reynal did everything he could to promote and introduce the book and during the months I was in New York, I gained an insight into the intricate business of book publishing. The book did better than Reynal expected, but it was far from being a best seller, though most of the reviews were good, including the New York *Herald Tribune,* which devoted an entire page to it.

Not all of my ideas in promoting the book were accepted by Reynal. Brentano's on Fifth Avenue were devoting a window to the book. I wanted to hire a Mexican and have him sitting in front of Brentano's with a serape over his shoulders and a large sombrero and he would be reading a copy of the book. But Reynal vetoed the idea and said it was undignified. Dag and I did visit bookstores, and whenever we saw copies of my Mexican book hidden away in a dark corner, or covered by other books, we surreptitiously brought them to the front.

A few days before Christmas, Reynal gave another party, starting at noon. It was the annual employee Christmas office party. I was invited because, having worked there, I was looked upon as an employee. There was plenty to drink but no music. Then when they were all gathered together, Reynal said he had an announcement to make.

As everyone knew, he said, his partner, Hitchcock, had died the previous year. The firm, Reynal and Hitchcock, had done well, but not well enough. It was losing money. He could no longer, he went on to say, justify its existence. It was merging with another firm. For a few, there might be jobs; for others, they would have to look elsewhere.

There was a depressing silence. I looked over at Reynal. There were tears in his eyes and in the eyes of almost everyone else. We had been invited, I thought, not to a Christmas party, but to a wake. None of them had realized, and neither had I, that my book—my first book—was to be the last one to be published by Reynal & Hitchcock.

"Well, let's get drunk," someone shouted. There was the clinking of glasses. People began talking and murmuring among themselves, first in whispers and gradually the voices grew louder.

I was glad I was having a session with Reik that afternoon. Perhaps he could explain how things like this happened.

Our three months in New York were about over. It was the middle of January and it was snowing and cold. I was on my way to a final session with Dr. Reik before we left for Guatemala.

"So tomorrow you leaf?" Dr. Reik said. "It vill be nice in Guatemala, no? The veather is varm, yes? You vill have a talk vid your brother. Then vat vill you do?"

"I have no idea," I said. "Perhaps return here for a while and then go on to California. I will have to look for a job."

"In San Francisco, perhaps?"

"I guess so," I said. "We will see what happens."

"You do not mind leafing Guatemala?"

"It will not be easy. But I do not mind it now. I think it is the thing to do."

"Vell, perhaps I see you again some day, yes?" Dr. Reik said, and I knew the session was over. I sat upon the edge of the couch but made no effort to move. Dr. Reik also stayed seated, instead of walking to the door as he usually did. This time the parting was not to be so abrupt. He knew I wanted to say something to him.

"I have been here with you close to three months," I said. "You have made many notes while I talked. Am I all right? Do I get some kind of a written report from you?"

"Vat? A written report? That is vat you vant? I give no reports."

"You mean I just leave now—just walk out?"

"You vant a diploma? Something to say how goot a boy you are? But you need nothing. Soon you vill see how vell you vill feel. Later you vill understand things better. I have done nothing. Perhaps my intuition—my third ear, I call it—has helped a liddle bit. Who knows? Only you. You feel bad about going, yes? You should not."

He took out a cigarette and began puffing on it. "I vill tell you a liddle story, yes? Ven I decided to go avay from Vienna, I vent to see Freud. I knew I vould never see him again. I felt very sad, for I had been vid him for many years. He knew how I felt. So Freud, he says to me: 'Reik, I tell you something. One does not have to be glued to one another to belong to each other.' Yes, that is vat Freud said to me. I repeat it for you. One does not have to be glued to one another to belong to each other. The trouble vid people is they vish to be too possessive—to be glued together. It is not goot."

He started walking across his office and I followed him.

"Vell, have a nice trip," he said at the door.

I went down the dark hall, rang for the elevator. It took a long time for it to reach the eighth floor. I got in.

"It's beginning to snow again," the elevator operator said.

I nodded and put on my heavy coat. I started down the street, the snow falling softly against my face. For three months, Dr. Reik had assumed the role of my father, and I was leaving him. A feeling of sadness and great emptiness came over me. Dr. Reik had opened a window into the past and now I saw everything differently and with deeper understanding.

CHAPTER TWENTY

All Twelve Survived

Everything, given time, Dr. Reik had once said to me, re-
solves itself soon enough. "The problems of others—vat are
they? They are not yours. No one is Gott. So, it is vid your
brother. He must make his own life—yes?"

During the months we had been away, my brother had
met a young and attractive Guatemalan girl. He had pro-
posed to her and by the time we returned even the date for
the marriage had been decided upon. His marriage also meant
that it would be easier for us to leave Guatemala—we would
not be leaving him alone. He had solved his own problem.
We had our own now to work out.

The wedding took place in the town of Tecpán in the
Guatemalan highlands where the bride's family lived. Her
friends and her family had prepared for it some time in advance. They had laid freshly cut pine needles in the patio
and on the floors of the house. It created a festive atmosphere,
and there was a wonderful fragrance in the air. From the
moment of our arrival in the late afternoon until the early
hours of the morning, there was marimba music and the long
tables of food, decorated with banana leaves, were replenished
continuously. Half the people from the town seemed to be
there; they sang and they danced, and there was the constant
popping of champagne corks throughout the evening.

My brother was happier than I had ever seen him. And, why shouldn't he be, Dag said—he was in love; it brought about a remarkable change in him. His young wife was strong willed and determined to bring contentment into his and her life, but like all Guatemalan women, she also appeared flexible enough to bend to his ways. It would not be easy for her, but we felt she could do it and that we were leaving him in good hands.

Time went quickly then. We were selling most of our furniture and packing only a few things to which we had become attached. The orchid collection was of considerable concern to Dag. She had taken the necessary precautions and had written to the United States Department of Agriculture asking permission to bring the plants with us. They had sent the necessary tags to attach and had assured her there would be no difficulty.

Then she learned that there was a Guatemalan law which prohibited the export of orchids without a special permission which was not readily granted. But just when it seemed a hopeless undertaking, the United States Air Force attaché came to the rescue.

"Give 'em to me," he said. "I'll fly 'em to Puerto Barrios and then put 'em on a boat for you."

And thus, the orchids reached the cabin of the S.S. *Talamanca*. They were there in six big cartons when we came on board.

As the ship pulled out, I wondered when, if ever, I would see my brother again. I thought of Guatemala and how loath one is to depart from the country of one's birth. Then as I stood by the ship's railing, watching the shoreline disappearing, I could hear Dr. Reik's reassuring voice: "You are not a child any more. Vat is that you leaf behind—the umbilical cord? Vat goot is that? You vill see—you vill start out fresh wid everything new before you. Vat is there to worry about— the future? You have done vell in the past—you vill do vell again. So, you leaf Guatemala—you start a new life. It is goot—very goot—to make the change."

It was a hot June day when the S.S. *Talamanca* tied up at the pier in New York. Dag was happy about the warm weather.

"It is exactly what the orchids need," she said.

We went through customs quickly, but then two inspectors from the United States Department of Agriculture moved in on us.

"We can't let these plants go through without placing them in quarantine," one of them said. "They'll have to be taken to the quarantine station in Hoboken."

"But the Department of Agriculture told us we would have no difficulty in bringing them in," Dag protested.

"Maybe so, lady," the inspector said, "but we got no authority to pass them. Besides, they are going to be fumigated —they have to be. They may be full of bugs."

"They are clean, healthy orchids!" Dag spoke up, her voice rising, "and if you fumigate them—why—why, you may kill them!"

"Sorry, lady, but that's what's got to be done," and he started to write out a card. "Here's a receipt. Pick 'em up in Hoboken in a week's time."

Florence had been waiting, and she now greeted us as we came through.

"What happened?" she asked. "They cleared all the passengers but you. They said you were being held in quarantine; are you all right?"

A week later we went on the ferry boat to Hoboken and then in a taxi to the quarantine station of the U.S. Department of Agriculture. We presented the receipt given to us at the pier and were taken down a hall and to a back room. The orchids were there spread out on newspapers and on tables. They looked drab and lifeless. Dag took one glance at them and then she turned to the agriculture inspector.

"You killed them!" she said. "You've poisoned them!"

The inspector was kind and understanding.

"I admit they don't look too good," he said. "But orchids are hearty. Maybe with proper care some of them will come through."

We placed the orchid plants in the cartons and brought them to Florence's apartment where we were staying. Only a dozen or so survived and the rest, gathered in the highlands and the tropical jungles of Guatemala, went down a Park Avenue garbage chute. If they had to be buried, I said, at least they went to their final resting place in style. It was not, Dag commented, a very amusing observation.

Now that we were in the United States for good—or so we thought—we wanted above all to feel again like Americans. So we did everything that was typically American. We bought a Ford automobile, took in a baseball game, ate hot dogs, and even went to the Brooklyn Zoo. Finally we drove across the country and through the middle west. We sat at lunch counters, drank milk shakes, ate hamburgers and apple pie.

On crossing the border into California, we ran into trouble.

"What's that you got in the back seat?" the border inspector asked suspiciously.

"Just a few orchids," Dag replied.

"Don't you know you can't bring plants from another state into California?" the inspector said.

"They are not from another state," she explained; "they are from Guatemala and have been thoroughly inspected and fumigated by the United States Department of Agriculture." She reached for her purse and brought out the papers that had been officially stamped in Hoboken.

The inspector went over the documents. "Sure, they got

the approval from the U.S. people," he said, "but that don't mean they can come into California. Who knows what bugs they picked up on the way 'cross country? Sorry, but they can't come in. They haven't a clean bill of health, as far as this state is concerned."

The twelve surviving orchids that Dag had taken so much care of on the trip were now removed from the car.

"What are you going to do with them?" she demanded.

"They got to be inspected and left in quarantine."

"Not again!"

"Yes, ma'am—for at least a week or so."

"You won't let them through?"

"Sorry, ma'm. I just can't."

"Where can we pick them up?"

"I'll give you this address. You get in touch with 'em in a week or so, and they'll tell you where they will be. Okay, now. You can pass on."

We left the orchids, our last link with Guatemala, at the border. We drove on through Southern California and up north and by the Big Sur country. At Parkington Ridge we drove up the steep hillside to visit Maud Oakes, whom we had known in Guatemala and who was living in a house next to Henry Miller. We stayed with Maud for three nights, then went on the coast road toward Monterey.

On the Monterey Peninsula we saw Sam Morse again, and many of our former friends. But somehow, everything had changed; It wasn't at all as it used to be. We found it even difficult to keep up a conversation with our friends.

"You must have had some interesting experiences," one of them said, "and you must be glad to be back in God's country and away from all that filth and dirt in Mexico. Was it as bad in Guatemala?"

At first, when we heard these comments, we tried to tell them about Mexico and Guatemala. But after a while, we knew we were not getting through to them. They would have to find out for themselves. Everyone made an effort to be friendly and kind, but we felt out of step; it was we who had changed and who had to readjust our lives and our thinking.

We drove to San Francisco, but after being away eight years it was not the San Francisco we knew. Everywhere there were freeways, and more being constructed; on sand dunes, where I had played as a youngster, there were now subdivisions. We were waking up from a Rip van Winkle dream and the reality, for the moment, frightened us. Why had we returned? Clearly, we no longer belonged here, we thought.

Nevertheless we rented a furnished flat overlooking the Bay and the bridges, and just a short distance from Fishermen's Wharf. We'd go to the Wharf to buy fresh crab, clams and shrimp, and frequently we'd walk through Chinatown or over to Columbus Avenue towards the Italian section where there was even a drugstore that sold leeches. Gradually we began to get into step and to accept the difference between living in the United States and abroad.

One afternoon when I walked into the flat, Dag's face was glowing and she seemed happier than I had seen her in a long time.

"Guess what?" she greeted me. "Look over there—on the table."

Then I saw them. Her orchid plants.

"They finally shipped them. All twelve survived."

It was difficult in the beginning, but after I had opened my office as a public relations consultant, business began coming my way and we soon had all the clients we needed. On weekends we visited our friends, Frank and Toni Bartholomew, whom we had met during our early days in Carmel. He was still with United Press, and about to become president. They had purchased land in Sonoma, fifty miles north of San Francisco, in the Jack London country. They had a vineyard and an old historic winery called Buena Vista, where some of California's best wines had been made before the turn of the century. It was Barth's dream to produce fine wines again.

We'd often spend weekends in their remodeled red barn and we'd have drinks at Jack's Old Fashioned Bar in an ancient wooden building on the town's square. Jack made the best old fashioneds we'd ever had.

We were determined that we were going to stay permanently in San Francisco; our days of living abroad were over and so, when a twenty-acre ranch, adjoining the property of the Bartholomews' became available, we bought it. There was an abandoned pear orchard in the front part, and in the back was a grove of oaks and madrones and a chicken house. The chicken house was falling apart, but it had been constructed of redwood. Dag thought of making it into a weekend cottage until we decided to build a house. Almost every Saturday and Sunday we would drive to Sonoma where we talked of what we were going to do with our newly acquired property.

Then a letter arrived at the office. I opened it, read it, went over it a second time and then phoned home.

"There's a letter from the State Department," I said.

"What do they want?" Dag asked.

"It's very flattering," I said.

"Then, they must be after something."

"They want me."

"You?"

"Yes."

"No!"

"Yes."

"The hell with them."

"That's what I think."

"Why should they write you now?"

"They need someone in Brazil. They came across my records and that letter Uncle George wrote long ago—seems to have impressed them. They think I would make a good diplomat. They want me to join the Department and then go on to the Embassy in Rio."

"Brazil?"

"Yes, Brazil."

"You're going to turn them down, I hope," Dag said.

"Sure. Don't want any part of it."

"I agree," she said with considerable relief.

"I'll bring the letter home and you can read it. If they had sent it a year ago when we were still in Guatemala we might have accepted. But not now. You in accord?"

"I certainly am. I don't want to leave the United States again. Besides we have the ranch and we are going to remodel the chicken house."

That evening we had some drinks and then I brought out the letter.

"You sure you want to turn it down?" Dag now asked.

"It would be fun to be a diplomat, and Brazil sounds interesting," I said.

"It would be crazy."

"I know. But it still is nice to be wanted."

"You and the State Department would never get along."

"I agree."

"You plan to answer them?"

"I'm going to send them a wire turning them down."

"When?"

"Right after we have another drink."

We had the drink, and then we wrote out a telegram and telephoned it in to Western Union. After dinner we went to bed early and went right to sleep. But I woke up. Dag was also awake.

"You're restless," she said.

"A little."

"You are sure you didn't want to go to Brazil?"

"I'm sure. Even if I did, it's now too late. They'll have my telegram."

It was after eight the next morning and we were having breakfast when the telephone rang. I picked up the receiver; it was long distance.

"They're calling from Washington," I said.

"What are you going to tell them?"

"I don't know."

"You really want to go to Brazil, don't you?"

"How about you?"

"Why not? If that's what you want to do."

The plane for Washington was late and we sat in the bar at the airport with Frank and Toni Bartholomew who had come to see us off.

"What are you going to do with your Sonoma property?" Frank asked.

"What can we do?" I said. "Just let it stay there until we get back."

Frank ordered a second round of drinks.

"The pear orchard isn't worth anything," he went on. "I could have our foreman run a bulldozer through it and yank the old trees out."

"That's not such a bad idea," Dag said.

"After we clear out the orchard," Frank said, "we could plant wine grapes. By the time you returned you'd have a vineyard producing grapes."

"What kind of grapes?" Dag asked.

"Traminer and Riesling," Frank said. "They're the best white wine grapes and they will do well on your land."

"You could even make some wine for us from our grapes, couldn't you?" I said.

"Sure, we could," Frank said.

"I hope," said Dag wistfully, "they're the kind with leaves that turn red in the fall."

Just then the departure of our plane was announced and we walked out to the airport gate.

On the plane I thought about our two years in San Francisco and the lucrative income I was giving up for a diplomat's modest salary. Friends and clients were against the decision we had made. "You can go away once," one of them had said, "but not twice and expect to return and pick up where you left off."

I knew that, but I had no intention of returning. I was now in the diplomatic service and we planned to stay in it for the rest of our lives. Working for the United States, selling our way of life to people of other countries, was important and much more satisfying than the corporate public relations work I had been engaged in.

It had not been an easy decision: at age forty-four one shouldn't just pull up roots and go off to a foreign country, knowing little of what to expect. For Dag it was probably much more difficult than for me. But she, too, had an adventurous spirit.

From the window of the plane we had our last glimpse of the Golden Gate and San Francisco Bay. When would we ever see it again?

CHAPTER TWENTY-ONE

Friends of the Tiger

The two assistant secretaries of state took me into the holiest of sanctums in Washington for lunch; the private dining room in the State Department building. There was Dean Acheson, the Secretary of State, sitting at a table near us; a little later I was introduced to him. He seemed pompous and as cold as a New England cod. What a difference, I thought, between him and Nelson Rockefeller.

I was to have two weeks of briefing before we left for Brazil. But the foreign service officers I talked with had little to tell me about Brazil, of our objectives there, or of what was expected of me. They agreed that the Communist threat in Brazil was serious and that something had to be done about it. Yet they had no plan worked out as how best to combat Communism.

"You'll just have to feel your way and do the best you can," I was told, and assured that I would have unlimited funds available and no interference.

Perhaps it was intuition, or just plain common sense. But I didn't like the whole thing. That noon, while having lunch in the State Department building, I knew I had made a mistake. I never should have left San Francisco.

Before our ship sailed for Brazil, we stayed with Florence

in New York, and I saw Reik twice. "Vell, so you tink you make the vrong decision—vy, vy? Tell me."

I told him.

"Who knows vat is the right or vize decision?" he said. "It vill be a new experience for you, yes? A new experience is goot for the heart. You vill see—it vill vork out."

It was cold and bitter that February morning as the ship left New York. In the dining room they sat us at a table with a Brazilian army general and his wife. They spoke some English and he gave me my first lessons in Portuguese.

"When I get to Rio," he said one evening, "I don't know whether they are going to throw me in jail, or run me for the presidency." Eventually he did run for the presidency, and almost made it.

There were few interesting people aboard ship. The Americans returning to Brazil hated the thought of going back. There are two kinds of weather in Brazil, we were told—hot and hotter. "Why does anyone want to live in that country?" the head of a U.S. corporation who had been in Brazil for 17 years said one night.

The ship's captain invited us for cocktails and dinner. "I just never get off the ship in Brazil," he said. "Now, in Argentina everything is different."

"Too bad you're going to Brazil—you won't like it," said the ship's barber cutting my hair. "Rio is a dirty, smelly city and most of the people are colored. I'll take Argentina any day."

I could never understand why Americans prefer police states, like Argentina or Spain. Cleanliness, I thought, was no compromise for dictatorship.

At seven in the morning, the day we arrived, I was up on deck. There was a heavy fog. The Brazilian general was up early, too. "Whenever it is foggy, it is terribly hot in Rio," he said. "It is going to be an awful day."

At breakfast the waiter said, "You better eat plenty; you won't be eating breakfasts like this in Rio."

About eight o'clock the fog lifted. Now we began sailing through the bay and we could see the skyline of Rio and Sugar Loaf.

"It looks beautiful," Dag said, and she gripped my hand reassuringly.

Protocol is the lifeblood of the State Department; to maintain protocol a diplomat will hide his resentment and do about everything that's expected of him. I was arriving in Rio with the title of Counselor of Embassy, which put us high in the Embassy hierarchy—just under the Minister-Counselor. This meant that we out-ranked most of the foreign service officers in the Embassy and they wouldn't like it.

But they were there on the pier that morning to welcome us, all smiles, bright with friendship, and quite ready, I was certain, to plunge a knife into my back at the first opportunity. Among them was one friend I could count on—Paxton Haddow, now a foreign service officer, who had worked for me when I headed the Rockefeller office in Mexico. There was also a man I liked right away, Al Neto, a Brazilian who was with the Embassy.

We found Rio and Brazil a pleasant surprise to what we had been told in Washington and aboard ship. Our hotel room was clean, the food excellent, the service impeccable. Apartments were difficult to find, but Paxton had located just what we wanted in one of the best buildings in Copacabana. It was spacious, overlooked the beach, and the cross current ventilation kept it cool.

Brazilian Portuguese is a language all its own. Our fluent Spanish helped, but not enough. The Brazilians could understand our Spanish, but we could not understand them. In time our ears became accustomed to these new sounds. We took lessons and also met many Brazilians.

We thought it important to know the language, the people,

and the country. Brazilians were different from the Mexicans; they seemed not as melancholy nor as repressed. Over the centuries there had been a harmonious blending of blacks and whites which was fully accepted. It was a *café au lait* culture. Our cook, Béni, was black, the granddaughter of a slave; our maid, Maria, was light. They shared the same room and they were friends.

While Mexico has gone through years of blood-drenching revolutions, wars, and social conflicts, there had been no great upheaval in Brazil, and seldom did it even resort to the firing squad. Mexican music is sad and has a mournful quality; Brazilian music is gay and stimulating. There is also nothing to equal Rio's carnival—rarely are there quarrels, knifings, or shootings and practically no drunks are to be found on the streets. The majority of Brazilians drink little and when they do, they prefer beer to *cachaça,* the native distilled hard liquor.

Copacabana is probably the finest beach in the world and it was at our front door. Each morning we rose early, played beach tennis, and swam in the ocean. Sometimes after a storm, we looked for mussels that washed in. We bought shrimp and fish from the fishing boats that came in during the morning hours. On the hills, behind the luxury apartment buildings, were the *favelas* where the poor lived. No white man, it was said, dared go there.

We were fascinated by Brazil and wanted to know more about it. Al Neto introduced us to Brazilians and we began making friends. One of them was in the Ministry of Education and we persuaded him to take us to a *macumba,* a native witchcraft ceremony. Although Brazil is a Catholic country, only a small minority go to church. Large segments of its population still practice voodooism and worship *Xango,* a legendary god. A *macumba* is a part of this voodooism.

Our friend warned us that it might be dangerous to go, that anything could happen, but we went anyway.

Around nine o'clock, we drove to a poor section of Rio, parked the car and walked for about half a mile. We reached a backyard and stood looking in the window of a room crowded with about twenty Negroes. The men, dressed in silk pajamas, were on one side; the women in sleezy silk or rayon dresses were on the other side. The master of ceremonies was very light in color, almost white. The *macumba* began when a huge fat Negro woman, puffing at a big cigar, started to moan and to cry out. Every minute the intensity of her voice increased. The group in the room passed by her and prostrated themselves on the floor before her. At the snap of her fingers they would be up on their feet, shouting, screaming, and singing.

Then a little man appeared in the middle of the group and he soon was dancing hysterically, jumping into the air, and at other times falling to the floor. He was the devil, we were told. This was the signal for everyone to participate more actively, singing, dancing, screaming, and sometimes barking like dogs. After a while, we walked quietly away, content to be back in the car.

Next I wanted to visit the *favelas*, to talk with the people. Once again, a Brazilian friend paved the way and we spent hours in the dingy houses, made of every possible material available. We never once were frightened or threatened; the people sensed that we were there as friends. They talked and they laughed, and a few sang and played guitars and drums for us. While they were poor, many had talent. The best samba songs for carnival almost always come from the *favelas*.

There was one group of Brazilians we did not meet. Among them were Candido Portinari, Brazil's leading painter, and Oscar Niemeyer, the famed architect who was to design Brasilia. They were considered Communists and not to be approached; we were not to be seen in their company. One evening at a party we met Dorival Caymi, who has written some of Brazil's best folkloric music. He sang and played on a guitar for us and later told me how much he wanted to go to the United States. I said I would do what I could.

Next day when I mentioned his name at the Embassy, I was informed that Dorival had been a member of the Communist party ten years previously.

"But he's not a member now," I protested, "nor has he been for years. How can we ever win these people over if we slam the door right in their faces?"

The American Consul was sorry. It was not he, he said, who made these decisions; it was Washington. I wrote a dispatch to the State Department, pointing out the importance of cultural exchange, of getting Brazilian intellectuals to know America and our way of life. Is our democracy so weak, have we so little faith in it, that it will topple because we let a few former Communists in? No answer came from Washington, nor did I expect one.

We had been in Rio but a few months, when Artur Rubenstein, on a concert tour of South America, telephoned at the suggestion of Nelson Rockefeller. We invited him to the apartment for cocktails. He was a small man, with tremendous energy and enthusiasm and a wonderful sparkle in his eyes.

We spoke of many things, and then rather naïvely (for I know little about music) I asked him about Heitor Villa Lobos and what he thought of him as a composer. We thought Rubenstein was going to jump through the ceiling.

"Good God, don't you know that Villa Lobos is one of the greatest contemporary composers?" he exclaimed.

Through Rubenstein we met Villa Lobos, who liked us from our first meeting. We developed a friendship that continued during the two years we were in Rio; hardly a week passed that he and I did not have lunch. We seldom talked about music and perhaps that was a welcome relief. Our conversation, however, touched on everything else, including why Brazilians prefer brunettes to blondes.

"We Brazilians are a mixture of color, predominantly on the dark side," Villa Lobos said. "We are not ashamed of it and blondes are not to our taste. They appear cold and foreign to us. But you Americans want to be dark skinned, too—if this is not so, why do so many Americans spend hours on the beach and in the sun, trying to get tan? 'Look how brown I am,' you say—is that not curious for a people who have so little tolerance for the Negro?"

On occasions we went to concerts with him and his wife, and also to one when he conducted the symphony orchestra playing only his music. I remember as he concluded, the perspiration rolled down his face, and the audience rose to its feet shouting and applauding.

Later that evening he said almost sadly, "This is the first time a Brazilian audience has fully accepted my music."

One night, about midnight, Paxton Haddow, Dag and I went into a *boite,* or night club in Copacabana. We ordered drinks and listened to music. I glanced about and saw at the table next to us a Brazilian man and a young, attractive woman. They seemed bored, and as I sometimes do, I began talking to them. Within a few minutes they joined us; we danced and sang to the music, and we probably drank more than we should have. It was four in the morning when we ended up in our apartment. Our new friend was one of Rio's leading attorneys; the girl was his mistress, and they were quite frank about it. I told her I wanted to know more about Brazilians.

"I live with my parents," she said, "why don't you all come for lunch next Sunday? We will have a typical Brazilian dinner."

The following Sunday we were there. It was a small but tastefully decorated apartment, and both her father and mother knew about her friendship with the attorney. For lunch, served about two, we had a *feijoada completa,* which is made of black beans, salt pork, dried meat, sausages, tongue, pork ears, pig tails, and ground mandioca. When well prepared, it is delicious and as Brazilian as Brazil. Later, after brandy with our coffee, she said:

"Antonio is going to invite you to a party he is giving at his home in Petropolis. You must accept and you will meet his wife."

Then she told us that along with many rich Brazilian women, his wife often telephoned Christian Dior in Paris to buy clothes from him.

In about a week a formal invitation came for the party. Many rich and not too rich Brazilians have weekend homes at Petropolis, because it is at an altitude of several thousand feet, much cooler and only a little over an hour and a half from Rio by car.

Upon arriving around nine o'clock, Paxton, Dag and I went into the huge hall. The party was formal and the butlers were in tails and white gloves. Already about a hundred people were there and in one of the reception rooms was the great-grandson of Dom Pedro, the last emperor of Brazil. We watched Brazilian women in their expensive gowns, curtsy to him and his wife; after all these years he was still addressed as "Your Highness."

Our host met us and introduced us to his wife, who appeared most pleasant.

"You look so wonderful in your Dior gown," I complimented her in Portuguese.

She was flattered. "How observing of you to recognize a Dior dress—so few men do. Come, you must join me for a toast of champagne."

I went off with her and we were joined by others. Soon I was drinking champagne and talking to a delightful woman

in her early thirties, rather slim and looking much younger.
The music had started playing and people were dancing.

"Do you samba?" she said.

"Not well."

"But you will samba with me?"

"Of course."

We went onto the dance floor and almost at once I noticed
people watching and giving us plenty of space in which to
move around. I could see they were staring at us. What was
I doing wrong?

Finally the music came to an end. I thanked her and
brought her back to the table. We had another glass of
champagne and I made as quick a get-away as I could, and
then ran into Paxton.

"Do you know who you were dancing with?" she asked.

"No," I shook my head.

"You are in, and how!" she said. "That's the daughter of
President Vargas and, they say, the real power behind him.
Also, her husband happens to be governor of the State of
Rio."

Occasionally it was fun, and at times we felt important
when we received invitations to receptions to various embassies including the French, British, and Indian. But we
also worked hard, as did some members of the Embassy
staff often until ten or eleven at night. With Al Neto's help
we had news and other informational radio programs on
several hundred stations at peak listening hours, following
a pattern we had started in Mexico. We cooperated with the
Ministry of Education and began an intensive exchange program; one of those who came from the United States was
Richard Feynman. He loved to samba and to play the bongo
drums. He was young, but already a top flight scientist but
we never thought that some years later this bongo drum
player would win the Nobel Prize.

We also brought Robert Frost, Louis Bromfield and, most important of all, Cardinal Spellman to Rio.

The Cardinal was astute in everything he did, from giving interviews to talking with Brazilians. One night in Rio's largest auditorium Catholic dignitaries were gathered from many parts of Latin America. Cardinal Spellman was to be the principal speaker. With him was a Monsignor, his assistant, and the Brazilian Foreign Minister. I sat in the box to the right of the stage with them. When it came time for Cardinal Spellman to speak, we left the box and accompanied him to a wing of the stage. After he finished and we started walking back to the box, he said he felt tired. He gave his cardinal cloak and hat to the Monsignor.

"You be Cardinal for the rest of the evening," he said, and went off to a waiting car. I returned to the box with the Monsignor and sat through the next hour and a half of talks.

Dag was in the audience and when I later joined her she said: "Toward the end, Cardinal Spellman looked terribly fatigued."

"That wasn't Spellman," I said. "That was his stand-in."

I knew when I went to Washington that I had made a mistake; I was not cut out to be a diplomat. To a foreign service officer, which I was now, the State Department is something of a mythical oracle which can do no wrong and which moves in mysterious ways, often groping in the dark for answers that are not there. A good and faithful diplomat worships at this prismatic shrine, accepts his role and never complains. He follows the Department's policy: "It's safer to do nothing."

But I couldn't conform and neither could Dag to the ways of the foreign service and the Embassy. So, while in Brazil I did what I thought was right, and more often than not I became angry at the stupidity of high ranking priests in

Washington. Dag shared this anger with me, bravely and understandingly, and we fought back until eventually we realized it was futile.

There is a saying in Brazil: *amigo da onza,* friend of the tiger. Well, the tigers in striped trousers were after me and I did not do a thing to stop them. It didn't matter. Long before, we had made up our minds that we were going to quit at the end of two years and return to San Francisco.

In November it was announced that Secretary of State Dean Acheson was coming to Brazil. It was to be the first official visit by an American Secretary of State in Brazil's history.

An advance brigade of Washington experts arrived to prepare for the visit. I sat in on one long conference after another. They planned a white-tie reception at the Embassy residence. I protested, pointing out that the *gran finos,* or rich Brazilians, were already on our side. Our appeal should be broader and geared more to the common people. I was outvoted.

Secretary Acheson arrived in the President's plane from Washington. We formed a cortege of cars and the whole thing looked as if we were going to a funeral.

We had lunch at the Embassy and then I spent an hour with Acheson, briefing him on what kind of local questions he would be asked at the news conference that had been scheduled. I have said that Acheson was as cold as a New England cod. He lived up to that description at the news conference. He spoke down to the forty people who were there. He acted as if he was doing them a favor to answer their questions. There was no warmth, no understanding— and the Brazilians knew it.

The following evening was the white-tie reception. All the industrialists, all the rich Brazilians were there, with the women in French gowns. There were no union leaders, no prominent educators, no writers, no artists, and even Villa Lobos was scratched off the guest list.

Two weeks later the Ambassador called me to his office in the late afternoon. I liked him and we got along well, though often I felt sorry for him as I knew how he had been pushed around by Washington. He had never married; his mother lived at the Embassy residence and there were few decisions he made without consulting her. As I came in, he asked me to sit down. We talked about many things, for he was well informed and understood Brazil better than Washington did.

But I could sense that he was concerned and I intuitively anticipated what he was about to tell me—it had been coming for a long time.

"Washington wants me to quit, don't they?"

"Well, not exactly," he said, searching for the right words. "They would like to have you go to Europe for a few months and talk with our foreign service officers there, and visit and report on our information centers."

"What have they against me?" I demanded.

"Nothing really—except you are always with Brazilians and you seldom mix with the Americans here."

"But, being with Brazilians—knowing what they think, what they feel—is essential. Do you know," I went on, "that your Minister–Counselor hates Brazil and considers Brazilians just a bunch of blacks? I am certain you are aware that your first secretary who is writing political dispatches to Washington can hardly speak Portuguese. And I guess not even the greatest optimist could say that Acheson's visit was an overwhelming success. He should have stayed home."

"These matters are beyond my control," the Ambassador went on, almost pleading for understanding.

"You could protest."

"It would be to no avail."

"All right. When do they want me to go."

"By early December."

He got up and shook my hand. Always a diplomat, he said, "I am giving a reception in your honor next Friday."

I picked up Paxton Haddow and Al Neto in their offices, and we went to the apartment to join Dag. We talked about it over some drinks. But there was really not much to talk about. My days as a diplomat were about over and Dag and I felt relieved. Soon now, very soon, we would be free to say whatever we wanted and go wherever we chose.

CHAPTER TWENTY-TWO

It Was Snowing in Norway

Just before we left Brazil we gave a dinner for Villa Lobos and invited a number of our Brazilian friends and members of the diplomatic corps, including our Ambassador. We had arranged to have some of the compositions of Villa Lobos played, and as the coffee and brandy were being served I asked him if he would make a few remarks about his music.

He was shy and seldom talked in public, but he was apparently enjoying the small group and he liked the dessert so much, Dag told me later, he had asked for a second helping. The Maestro rose to his feet, then selecting French as the language in which he would be best understood by everyone, he said:

"People talk in order to conceal what they are really thinking. But music is the only truthful avenue of communication that has ever been created. It does not come from the mind, but from the heart. It conceals nothing and there is no language barrier. My music has been inspired by the folk songs of Brazil and the sounds of the jungle—there is nothing as beautiful as the jungle in the early hours of the morning or in the late afternoon, after the sun has gone away for the night. The music I have composed is but an interpretation of the sounds and rhythms of the jungle. I am a religious man. I have also been influenced by Bach; of course some of my music *c'est moi*."

We were the only Americans on the French ship going from Brazil to Europe. Because it was off-season we were given a spacious cabin and we also had an opportunity to practice our French. The food could not have been better, and vintage wines were offered at reasonable prices.

We had good weather, but as we approached Marseilles it turned cold; after two years in the tropics, we felt the icy wind cutting through us.

We arrived late in the day and after clearing customs, went from bar to bar, drinking hot coffee and brandy and trying to keep warm while we waited for the train to Paris. We had a leisurely dinner and finally when it was close to midnight we drove in a taxi to a small railroad station on the outskirts of Marseilles where we picked up the *train bleu*.

We were in Paris the next morning eating croissants and drinking *café au lait*. Later in a taxi loaded with our baggage we went to a small hotel, the Castiglione on Rue Faubourg Saint Honoré, a short distance from the American Embassy. How wonderful it was to be in Paris—the gray skies, the old buildings, French policemen with white gloves directing traffic, the smart shops, the crowded sidewalks, and the men and women in heavy coats. It was all so new to us, so different from Rio. In our room were flowers from our friend Serge Arvengas, whose father had been the French Ambassador to Brazil. Serge invited us to his apartment where we had dinner together.

We were in Paris only briefly, for we had plans to spend Christmas in Norway.

Always in the past, it had been trips and long stays in Latin America. Now it was time for Dag to go home—to visit the country of her own people.

We arrived in Oslo the night before Christmas Eve; in

our hotel room we found a small Christmas tree and fresh fruit and candy. The following day I reported in to the Embassy as I had done in Paris, and spent most of the day there. I returned with two bottles of Scotch, for all the bars in Oslo would be closed during the holidays.

As we were having a drink and eating our open face sandwiches sent up by the management, Dag heard music and the clapping of hands. She said, "They are going around the Christmas Tree. Let's go and see."

We left our room to find the gathering, only to be told that it was a private party for the hotel employees and their families. But they suggested that we go to a balcony where we could watch. A hundred people or more were seated at tables while the children joined hands and went around the decorated tree, singing traditional Christmas songs. Everyone was drinking chocolate with whipped cream and eating Christmas cookies. Then came the big moment with the entrance of the *Jule Nisse* the Norwegian Santa Claus with a pack on his back. He greeted the children who then followed him as he went around the tree.

Later we went for a walk in downtown Oslo. We had the streets to ourselves. We happened on the City Hall, and by the reflected light from the snow we could see the dramatic colored wood sculptures which were on one side of this modernly designed building. We walked back to the hotel, over thick snow, throwing snowballs at each other.

On Christmas morning we went to the Lutheran Cathedral where the Bishop conducted services. It was moving to see these people who had withstood so much from the occupation and who sang with steadfastness and faith.

In the afternoon we took the ski train to Frognesaeteren where we watched people of all ages, from tiny tots with their parents, to teenagers skiing so freely through the pine forest. We had beer and sandwiches in a ski lodge where we were served by an older waitress who told us she had waited on Mrs. Roosevelt and Winston Churchill.

As Dag had not met or corresponded with any of her relatives, she felt it would be an intrusion to call upon them and be entertained on Christmas Eve and Christmas Day. For this reason we waited until the second day of Christmas, as it is called, to visit them. They were most cordial and pleasant although I thought they were rather reserved as compared to our Latin friends. They were interested in modern art, and one had been a tennis champion and the other an amateur exhibition ice skater. We asked Edna, Dag's cousin, at what age their children start skiing.

"As soon as they can stand up, they get on skis, and at three, they go to ski school," she said.

We had dinner with her and her husband and other cousins, and then we left for Denmark, England, and back to Paris.

In Paris we rented a car and drove into the Burgundy wine country. We had reservations in Baune, but before reaching our destination it began to rain so hard that when we came to the town of Saulieu we stopped in front of the Hôtel de la Côte d'Or. It looked modest and almost shabby in appearance, but we decided to spend the night there if they could take us. As it was the middle of January, we had no trouble getting accommodations.

We went to our room, changed clothes, and walked down to the bar. We were having a brandy when a ruddy-faced Frenchman, wearing a white apron and a chef's hat, came to our table. He welcomed us and we invited him to sit. Soon we began discussing what we might have for dinner. At first he suggested *grenouille de brochet*, or a young wild duck.

"*Non*," he finally said, "I think I will prepare you some *gratin de queues d'ecrevisses á la crême*, and to start with perhaps some eggs with ham *á la gelée. Bien?*"

We answered, yes—why not? Another ten minutes went
into talking about the wine. He chose two varieties, one with
the *commencer*, and another with the *entrée*.

"I will have everything ready for you at eight o'clock," he
said, and left us.

"I don't know where we are, but I have a feeling we hit
on something good," I said to Dag, and then told her I was
going upstairs to look up the Hôtel de la Côte d'Or in our
Michelin Guide.

I rushed back in a few minutes.

"It's a three-star place and there are only four restaurants
in all of France with that rating," I said. "And that man we
were talking to must be Alexandre Dumaine, who is considered one of the greatest chefs in France."

It was M. Dumaine, all right, who prepared our memorable
feast. As we sat down in the small dining room, we noticed
that the table cloth and napkins were linen; the silver had
been recently polished; the wine was served in huge wine
glasses. The ham *á la gelée* was delicious and the *queues
d'ecrevisses* were superb. I don't know when we had a better
dinner. For dessert we had chocolate cake made with ground
almonds; as full as we were we had second helpings.

In the morning we bade him goodbye. We asked him for
the names of the dishes we had for dinner, and he wrote
them on a card.

We went on to Italy and to Rome where we met Art
Mencken, who had been on the boat with Spike and me
going up the Pearl River to Canton when we had been
bombed by the Japanese. He was now working for the Embassy. Also in Rome we found Dixon and Lucia Donnelley,
who had been in Brazil about the same time we had been
there. Lucia was Brazilian; her mother was Maria Martins,
a noted sculptor, who was married to the former Brazilian
Ambassador to the United States. Lucia spoke fluent Italian,

Portuguese and French. With Lucia and Dixon we went on to Naples, Sorrento, and Capri.

In each of the countries—France, Sweden, Norway, Denmark, England, and Italy—I spent time in our embassies and consulates, talking to foreign service officers and going over the United States information program being carried out. In some embassies and consulates there were a few dedicated people, working hard to achieve results, but generally receiving little support from Washington and not much understanding of what they were trying to do. These visits were disappointing and discouraging and I was glad when they were over.

Our trip with the Donnelleys was something of a holiday. When we returned to Rome, we booked passage on a small Danish freighter leaving Genoa for New York. On our way to Genoa we stopped for a few days in Florence, in Venice and then in Milan where at La Scala we sat up in the gallery and watched the premiere of Carl Orff's *Trionfo d'Afrodite* with Herbert von Karajan, conducting.

The trip on the Danish freighter, the *Ragnild Torm* was to have taken 12 to 15 days; instead it took 22. For a time we were not certain we would make it at all. Our first stop was at Marseilles where Dag found out they were putting 50,000 gallons of kerosene on the forward deck. Longshoremen lighting and smoking cigarettes walked by the five-gallon tins of kerosene without giving it a second thought.

But it was as friendly a boat as anyone could travel on. Captain Jensen usually had us up in his cabin for aquavit or Scotch at eleven in the morning, and again at five in the afternoon. In between, we'd go down to the engine room and drink Danish beer with the chief engineer.

At Casa Blanca the kerosene was unloaded and less flammable freight was taken on including three passengers. Then we sailed on to Agadir.

Five days after Agadir, somewhere in the middle of the Atlantic, we hit the worst storm of the year head-on. The *Ragnild Torm* rolled and pitched, and on the third night the violence of the storm was so great, we had to hold on firmly to our bunks to keep from being tossed out. I wondered how long the little freighter could take this kind of punishment.

At midnight the ship's whistle began blasting off. It was frightening to hear this ghostly sound in the middle of the Atlantic. If we'd run into trouble we'd have no chance on life boats in a heavy sea. Suddenly there was a knock at our cabin door. We knew what it meant. Into our clothes and up on the deck.

"Yes?" I shouted out.

Then came the reassuring voice of Captain Jensen, telling us that a short circuit had caused the ship's whistle to go off—and the storm, he added, was about over.

When we finally docked in New York, we had become so attached to the *Ragnild Torm* and to Captain Jensen that we hated to get off and face reality again. It was not a pleasant thought, either, of going to Washington, where I would have to resign officially.

All the anger at the State Department which I had repressed for so many months was beginning to come out. We should have recognized China from the very beginning and if we had, the war in Korea might have been prevented. I blamed the State Department for its naïve attitude in the Far East and I was concerned about our attitude toward Latin America; unless we changed our attitudes in dealing with the Latin Americans, we could and will have serious troubles with many of our neighbors. We have, I thought, taken for granted the friendship of countries like Brazil and Mexico and Guatemala. While Dag and I lived there, we saw that the Communists were gradually winning favor.

I wanted to hit back, to tell about the weakness in our foreign policy and of the inadequate representatives we had abroad. Dag knew what I had in mind and she suggested I talk it over with Dr. Reik.

Next morning I went to see that wonderful old man, to tell him everything that had happened and what I planned to do. He listened for a long time and then sat back in his chair.

"So you vish to be Jesus Christ, or perhaps maybe Albert Schweitzer, yes?" he said. "I tink not. No, you vill just go with a smile, shake everyone's hands, and tank 'em. Yes, tank 'em for dat is not vat dey vill expect." Then he went on. "You vill be a bigger man for it—besides, vat goot is a satisfied ego? Vat can you buy vid it? Now you tell me."

Reik sent me to Washington with the youthful confidence of my twenties. I was suave and smiling as I spoke with key people in the State Department. Reik had mesmerized me, or perhaps had just put a lot of common sense into me. I realized later it was wise advice for that was the McCarthy era of witch hunting. Whatever I might have said could have proved damaging and could also have hurt many innocent people in the foreign service.

We returned to New York, had Easter breakfast with Florence, and watched the Easter parade on Fifth Avenue in front of St. Patrick's Cathedral. Several days later we flew back to San Francisco; we were home once again and looked forward to seeing our vineyard in Sonoma.

April can be one of the nicest times in California. As we drove across the Golden Gate Bridge, the Amalfi Drive and Capri couldn't compare with the blues and greens of the sea and the hills.

In the back seat of our car was a lunch basket of fried chicken, pickles, potato salad, and apple pie. We planned to picnic somewhere on the edge of the vineyard, perhaps by the creek which passed through our property. When we arrived in Sonoma, we turned right at the plaza and went up the valley a few miles. Soon we caught the first glimpse of the vineyard. We drove down the roadside, which was full of ruts and puddles. We stopped the car and climbed out.

How different the property looked now. There were no signs of the old pear orchard, and, as far as we could see, there were young vines. We were excited and thrilled. How pleasant and peaceful everything seemed.

"It won't be long," I said, "before we'll be drinking wine from these grapevines. Think of it! Our own wine, just like a French chateau owner!"

I walked into the vineyard and suddenly felt my feet sinking. I was covered with mud to my ankles and had to reach for a grape stake to pull myself out, only to sink again. Then I saw a man a few rows away who had on rubber hip boots. He stopped working and glanced over at me.

"Hey, don't you know better than to walk into a wet vineyard?" he yelled.

I didn't pay any attention to him. I was having a time getting out of the mud, and eventually got back to the solid ground on the road. My shoes, socks, and trousers were thick with mud.

The man left his work and came toward us. "I wouldn't try to wash it off," he said. "In a couple hours you will be able to brush it off."

"Is this vineyard always this muddy?" I asked.

"Sure, whenever we have lots of rain. But by summer the ground will be as hard as rock. Damn fool people put a vineyard here. Should have planted the land in hay and oats. Something useful horses and cattle can eat. Not grapes. Cost too much to take care of 'em."

"You work here?"

"I'm the part-time caretaker. You looking for somebody? Because if you are, there ain't nobody around."

He was short, with a heavy frame and thick arms. He had a ruddy complexion and blue eyes shaded by the turned-down brim of an old felt hat. As he stood there, he lit a half-smoked Italian stogie.

We told him who we were. He didn't crack a smile or show the slightest interest.

"Heard you was coming," he said. "But wasn't expecting you until the weekend. City folks always come on weekends. Not in the middle of the week like you done." Then he added, "Make yourself at home," and went on back to the vineyard.

I had closed my office and given up a lucrative business to go with the State Department. In Brazil our expenses had gone far beyond a diplomat's salary and had cut into our savings. In addition there were the growing costs of maintaining the vineyard. I knew, of course, that it would not be easy to start over again in San Francisco; we might have a rough time of it. Reik had suspected as much and one of his parting remarks had been: "Ven you go to the poor house, I vill go vid you."

It wasn't necessary. As it turned out, the stars were in the right places, and we also had a few good friends who remembered my skills and experience and who recommended me to corporations and industries. In a brief time I was doing much better than before, and I had learned by now to demand and to get larger fees. I had finally come to realize that corporations and others in need of assistance did not seek bargains; they sought performance. Orson Welles once said, "If it is expensive, it's cheap." I remembered that when talking with clients.

It felt good to be successful and after a time not to be concerned about money. As a matter of fact, looking back on the past, money in itself has not been too important to us. Perhaps it was H. L. Mencken, or someone as astute as he who said that any fool could make money, but only a wise man knew how to spend it. Most of my life I have been associated in one way or another with millionaires and more often with multi-millionaires. Yet there is little that they have that we have ever wanted and I believe they must sense this, for suspicious as millionaires are and probably have a right to be, they have trusted and confided in me.

And at times, because money does not bring a feeling of security, I have had to hold their hands and reassure them. When on occasion I have lunch or dinner with them, I usually pick up the check; when I do, their faces glow.

Just a short time ago, I took a multi-millionaire from New York with his son and daughter-in-law for a tour of San Francisco. As we drove on Post Street, I suggested they might like to stop and look around Gump's, a famous San Francisco store. "What for?" he said. "To buy things?"

These are accumulators of money and they have very few, if any outside interests. There are also millionaires who have great dreams. A number of them, such as S. F. B. Morse, Louis Petri, and T. Jack Foster, have been my friends and clients; they are people of warmth and compassion. They are also men of vision. Louis Petri designed and built the first wine ship in the world—a ship which transports millions of gallons of California wine to the East Coast. T. Jack Foster had retired and was living in Pebble Beach when, at the age of sixty, he plunged into the biggest project of his life— Foster City, a 650 million dollar development into which he risked all his own capital and that of his three sons. What makes people turn from security to new ventures that they cannot possibly resist? Are they also searching for something?

Sometimes, I am asked why, knowing so many millionaires, I have never become one. I have a ready answer: I have never made a million. Besides, I don't have the desire nor the drive. Our best investment, it seems to me, has been neither in the bank nor in the stock market, but in ourselves. Florence once said that you get out of life exactly what you put into it. We have, I hope, always done that.

CHAPTER TWENTY-THREE

Tomorrow Is Not Today

For a time my work as a public relations consultant was interesting and occasionally challenging. I was able to help clients in trouble and that in itself had its satisfaction. As important, too, were the many new friends I made. San Francisco was changing fast; the old guard which had for so long controlled and run the city was disappearing. There was a different group moving in, although the scions of the establishment had still much to say about what went on or didn't in Montgomery Street's financial district, the opera, the symphony, the museums, and of course, the Republican Party.

In the beginning I was on the move too much—two or three times a week to Los Angeles, and frequently to New York and Hawaii. In recent years, I have reduced most of this traveling, spending more time in Sonoma, getting away from the telephone and doing some constructive thinking. But I still go to New York and it was on one of these trips that I saw Nelson Rockefeller again. I had tried to do what I could in California to persuade some members of the Republican delegation to come out for Rockefeller instead of Nixon, but I didn't get far.

After Kennedy was elected, Rockefeller was finally being talked about as the logical presidential candidate; some Republicans were even saying nice things about him.

On the day I went to see him he appeared preoccupied and lacked his usual warmth and smile. I was certain something was troubling him and he wanted to talk about it, and yet he didn't. We were together less than ten minutes and I had a terrible letdown feeling when I left him.

That night on the way to the hotel from the theatre, we picked up the New York *Times.* We went up to the room, and as I dropped the paper on the desk, the headline hit hard.

"That's done it!" I said to Dag. "Rockefeller's getting a divorce."

At first Dag couldn't believe it. "He's thrown away all chances of ever becoming President," I said.

"But at least he's being honest about it," Dag said, "although I suppose most Americans won't feel that way."

Whether or not Nelson Rockefeller did the right thing and has not regretted it, only he knows. He would have been great as President, and had he been elected the first time around, there might never have been the Cuban crisis, nor a further involvement in South Vietnam.

The last time we saw Rockefeller was in San Francisco; he was then re-married. We were invited to a reception for him at the St. Francis Hotel. When he saw us he gave me an embrace, a Mexican *abrazo;* and then introduced us to his wife. "These are *really* old friends," he said. He was smiling and there was that wonderful warmth back again. Even so, we thought he was lonely—it is very lonely to be a Rockefeller.

Nelson Rockefeller and I were rather close at one time and we had always been on first name basis; we are about the same age. His brother, Laurance, I hardly know, although for half a dozen years or more we have done the public relations work for the Grand Teton Lodge Company, a part of the Jackson Hole Preserve, Inc., a non-profit operation of which he is president.

One morning in late September, I received a call to fly to Grand Teton National Park in Wyoming. Jackson Lake Lodge, which had been closed for the winter, was being re-opened to take care of President Kennedy and his entourage of some eighty persons, including Cabinet members, Senators and Washington correspondents. I was asked to be there to assist in any way I could.

Raymond C. Lillie, executive vice-president and general manager of the Grand Teton Lodge Company, met me at the airport.

"You've never seen anything like it," he said. "The Lodge is like an armed fortress. There are Secret Service and government people everywhere.

With his wife, Vivian, we went into Jackson, a small frontier town, where I had a quick lunch. Later we went to a western outfitting store where Vivian was having a leather jacket made. They had a large selection of western hats, and I tried some on. There was one I liked. I bought it because I thought it would go well with a suede tie I had purchased at the Christian Dior boutique in Paris the previous year; until now there had never been an appropriate occasion to wear it. I told Ray and Vivian about the tie and we laughed about it.

On the way to Jackson Lake Lodge, Ray described the hush-hush manner in which the President's visit was planned. First, he said, he had received a call from a Jerry Bruno who informed him that he and a group from the White House wanted to visit the park; they would be arriving on September fourth in a military plane.

"I thought there might be eight or ten in the group," Lillie said, "but there were seventeen. As we drove from the airport in the bus, Mr. Bruno looked at his watch and said he wanted to time exactly how long it took to go from the airport to the Lodge."

The visit was short, but before they left they asked for a blueprint of the Lodge. Just before their plane took off, Mr. Bruno told Lillie there was a possibility that the President might come to the Park. This was later confirmed, and the date was set for the twenty-fifth of September. I arrived two days before.

Now, as I walked down the hall to my room, there were two men inspecting an alcove. "I don't think we'd have any trouble here," one of the Secret Service men was saying. "Not even a midget could crawl through that hole."

There was every precautionary and safety measure taken; I was even told that the rangers were being brought in from Yellowstone. The morning President Kennedy was to arrive, we heard that two helicopters had flown in from Washington. One would pick up the White House staff from the airport, and the President would ride in the other. We also learned there would be a helicopter landing rehearsal in the parking area in front of the Lodge.

At three-thirty in the afternoon as Lillie and I were standing in front of the Lodge, a government car arrived from the airport. In the car were the President's valet and two secretaries. A Secret Service man accompanied them up to the President's room, the entrance of which was now guarded by two Secret Service men. The President was due at six o'clock. But at five-fifteen we learned that he was ahead of schedule and would arrive at five-thirty.

At five-twenty-five we saw the first helicopter coming in from Jackson, and it landed in the parking area. Five minutes later, the President's helicopter came in. One of the Secret Service men and Lillie started walking in the direction of the second helicopter, and they reached it just as President Kennedy walked down the small ramp. Lillie shook his hand and they started walking toward the Lodge. As they reached the entrance, Lillie introduced President Kennedy to a small group, including myself.

The President shook hands with each of us and as he came to me I became aware that he was looking directly at me. Then suddenly he was talking to me.

"I like that tie you're wearing," he said. "Where did you get it—here in Wyoming?"

"No, sir," I said. "It's from Christian Dior in Paris."

"I thought so," he laughed, and he went up to his room.

With him in the Presidential party were Pierre Salinger, whom I had known for many years, and Edward P. Morgan, who had been bureau manager for United Press in Mexico during the period we lived there. There were about forty additional correspondents at the Lodge, and I thought Pierre handled them well. He must have been extremely helpful to President Kennedy.

I don't know why I did it, but often I seem to do things on impulse. That evening I took off my suede tie. I went to Lillie's office, got some tissue paper, wrapped it and placed it in a small manila envelope. I gave the package to one of the Secret Service men, for I knew that otherwise the President would never receive it.

The next morning when the President was being photographed on the terrace of Jackson Lake Lodge, he caught a glimpse of me and walked over.

"Thanks a lot," he said, and there was warmth and firmness in his handshake.

I didn't think I had done anything unusual until I returned to San Francisco and told Dag about it.

"You didn't!" she said rather startled.

"But, why not?"

"Because you just don't give the President of the United States a used tie," she said.

A month later, President Kennedy was gone, and somehow the world has never been the same since.

That December we went to visit Paxton Haddow who had resigned from the foreign service and was living in Cuernavaca. We drove on to Taxco to spend the day and have lunch with Bill Spratling. Bill, who is now in his early seventies, came to Taxco in 1933, and did more than anyone else to revive the silver making industry in Mexico. Every Mexican shop that sells silver owes a debt to Bill Spratling who, as Diego Rivera once told us, did more for Mexico than any other American. We had three tequilas before lunch, which consisted of soup and avocado, and *chiles rellenos*.

On the way back to Cuernavaca, I decided we should spend Christmas with my brother in Guatemala. Dag agreed. I sent a telegram, arranged for plane tickets, and went on to Mexico City where we had lunch with Dr. Mario Gonzales-Ulloa, one of Mexico's leading plastic surgeons and a friend of Dr. Eugene Kilgore's in San Francisco. Our lunch began at three and we finished at five. Next day we were in Guatemala with my brother, his wife, and their two children, Alfredito and Anna Cecilia.

We were in Guatemala but a day when Juliana, our former cook and Felipe, who had been our houseboy, came to welcome us with a huge bouquet of flowers and a hand embroidered table cloth. Juliana is of pure Mayan descent and in her native clothes, which she always wears, she possesses great dignity. Felipe had become a tailor and operated a shop with his brothers. They invited us to visit them which we did one afternoon.

Their home was small but immaculate. In one corner of the house, they had arranged a Nativity scene as is the custom during the Christmas holidays. Juliana brought us into a tiny dining room to sit at a trestle table. The tea set was obviously new, a good copy of Spode. She served us tea and home-made cake and cookies. No wife of an Ambassador could have poured tea with more grace than Juliana.

When we were leaving, Juliana said to Dag, "I know you need me and I would be glad to go with you, but I am too old to be of real use. Besides, I can't talk English or read and write."

Juliana broke into tears, and so did Dag; I embraced Felipe and he embraced me. Our visit with them had brought back many memories of our former days in Guatemala.

Our stay with my brother and his family was a pleasant one. On Christmas Eve, various friends came by to leave gifts and join in on a holiday drink. At midnight we had tamales for supper, sent over by Juliana, as well as turkey and other festive dishes.

On Christmas Day, we drove to Antigua, and stopped at a place where Americans seldom go. There they serve such unusual native dishes as *gallo en chicha*, a rooster cooked in native rum; *pepian en espinazo*, a pig's spine in a sauce of toasted squash seeds and chile; *longanizas con chirmol*, sausage in a piquant tomato sauce; there were also *chuchitos* and *enchiladas*. There was a marimba band and it was all very gay and the food delicious.

Eventually we left Guatemala and within an hour by jet plane we were in Merida. Not too far from the hotel we stayed in were the Mayan ruins of Chichén Itza which we had visited years previously with Dr. Sylvanus Morley, who was responsible for their restoration. Next day we went to the Island of Cozumel, off the coast of Yucatán, where the water is of a magnificent aquamarine color. It was at Cozumel that Cortéz and Bernal Díaz landed before going on to Vera Cruz and what was to be the Conquest of Mexico. But today Cozumel is expensive and with hotels for American tourists. We did charter a small one-engine plane and looked over some Mayan ruins we had always wanted to see. On another day in a fishing boat we had the Mexican boys dive overboard for lobster and sea snails, which we later cooked on the beach.

It was early in February when we came back, and San Francisco was cold and foggy. Just before Washington's Birthday, Dag, Gary, from my office, and I drove up into the snow country—Gary to ski and Dag and I to take lessons. We were away for several days and then came back to spend the weekend in Sonoma. Dag seemed tired and not well, and she rested most of Sunday. On Monday morning Gary took her car and later I drove her to San Francisco. As we came up the Waldo Grade approaching the Golden Gate Bridge I realized she was ill, but how ill I had no idea. We went to our apartment on Russian Hill where Dag said she just wanted to rest. I drove to the office and put in a call to Monterey for Mast Wolfson who had been our doctor and friend for many years. Mast suggested that certain tests be made, but there didn't seem to be any urgency about it.

When I phoned later she seemed better. By late afternoon she was feeling bad again; this time I phoned Dr. Eugene Kilgore who joined me at the apartment in a short time. He decided she should go to the hospital for the tests Mast had suggested. Eugene brought in Dr. Joseph Dobos, who examined Dag for over an hour while I waited in the hospital corridor. Both doctors called me in.

Dag was half-sitting up on a gurney. Joe was blunt and came right to the point. Dag had suffered, for reasons that no one can explain, a massive coronary. She took the news calmly and with great fortitude; she seemed then like a Norwegian captain whose ship had run into a storm. All the strength of her Norwegian ancestry was in her face as they wheeled her into Intensive Care.

Eugene drove me to the apartment. We didn't talk for quite a while, and then I said: "How bad is it?"

"Bad."

"What are the chances?"

"Small."

"That bad?"

"Yep."

He pulled up in front of the apartment. "You're all right?"

"Sure, Eugene."

I went into the apartment, poured myself a half a tumbler of Scotch, and drank it down. I had given up smoking, but now I searched in the bureau drawers and found an abandoned pipe and some old tobacco. I poured myself another drink. I thought of Dag and our life together and what it would be without her. I had enough barbituates in the apartment, but then I thought of the rifle and shotgun at the ranch. If I was going to do it, I was going to do it well.

Then Mast phoned from Monterey; he must have suspected how I felt for he talked for a long time.

After a while the phone rang again. This time it was T. Jack Foster, a client and friend. Jack talked to me like a father to his son. It seemed to work; I returned to reality and began to think. Then I remembered John Sampson. He was one of the great heart men in the country and at the time president of the American Heart Association. We had entertained him long ago in Brazil. I reached him by phone that night; he was leaving San Francisco for Chicago, but promised to see Dag before he left.

Next morning when I was at the hospital, Dag was under an oxygen tent; she squeezed my hand and I squeezed hers. "I have no intention of croaking," she said, and after that I knew she was going to fight. Mast, Eugene, and Joe said that was half the battle. But it was going to be a long pull and we all knew it.

Gary was outside waiting in my car and as we drove toward town from the hospital, I asked him to take me to a little Mexican church I knew, not too far from the apartment. He drove me there and I went in.

When I was a boy in Guatemala, my Indian nursemaid, Chenta, would take me to church every morning. But Chenta didn't pray like anyone else. She talked to God as if He were a person; she demanded action and asked Him to get busy and do the things that were necessary. As I sat in the little Mexican church, I remembered Chenta and the way she talked to God. And now I talked to God as she had: "You can't do that to Dag and me. Get busy, before it's too late. But hurry, please hurry . . ."

The following day she was better, so much better in fact that she asked me to get her a copy of Genet's *The Thief's Journal,* and a copy of *Our Lady of the Flowers.* "After all, I might as well get some reading done."

Dag's illness shook me as nothing before had, and yet this was life, full of uncertainties and ever challenging. There are, I am told, two kinds of coronaries—the one you never know you had, and the one from which you recover. It was slow going for her at first, but by summer she was swimming in our pool in Sonoma and in December we went to Paris to spend Christmas in our favorite city—and with two of our favorite friends, Bob and Hélène Gollum. We went to Notre Dame and burned candles for Patricia Johnston and for Linda Capurro, for they had burned candles for Dag when she had been so ill. Then we saw Serge Arvengas and a charming French girl friend, and we all went to a Brazilian night club where a Brazilian musician with his guitar sang and played some of Dorival Caymi's songs.

We also went to Mère Michel's for dinner in her tiny restaurant at 5 rue Rennequen. She remembered us and invited Dag and Hélène into the kitchen to show them how she makes her *omelette soufflé au grand marnier.*

In New York on our return trip we had breakfast at the Plaza and looked out at the park, white and beautiful with snow. While we love Paris, we thought how good it was to be back in the United States; we might someday live abroad again, but we could never be expatriates.

I think of the "to have and to use" philosophy that Dag

evolved long ago and which we try to follow. We never save anything for special occasions; we use our silver and china (some of it almost museum pieces) every day. We drink white wine from our vineyard and the best red wines we can get. We go along whole-heartedly with Michael Arlen who once said, "I want very little in this world. All I want is the best of everything, and there is so little of that."

I have tried to be objective in this now rather long documentary of events that have gone by, but perhaps in summing up I should tell a little more about myself.

It may seem strange to those who have read so far to hear me say that I am shy, yet it is true. I dislike talking to groups or belonging to clubs; I hate the telephone and talking to most people. It is, of course, my curiosity and impulsiveness that compensates for my shyness.

I was eleven when my father died. My father was an adventurer who, at the turn of the century, booked passage on a ship going to Latin America; because Guatemala was the first port, that is where he got off. My mother, born in Guatemala, was seventeen when my father married her. In time he became financially well off and important in Guatemala. His biggest mistake was in returning to the United States where he promptly went broke and died when he learned of it.

My brother, seven years older than I, took on a full-time job while I worked in the afternoons and on Saturdays. It was not enough to get us by. Mother thought of opening a tamale parlor or concentrating on her poker playing—which she had picked up from father, and in which, by now, she had become quite proficient. Her friends told her she put too much butter and chicken into her tamales to make money; so she went to poker games three or four times a week and managed to put me through school from her winnings.

Such ability as I might have in making friends must come

from my mother. She made friends with everyone, including street car conductors on California Street. They would stop the cable car in the middle of our block to let her off. No one could refuse her; everyone did things for her.

She had learned English by going to the movies, and she used movie clichés. If there were difficulties she would say, "but then came the dawn and everything was all right." At almost every turn, the Marines arrived and set things straight. Tom Mix for her was a salad, not a cowboy. She combined words delightfully and she seldom ever got names straight. When she met Dag, whose name is Dagmar, Mother immediately called her Denamark, and Denamark she was after that. To her an onion was the sister of garlic, and one morning I heard her on the telephone telling a friend that her neighbor had turned on the gas on the stove and had "almost become sophisticated."

But there was nothing naïve about her; she was wise in many ways and few people ever impressed her. She enjoyed playing poker more than anything else. Before she died she told me she did not want flowers at her funeral; just decks of cards strewn over her. Unfortunately it was war time and I was away and could not follow her instructions. She died, as she always hoped, playing poker, holding in her hand, I was told, three queens and a pair of tens.

I have missed her; she lived as few people know how to live. If I inherited some of my mother's warmth and her ability to make friends, I also owe to my father his deep interest in reading and his drive for adventure. He taught me early to be appreciative of other people.

When we are not in San Francisco or off somewhere, we enjoy best of all, either in summer or winter, our home and vineyard in Sonoma. It is never dull or quiet there, and we like it that way. But I suppose, looking back, our happiest days were probably those spent in Carmel, when we had so little money and it made no difference.

We have no plans for the future and seldom make any. We know where we were yesterday, but we don't know where we will be tomorrow. Perhaps in Paris, or maybe in Rio—it could even be Peking. Have we found what we were searching for? We think we have.

Tomorrow, say the Mexicans, is not today, and on this we must agree. The very fact that life is so unpredictable, so full of uncertainties, is in itself what makes it exciting and worth the whole effort.

Who would want it any other way?